PRAISE FOR JANE MEREDITH'S
Circle of Eight

I love Jane Meredith's focus on local magic and her tools
to help us take root in place and weave new traditions out
of the strands of our own authentic experience. Meredith
is a graceful and poetic writer, and a true originator of
approaches to magic and spirit that can inspire us in these
times. Her beautiful, descriptive nature prose is interwoven
with stories and recipes that allow the reader to discover
their own deep connection to the land, the seasons, and the
particular energies of their own land. She also honestly
wrestles with the dilemmas of being a nature-worshipping
Pagan in a land that is not the land of one's own ancestors
and that has been stolen from its original owners. She offers
a path to our authentic connection to the deep forces of
nature as our guides and teachers.

—Starhawk

We live in a time of radical change—in our climate, our
environment, and ourselves. In a gentle but insistent and
courageous voice, Jane Meredith teaches us how to bend
our spirit to listen to what the sacred land is telling us about
itself and to create ritual that is alive, vibrant, and flexible
enough to adapt to whatever comes with honesty and
grace. Recommended.

—Anne Newkirk Niven, editor, *Witches & Pagans* magazine

What *Circle of Eight* finally does is address *witch* as utterly involved with *place*. This is fundamental. People suffer the sickness of the illusion of separation and wonder why they are unhappy. In Australia "crossing country" is to travel from one myth to another. In this work Jane involves those with whom she works magic in an awareness-raising practice that nests them within a recognizable environment. This invokes contact at such depth. I admire her breakaway method, a magical deep ecology that recognizes the mutuality that exists with all life.

—Ly de Angeles, author of *Witchcraft: Theory and Practice*

It's easy to forget that while acknowledging its ancient heritage, Paganism is a relatively young spirituality. We are still finding our way with modern tribes and traditions, but no matter where we are or how we connect with the world, Paganism is about learning from the land. The heart of our practice is as simple as stepping outside to breathe and to listen. *Circle of Eight* is a breath of fresh air. Jane Meredith wakes us up to the dangers of getting stuck in a "spiritual rut"—that what's taken for granted as Pagan practice in the Northern Hemisphere is very different in the South, while still remaining equally valid and true.

As our personal practice joins with that of others, so our homelands connect to our ancestors and we move forward, exploring the way together. *Circle of Eight* provides real, heartfelt, and practical methods of living our spirituality, of reminding us what our Paganism truly means while keeping open and inspired by the lessons around us.

—Cat Treadwell, Druid priest and author of *Facing the Darkness* and *A Druid's Tale*

These are ritual practices for our times. Jane Meredith provides a beautiful and evocative introduction to learning to relate to the Australian land with love and respect.

—Douglas Ezzy, author of *Practising the Witch's Craft* and *Sex, Death and Witchcraft*

Jane weaves together the ancient and modern to create a beautiful resource for those who want to create rituals and rites of passage to honour the cycles of life and the turning wheel of the year. A book bursting with helpful ideas on how to create ceremonies that are fresh, alive, and of the moment.

—Chris Waters, founder of Spirit of the Inca:
Shamanic Training

Praise for Jane Meredith's
Rituals of Celebration

Rituals of Celebration serves as a thoughtful introduction for those coming to magic and Earth-based practice as well as a handbook for those seeking to create intentional community through ritual.

—George Franklin, coordinator of
Reclaiming Quarterly magazine

Filled with beautiful personal anecdotes and practical steps, this book is accessible and user friendly… At every turn this book is inspiring, confronting, vulnerable, and courageous…I can't recommend this book highly enough.

—Rachel Zinman, international yoga teacher and trainer

Rituals of Celebration is a very real and magical read, poignant and totally soulful. I love the simplicity of being able to create rituals in the moment, and Jane gives us plenty of ways to celebrate the ever-changing seasons and cycles of life.

—Chris Waters, founder of Spirit of the Inca:
Shamanic Training

If you want rituals that will be real "I wish I'd been there" ones, then use this…an important book.

—Geraldine Beskin, owner of
The Atlantis Bookshop, London

CIRCLE
of
EIGHT

Photo © David Brazil

About the Author

Jane Meredith is an author and ritualist who lives in Australia and presents workshops worldwide. Her interests include mythology, magic, and ritual. Sign up for Jane's e-zine, learn about upcoming workshops, and read more by visiting her online:

WWW.JANEMEREDITH.COM

CIRCLE
of
EIGHT

Creating Magic for Your Place on Earth

Jane Meredith

Llewellyn Publications
Woodbury, Minnesota

FIRST EDITION
First Printing, 2015

Cover design by Kevin R. Brown
Cover image: 151149986/©Elena Schweitzer/Shutterstock.com
Interior illustrations by Llewellyn Art Department

Llewellyn Publications is a registered trademark of Llewellyn Worldwide Ltd.

Library of Congress Cataloging-in-Publication Data
Meredith, Jane, 1964–
   Circle of eight : creating magic for your place on earth / by Jane Meredith.—First Edition.
      pages cm
   ISBN 978-0-7387-4215-1
1. Magic. 2. Ritual. 3. Fasts and feasts. 4. Geography—Miscellanea. I. Title.
   BF1623.R6M47 2015
   133.4'3—dc2

                                                                      2014042212

Llewellyn Publications
A Division of Llewellyn Worldwide Ltd.
2143 Wooddale Drive
Woodbury, MN 55125-2989
www.llewellyn.com

Printed in the United States of America

Other Books by Jane Meredith

Aphrodite's Magic: Celebrate and Heal Your Sexuality

Journey to the Dark Goddess: How to Return to Your Soul

*Rituals of Celebration: Honoring the Seasons of Life
Through the Wheel of the Year*

To everyone who was ever a part of the
Circle of Eight and the Phoenix Circle: thank you.

For bravery, creativity, persistence, trust, and brilliance.

Anna, Cathryn, Damon, David, Eli, Elvian, Emily, Emma,
Glenn, Ian, Jonah, Michael, Roshana, Ross, Trinda

And in memory of Ross Pepper, 1965–2013

All land is sacred land.

The Circle of Eight described in this book took place on Bundjalung land. It is a landscape filled with natural beauty: rich soil, gorgeous forests and beaches, and amazing flora and fauna. Wollumbin, or Mount Warning, is in many ways the heart and source of this area. I am very grateful to have been able to live on this land, to hold circles there and to relate with its intrinsic magic.

I respectfully acknowledge the past and present traditional owners and custodians of this land.

Contents

Introduction

Local magic is powerful magic. It rises up through the earth under our feet. It whispers and sings to us in the winds and the air we breathe. It can be found in the waters nearby and the ways fire touches the land. As soon as you step outside the door you have access to local magic, and even indoors you can see and feel its influence in a hundred ways. The Circle of Eight is a magical system that bases itself on your location. You will create a unique version of the Circle of Eight directly related to where you live: the weather and seasons, flora and fauna, and the special conditions that exist around you. When you celebrate the seasons as you experience them, when you work with the elements as they manifest locally, and when you relate magically to the landscape, plants, and animals that live where you live, you become an active part of local magic—not as an abstract concept but as real, lived, and immediate experience.

The Circle of Eight begins as a structure for magic and ritual. It is ideal for eight people but can be worked solo, with just a few others, or with a larger number. It is made up of eight positions that are the cardinal and intermediate compass directions; that is, North, East, South, West and North-East, South-East, South-West, and North-West. Each person in the circle holds one of these positions. When the Circle of

Eight meets, you literally sit or stand in the direction you are holding, so if you are holding East, your place is in the East point of the circle. The person holding that direction is responsible for bringing its magic and flavor into the circle's workings.

The Circle of Eight relates fundamentally to your local surrounds and conditions, creating an in-depth local magic. This is discovered by turning to face outwards from each of the eight positions into the directions themselves, and exploring magically, energetically, and literally what that direction contains and what it represents in your location. This takes place during circle work but also between circle meetings as you continue holding and working with your direction. Coming together again, each person offers what they have learned. These explorations help create the overall composition of your Circle of Eight and change your magic and ritual from generalized to particular—from generic to local. Usually people move one place further around the circle at the end of each meeting, so everyone cycles through all eight directions.

The Circle of Eight's positions are also aligned with the festivals of the Wheel of the Year. When these two things are layered together, a local relationship is created with each festival. The festivals are revealed as belonging to and arising from the land they are celebrated on, taking on the flavor, references, and energies of local magic. Books become a secondary reference as the land all around offers us direct learning, letting us know not just the character of that direction in our location, but also guiding us in the lead-up to each festival. In turn, your experience of the festival will feed back into your Circle of Eight, continuing to inform you about that direction.

This local magic can be expanded onto the land around you to create a vast three-dimensional ritual landscape. To do this, you find eight locations in the appropriate directions that you already have or can form a magical relationship with. These places might all be on one rural property, for example, or spread out over a much larger distance in a cityscape or local area. Each place then further informs the character of the direction it represents. Combined together, these layers—the circle with its directions, the festivals, and the geographic Circle of Eight—

form a complex and truly local model for your magic and ritual. The structure of the Circle of Eight remains the same wherever it is worked, but the character of each circle and of each direction within that circle is dependent on where you are creating magic, on your place on earth. The Circle of Eight arises from, reflects, and is embedded in local magic.

Local magic is both a revolutionary concept and what people have been doing all along. Paganism is based in close relationship to nature; recalling a time when what was happening in the sky, in people's fields and gardens, with the animals and plants and the cycle of life in their own immediate surrounds was essential knowledge for human survival. Any grand theories modern Paganism claims are born out of these simple observations and our experiences treading through the cycles of life and death, participating in the great turning wheel we are part of. Yet somehow, recently, the experiences and observations of a relatively small part of the world—England and parts of Europe—assumed such authority within Pagan culture that they were received as wisdom and lore for Pagans everywhere. It's a kind of colonialism; regardless of where we are, we attempt to impose the truths of one place onto every other place. It doesn't work.

Local magic has another beauty. As well as being directly relevant to the people and places where it exists, if you add it up—including all the local magics all over the world—it results in the whole of the earth being celebrated and engaged with both magically and spiritually. In local magic we are honoring the complexity of the earth, and this planet-wide aspect is infinitely more complex than we can take account of in just one set of magical or ritual workings. For the earth, night and day exist simultaneously; whenever it is day, it is also night. Whenever it is winter, it is also summer. When it is Samhain, it is also Beltaine. Earth-wide, opposites coexist; they hold hands. When everyone celebrates the Winter Solstice on the same day in the same way, regardless of local conditions, we are not truly engaging with the earth. We are following a dogma that doesn't align with the most basic understandings of Paganism: that our spirituality is earth-focused and rests on lived experience.

Creating magic where I live, in Australia, raised questions for me, and the Circle of Eight came out of my dialogue with those questions. Magic in the Southern Hemisphere can be puzzling. Although the sun rises in the east, exactly as it does in the Northern Hemisphere, it then moves anticlockwise through the northern sky before setting in the west. North is our direction of heat, light, and the midday sun. When Europe and the United States are celebrating the Winter Solstice and Christmas, Australia is in the hottest part of summer, facing threats of drought and bushfires. At Easter it's mid-autumn for us, so while there's springlike imagery of bunnies and eggs in the shops, outside there are autumn leaves and cooling weather. Books on magic and ritual, unless they are specifically written for the Southern Hemisphere, take no account of this. Those books and teachings present the Northern Hemisphere directions, magic, and festivals as if they were the only reality, rather than showing only half of the earth's patterns and balances.

Australia isn't unique in being unrepresented in the commonly taught alignment of directions with elements and the content and timing of the Wheel of the Year festivals. I've been told by people who live in Switzerland, California, Malaysia, and the Middle East that the books don't describe what it's like where they live, either. And what if we were to look at South America, India, China…? The list goes on. Mid-December will only have the longest night for half of the globe, and around the equator longest nights aren't even discernible. Only in a few places will the time of Imbolc be linked to the first green shoots pushing through snow; many places don't have snow at all, and in others the snow hasn't yet begun to melt or give way to spring. The Summer Solstice is not necessarily a benign time of the year, bringing welcome warmth and sunlight. It can be a ferocious, destructive time heralding months of worsening conditions as the country bleaches, dries, and burns.

But there is no puzzle to understanding magic or the Wheel of the Year if we stay local. It's obvious to anyone when winter and summer are or where fire manifests in the circle. If you're in the Southern Hemisphere, the tropics, or an extremely cold place, you can tell as soon as you open a book on traditional magic that what's written there doesn't apply to the landscape or the conditions around you. When we stay local, we walk on the land and watch the weather; we observe the sun's risings and settings and the direction it moves through the sky. Nature speaks to us, and when we make magic, we speak back. So our magic is intrinsically local, born from and reflecting the place where we live.

To be engaged in earth magic in Australia is to return to the tenets of Paganism. We have to open our eyes, see what is here: observe the animals, birds, and trees. We get to know the elements—not as they are written of in any book, but as we meet them here: earth, air, water, and fire, and in that meeting we reach towards the fifth element, aether or spirit, a blending and meeting of all the elements. We learn from simply being here what the Summer Solstice is about—or Beltaine, Lammas, or the Autumn Equinox. I believe we don't just need to do this in Australia, but everywhere. Pagan magic is, essentially, local magic. What's the point of burning sage for its cleansing smoke, for example, if sage doesn't grow here? For uncounted centuries eucalyptus leaves have been burned in ritual on this land. Why wouldn't we do that?

The Circle of Eight arose from these understandings. I wanted to create a structure that would support local magic—that would enable us to learn and embody a system of magic and ritual that was true to the place we lived. I was inspired by what I understood of the Australian Aboriginal relationship to the land. What has filtered down to me from their heritage is that all land is sacred, and our relationship to it is paramount. Further, each piece of landscape is exactly what it is; it does not need to be changed, built on, or terraformed to become more sacred. If a watercourse runs only during the wet season, it does not mean we should dig it up to try to make it run all year. It is sacred for running only in the wet season. The rocks that belong to one part of the country do not need to be moved to other parts of the country—and, perhaps, absolutely should not be moved—because they are sacred in their own landscape the way they are.

In spite of living in Australia, my own magic and heritage are European. I wanted to find the cross-over point of these two realities; how to engage with my magic and ritual, but locally. I adopted a simple structure—the neo-Pagan Wheel of the Year, with its eight celebrations—

and superimposed it over the compass directions. Diagrams showing this for both hemispheres can be found on page 12. The Circle of Eight came alive when a group of us literally placed eight cushions down in the compass directions and sat on them.

Our Circle of Eight worked with the Southern Hemisphere model, but apart from that we assumed nothing. We met once a month, and during the time between our meetings we each worked with the direction we had been sitting in. Thus I would spend a month exploring the concept of North in the place where we lived and also within my own life. I would invoke North, call to it, invite its energies into my life, look at my relationship to it and the ways I loved and feared, denied and welcomed it. At our next meeting I would contribute not just my feedback for the month on what I had learned, but as well I would deliberately feed that North energy of our Circle of Eight into our ritual and process.

Towards the end of our meeting we turned the wheel, energetically and physically moving around the circle one place so that I moved from the North to the North-West. Then I would spend the next month with the North-West. Over the years we built up a deep, layered understanding of each direction both as it applied to us individually and as it existed in our location. Each person experienced each direction differently, and often differently each time they held it, but the commonalities also came through as we listened and observed over months and years. In the end the commonalities became more powerful than any single particularity. We experienced from the very beginning that the circle and the directions spoke directly to us, and this only strengthened as we continued.

We made many discoveries concerning interpretations of the festivals as well as the structure and dynamics of the Circle of Eight. For example, the North-East—our Beltaine position—was characterized by the unexpected. It seemed that no matter what anyone anticipated or wanted when they moved into that position, that never happened. The North-East always had a twist to it. We understood this slowly, over years, watching person after person hold this direction and listening to report after report of what had happened to them. Even if it's not the first thing I think of for Beltaine—that it contains the unexpected—it fits very well with the deeper resonances of the festival. More than the romance or love Beltaine's often associated with, this theme harks back to the random nature of fertility, Beltaine's older association.

Another discovery for me was the importance and excitement of the cross-quarters. In the Circle of Eight they sit as equals with the more traditionally observed quarters of South, East, North, and West. The festivals of the cross-quarters—Imbolc, Beltaine, Lammas, and Samhain—are usually considered both equal to and different from the quarter festivals of the solstices and equinoxes. Sitting in the cross-quarters of the Circle of Eight, alternating with the quarters every time we moved position, we experienced them as far more dynamic and layered than the quarters. This was so continual and powerful, it changed all of our magic—to the point where if we were casting a circle into only four directions, we would often choose to cast to the cross-quarters, particularly at a cross-quarter festival.

After the Circle of Eight had been running for a couple of years, I began to want some physical manifestation of our circle; not just a ring of cushions or a small group of humans creating local magic together but something large and solid that represented and amplified this energy—something like a stone circle, a ceremonial ground, a temple laid out on the land. Sensitive to what I felt were the teachings of the Australian landscape, I didn't want to build, impose, or install anything not already there; rather, I wanted the local area to speak to me, to show me how the circle could expand around us. I started looking at landforms and places, as well as the characteristics of our locality.

Our shire, the local government area, has strong Green politics, although it exists in and amongst what is historically a farming area that retains an entrenched conservatism. To the north there are high-rise developments practically on our doorstep. But in a few small towns on the north coast of New South Wales and in inland remnants of rainforest, there's an oasis: large numbers of alternative, healing, New Age, sustainably oriented, and Eastern spiritual practitioners live and work here. The soil is rich, as our shire is part of a huge volcanic caldera. The waving line of the coast's bays and headlands ripples along its eastern edge.

We began looking for eight places on or near the edges of our shire that would hold the energy for a magical circle: being powerful in themselves, in the correct direction, on public land, and containing some part of what we now thought of as intrinsic to that position. As we slowly found them we continued our ritual and magical practice, visiting each place many times both individually and as a group. Four of these places were on or near the sea's edge, befitting the idea of our geographical area as being closely connected with the ocean. And someone had built a labyrinth in the middle of the shire, which seemed divinely given to be the center of our geographic Circle of Eight. The places informed our practice, deepened tremendously our understanding of each position in the Circle of Eight, and strengthened our rituals. We came to feel the individual nature of those places whenever we cast a circle. We could send the magic out to them or call in their presence to strengthen and inform our work.

Many things became clear during this time. The North-West, our Lammas position, had always been inexplicably powerful in our rituals; stronger than the North, which didn't make sense to me. When we started working with the land, we realized that the volcano itself, which had literally formed our fertile earth, sat directly North-West of us. The North-West had birthed our whole landscape, our entire circle; no wonder it came through as powerful. As we worked with the geographic Circle of Eight, we came to have a sense not just of a small circle in my living room, with its eight distinct but endlessly linked directions, but of the stretch and expanse of the geographic circle, from each of those eight cushions out onto the land. Beyond that, we felt the grandeur of the wheel turning endlessly—our little locality held within the cycling of the earth and stars.

The Circle of Eight taught me about the wheel itself: its turnings and contradictions, its patterns and beauty and grace. It taught me that whatever despair or joy I am experiencing is purely local, the conditions of the place I am in, and because the wheel endlessly turns, I need not be unremittingly attached to it. It taught me that dark is half and light is half and everything looks different depending on where you are. The circle taught me the essence of *parts* and *whole*; it showed me how each aspect of the whole is essential to that whole, but each part is also a lens through which the whole can be viewed. I came to understand that only when all those different perspectives are added together is anything approaching the entire wheel even glimpsed. It taught me about the vast celestial magic our earth spins within.

One time I fell into absolute despair that there were no teachers available to me in this tradition. Not other people who were making it up as they went along, the way I was, but wise elders who had done all this long before and could guide me where I wanted to go. As I was sitting in this loss, this great gap in my life, I felt something—almost a physical sensation. It was a small energetic draft blowing past behind my back, inconspicuous and not concerned with me. When I opened myself to it—when I bent my mind towards it to discover *what is this?*— I caught a glimpse of the wheel turning: just turning, as it always, endlessly does; nothing to do with me. But I grasped it in that moment and have never felt alone, abandoned, or unguided since; the wheel itself, and the structure of the Circle of Eight, was my teacher. Everything I needed to know, it would teach me. Its eight directions described all there was. And it could be studied; it could speak to me; it could take me as deep as I had patience or time or strength of enquiry for. There would not be an ending to what I could learn or how I could be supported.

We began this work to learn about our own local magic, and certainly the Circle of Eight taught us that. We would look into the South-East, our direction of Imbolc, down the valley where the fresh wind blew towards us, along the cliff edges, through the narrow gorge, and we would remember that this was where changes in the weather came from; it was the beginning of the new. We met on the new moon and we could see out the tall windows in our Samhain direction of the South-West the moon's crescent setting in the Western sky, and so were endlessly reminded of the conflux of endings and beginnings.

If you create a Circle of Eight, your circle and its magic will be relevant to the place where it is formed. If you are working in the Southern Hemisphere, your magic and ritual will be different than if you are in the Northern Hemisphere. If there is a mountain to the south, your circle will have a different flavor than if there was desert or sea. Indeed, mountain magic will be different than river magic or plains magic. And doing this work will create local magic for those who live there, based in relating to the land. But local magic is ultimately global magic; from the particulars of our place and when added to all the other local magics of the earth, together we are living an earth-wide, earth-honoring spirituality. When we are working local magic all over the earth, we will have a Paganism rooted in its strengths of lived experience and earth-honoring, and between us we will be weaving a global network of living magic.

How to Use This Book

Circle of Eight: Creating Magic for Your Place on Earth will teach you how to work with local magic, the magic intrinsic to the place where you live. In this book you will find an overview of the Circle of Eight, beginning with instructions for setting up a Circle of Eight with a group of people and learning to relate to the energies of the directions and elements as they exist wherever you are. This system can also be worked on your own; the word "eight" in Circle of Eight refers to the number of directions or places in the circle, not necessarily the number of people. This structure can be used by a small or larger group, combined with any type of Pagan or earth-based magic, anywhere in the world. There are many ways to explore this system; some of them are outlined here, and others you will discover for yourself.

Included in this book are memoirs from my own experience in the Circle of Eight, as well as the background behind its different aspects and instructions for creating your own Circle of Eight. The memoir pieces and introductory segments to each section describe the places of our geographic Circle of Eight; the beautiful waterfall, mountain, headland, beach, and other locations that for us came to represent local magic at its most immediate and intimate. I hope they inspire you to

Circle of Eight in the Southern Hemisphere

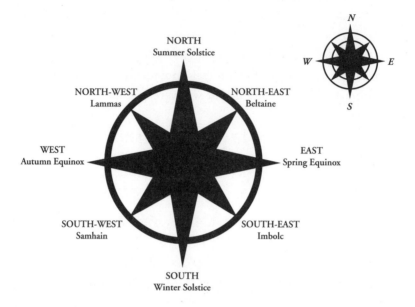

Circle of Eight in the Northern Hemisphere

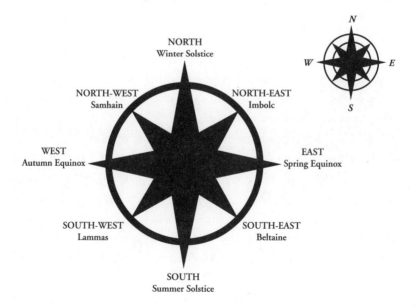

seek out places in nature, whether they are parks, skyscapes, your back yard, wild places, or special trees or walks that are sacred to you and support you in your spirituality and your exploration of local magic. The geographic Circle of Eight, laid out on the landscape of our local shire, was what transformed this system from an abstract concept to a solid, earth-based magic that was real—not just in our heads and in ritual, but actually real—and meant we were talking actively with the earth we lived on.

The book is divided into sections that cover how to begin, invocations, elemental associations, working both with myth and the festivals of the Wheel of the Year, inner work, creating your own geographic Circle of Eight, and endings. The descriptions of how things worked in my own Circle of Eight are intended only as examples to let you know one way that it has been done and to inspire you in your own experiments and investigations. The whole spirit of the Circle of Eight is that you take what is a very basic structure and let it fill with your own meanings.

Perhaps you already belong to a ritual or magical group that is looking for more direction. Perhaps you're starting out and have never cast a circle before. Perhaps you're arriving into earth-based spirituality from permaculture, earth activism, Eastern-based practices, chaos physics, self-help groups, parenting young children, conventional religion, or some other place, bringing both skills and questions with you. Perhaps you've worked with many different magical systems or you're not entirely sure what a magical system is. Probably, though, you'd like something that will provide both some structure and then a whole lot of freedom. Hopefully you're open to doing some exploratory work and testing things out to see what works for you, and ideally you're either searching for or open to evolving a local magic, something immediately relevant to the place you live: its climate, seasons, landscape, and community.

I expect your Circle of Eight will look different than my Circle of Eight. You may have different inclinations, pursue different areas of interest, live in a completely different place with different demands and potential, and have different reasons for exploring this work. That is all a part of local magic—that what you are doing is appropriate to your circumstances and locality. You might choose to work through this book in a different order than how it is laid out here; for example, your primary interest might be in a geographic Circle of Eight, something we didn't do until quite a few years into our Circle of Eight and that is described about halfway through this book. Or you might have little interest in the geographic circle and be much more concerned about how to combine the Circle of Eight with celebrating the Wheel of the Year. Feel free to skip around in the book to meet your needs.

One of the most exciting things for me is that the Circle of Eight teaches itself. As soon as you have laid out a circle and begun working it—as soon as you have stepped into one of the positions and begun holding it—as soon as you have turned outwards to face that direction and asked what exists there, you will be learning in an immediate, bodily way, and this book (or any other book) will become a secondary resource, a reference book. The real event—lived and happening all around you—will be your interactions with the directions, the circle, the people you're working with, and your own brand of local magic. You might receive this information in any number of ways, including in ritual, through dreams, through the land or its inhabitants speaking to you, through research, and through observation.

The tools for working local magic and ritual, and thus for the Circle of Eight, are tools we have had all along. They include practices such as grounding, being present with nature, revering the earth and all the elements, seeking the Divine in the everyday. They include your life experience—and the experience and knowledge of others in your circle—from previous rituals and magical groups, from work, and from personal interests and areas of expertise. They include your curiosity, your willingness to learn, and your hopes and desires for a working system of local magic. Along the way you might develop a lot more tools, skills, and understandings; things that others will share with you or teach you in circle; what you learn from the land around you and what you discover about yourself and your own brand of magic.

I've written this book not just to offer you my experiences with the Circle of Eight. I've written it to inspire and encourage you to take the Circle of Eight for your own, to engage as deeply as you can in local magic; to learn from this system and grow it in your own directions. I've written it because I deeply believe that local magic is the real Paganism and that global magic stems not from everyone doing the same thing in the same way regardless of local conditions or where they are, but rather from everyone working magic and ritual consciously in concert with their own place while honoring the whole earth.

The Circle of Eight is a magical model that blends the global with the local; it's a generalized structure that adapts to wherever it is placed. I encourage you to use it to explore, to ask questions, to discover and create your own magic, and to add your local blend to the worldwide mix of local magics that together can encompass and celebrate the whole of this sacred earth.

Our Geographic Circle of Eight

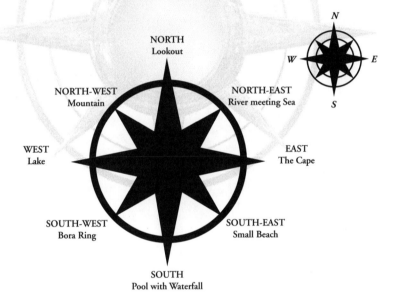

NORTH
Lookout

NORTH-WEST
Mountain

NORTH-EAST
River meeting Sea

WEST
Lake

EAST
The Cape

SOUTH-WEST
Bora Ring

SOUTH-EAST
Small Beach

SOUTH
Pool with Waterfall

Grounding

I clamber down the steep incline, hanging onto rocks and trying not to slide on the pine needles. It's been raining for most of a week, but right now the rain has stopped. I try to go slowly, slower; it doesn't matter if it starts raining again, but it will matter if I fall. Not that I am such a long way from civilization, but if I hurt myself it would be difficult to get back up; this path is nearly vertical. I know it will be worth it; just the thought of the waterfall in these conditions pushes me onwards. Of all the places in the Circle of Eight, this is the one I think of as grounding the whole circle; the beginning place from which everything else is born. Here I feel at the nadir, as if this waterfall and its pool pin the whole circle onto the land, and so it has my special loyalty.

Near the bottom I stop. The river bank that we walk along to reach the falls is gone, submerged under swift, swirling muddy water. This river has no bank, only a steep side I will have to clamber along: a mass of loose jumbled stones, all of them on their way down, towards the water. I scramble sideways, using hands as well as feet to jam myself into temporary crevices. The waterfall is only a few hundred meters upstream, but with this level of difficulty it will take me a while.

Even from here I can hear it roaring. It crosses my mind that probably no one else would do this—come here in a week of torrential rain. It would be considered dangerous, mad, inconvenient, unnecessary. But I have been waiting days for the rain to let up a little, feeling the call of the waterfall singing to me, beckoning; I have delighted in those masses of water closing roads and swamping everything, feeling this glory ahead of me. I was here once before when it was in flood, but not after as many days of rain; then I still walked along the path.

When I get there it is amazing, certainly worth this little effort and concentration it has cost me, and I am laughing and shouting up at the smashing torrents of it, the usual two streams of this waterfall merged to one thick, curling torrent out over the lip of rock and bellowing down into the round pool. I have never seen it like this. The air is filled with spray; water fills my mouth when I open it. The waterfall has overtaken the land and the air, and water leaps everywhere, temporarily escaping the huge downwards force. The photos I take are blurred with water.

The pool is alive, rapid ripples of waves quivering out from where the falls thunder down. I take off my clothes and go in. It's alive and fresh, not even very cold; this is a summer storm. The water pushes at me, pulses at me; I stumble past the shallows, hurting my feet on the sharp rocks, but I don't care, I just want to be in it. Once I'm deep enough I turn to face the cascade and swim. It takes all my strength to stay in one place, but laughing with it, playing this magnificent game, is like swimming in liquid life force; I'm tiny in this shouting, dancing water held within the circle of the pool. I look up at the rock walls and the trees that top them; watch the water lilies wrenched from their bed and pouring past me in the current; feel the fertile earth all around me, sheltering and breathing in with wet breaths; and know that even though I am half-submerged in water, this place is my ground, the earth; the anchor place of the circle.

The Circle of Eight Is Born

I was on a bus in England, leaving Glastonbury and musing about the land.

In England it seems people have such strong relationships to the land, not just the land in general but specific land, local land: *this* hill and *this* tree and *this* rock. In Australia we have a great generalized love of the Australian landscape, but it seems different than what I hear about in England. It can be related to those special places of forest and river and ocean each of us makes secret alliances with, but it's not as particular as the European way of relating to locality, of belonging to it, as if we don't care to trespass too heavily, to lay too great a claim to any magical relationship with this more recently invaded land. In England and Europe it sounds like a deep knowing of the land is in the bones, with generations living in one place and learning it over time more closely than a lover, speaking with it in an ongoing story that only deepens.

In Australia that had been done already, before us. Unlike England and Europe, more like the history of the United States, invading waves of people were not integrated piece by piece into the population but imposed themselves over and attempted to entirely replace what had gone before. The people who were the guardians of this sacred land— its Dreamings and knowledge—were slaughtered, persecuted, and largely disinherited. Out of respect, then, those of us who work European or other imported magics do not claim too great a belonging to this place. We try to live lightly, respecting what is here and hoping not to offend, not to transgress the invisible lines we don't know how to see. We marvel at this land—are amazed and awed and cowered by it; we love it and offer it allegiance, but we don't allow ourselves to think that we were *formed* from it; we are not intrinsic to it, and only at the edges has it touched our mythologies.

I envied Europe the obviousness of its stone circles, those bold declarations of ground dedicated to the cycles of turning sun and earth, those open invitations to magic and ritual. I wanted to have them, or something like them, in my own land. And yet…one of the great differences I had always seen between England and Australia was that in England it seemed everywhere I looked, I saw the landscape of humans. Each field, each slope and mound and rock—almost each tree—had been placed there by human hands, human design and labor. In the Neolithic era, humans had built those high earthen walls that now look like folds in the land, using hipbones of deer as their digging instruments. Humans decided the river should run over here, not there, and made it so; they carved a horse into the side of a hill; they transported massive stones from four hundred miles away to make a circle.

In Australia, outside of cities and relatively small areas of intensive agriculture, things are there because they've always been there, because that's the way they are. With the exception of managed fire, Aboriginal people who lived on and with this land for what's now thought to be between forty thousand and a hundred and thirty thousand years did not seek to shape or change it, but to understand and live in synchrony with it. If the river ran over here, that's where it ran. If those stones were found only at that mountain, that's where they belonged. If bunya nut trees grew over here but the fish were over there, then people traveled from the bunya nuts to the fish. They did not dig up pieces of the land and reshape them, they did not dam the rivers or reset their courses, they did not build pyramids or castles or sacred groves or underground cities.

England's magical and worked landscape enchants me like a fairy tale. Australia's raw, unapologetic, and stark this-is-what-is strips back my mind to ancient times. It does not talk about human landscape. It seems to say, *Here is a mountain; it is sacred. Here is a creek that runs only in the wet season; it is sacred. Here is a tree; it is sacred. Here, a mob of kangaroos, a flock of galahs; they are sacred.* Each and every piece of Australian land has been understood as sacred just and exactly for what it is, in itself. I felt I could not go around building stone circles on Australian land and stay true to it, even on any piece of Australian land that I imagined as my own. What I could do was learn from this understanding and seek sacred relationship with what was there.

Every part of Australia seeks to teach this lesson. Our terrains are so varied—coastal scrub to rainforest to desert to sclerophyll, or eucalypt forest—that what grows in one place will not grow in another. Wild animals and birds move through the landscape in vast numbers, ignoring roads and fences; ten thousand pelicans mysteriously gather together every so often. Kangaroos own the plains and paddocks, culled sometimes to reduce the numbers, escalating due to the encouragement of rich pasture where once there was only native grass, but essentially wild, unmanaged, unaltered by humans. Black cockatoos flock in Sydney as the weather turns, no longer appearing in threes and eights but now in dozens, then hundreds, sweeping across the sky on a mission, involved in their story with the land just as they presumably always have been.

And yet my mind and my magic was not as vast, as free-flowing and connected as that pre-European, pre-invasion connectedness; a connectedness that is expressed in the Aboriginal Dreamtime, a continuous and concurrent stream of existence where everything is in the act of becoming, right now. I believe this is also how much earlier European people—and maybe people everywhere—understood their land: that they were in community with it, journeying together; that they sought understanding and right relationship rather than dominion. But my mind is too filled up with systems and models and definitive absolutes; to create or discover anything like a stone circle in Australia, I would have to attempt some level of integration between the two systems.

I let my mind drift among all these potent, fermenting concepts. The image that presents itself to me is the simplest of structures: a circle segmented into eight. It represents not just the main compass directions but, underlying that, the basic turnings of the earth: the solstices and equinoxes that are known all over the globe and the cross-quarters that lie between them, which were the celebrations of the Celtic calendar. In modern Paganism this structure is the fundamental pattern of every year. I let this image of a circle, quartered and cross-quartered, drift across the landscape of my mind and the landscape of Australia, and I saw it settle, lightly.

I would start working with a Circle of Eight. The eight directions would correspond to the compass points as well as the solstices, equinoxes, and cross-quarters, but their nature would not be prescribed. We would no longer say *the North means this, and this and this;* instead we would look to the North and mark what was there, and we would name it sacred. We would say *in the South-East, here, this happens—and this— and it is sacred.* We would make ritual with what we found. When we turned to the East or to the South, we would not close our eyes and invoke what we had been taught; we would open our eyes and call to what we saw. And we would call it sacred because it was part of the land and was already sacred, just for existing. Within that we would create our magical circle.

The Waterfall

. . . .

Memoir

I've come to visit the waterfall on a full moon—the waterfall that holds the South in our Circle of Eight. I move cautiously on the rocks above the falls; there is still some light though the sun set a while ago. I have a good flashlight in my pack, as well as insect repellent and drinking water. When I get to the top of the track to the river, I turn so I am climbing backwards, like going down a ladder, and I go extra slowly. No one actually knows I am here, though my car is in the parking area, and eventually—tomorrow, probably—someone could find it and begin to wonder where the driver was.

The moon rose over the horizon while I was driving, full and luminous white, but here among the hills it can't be seen yet, and once I am down at river-height it will take even longer to be visible. I tell myself I have a lot of time; it doesn't matter how long it takes me to get there, even an hour would be fine, and I have no reason to rush. I'm glad I'm alone, that I can talk to myself and take my time, placing each foot carefully on the pathway along the water's edge, a pathway that is mostly walking round the edges of rock pools, jumping sometimes from one to the next or clambering along the bank between saplings and overhanging branches for a while before returning to the rocks.

Time stretches, gently. When I'm moving, I use the flashlight to see where I am going, but I also stop and turn it off for minutes at a time, listening, quivering with the night. I've been here many times during the day, dozens of times, but there's something about this round pool that suggested to me it might be a mirror under moonlight, a pool for scrying or just singing to the moon; a place that would be transformed from one set of realities to another if a human were to venture down here. The waterfall comes down in the west. The water heads east towards the sea; there's no cliffs in that direction and there's a general clearing of the larger trees. While the moon is still relatively big and low to the horizon, I'm thinking I will see it rise in that gap above the stream.

I imagine that if I stayed the whole night I would see the moon cross overhead; at midnight one could get into the pool and have the full moon directly above, though I'm not planning to do that this time. When I stand still there are mosquitoes and probably ticks and leeches as well; I try not to brush against the trees. I'm wearing walking boots to protect my feet, which seems extreme since often I come here in sandals, but my ankles feel supported and I step strongly over the uneven terrain. Even though I take twice the time I normally would, I feel steady and purposeful; anticipatory.

When I reach the waterfall, everything is still dark. I pick my way carefully around the side of the pool, in among all those loose and sharp rocks that have tumbled down from the walls over the years. There's a grass snake who lives here—I've seen it three times—or possibly there's more than one. It's longer than my arm, slender and greeny, with a narrow head and yellowish belly. Grass snakes are not dangerous and either it's not afraid or else the vibrations of the waterfall throw it off balance; I've come close enough to touch it every time I've seen it. It ribbons itself over rocks, and once I saw it flowing down the bark of a tree to the ground, as if it were coming to check me out. I think of it as the guardian here, the one left on watch when the humans—water catchment authorities or bush regenerators or just visitors like me—aren't here.

In the Circle of Eight this is the direction I associate with the element of earth, so I love that there's a snake here. There's also a cave—big enough to camp in—in the rock wall behind and beyond the waterfall, and often there are one or two fish jumping in the pool. They jump completely out of the water; you can sit and watch them doing it, and I always think it can't be for oxygen since the waterfall is pounding down, surely aerating the whole pool. The stream of water that leaves the pool is quite shallow; this must be the end of the line for fish that size, so perhaps they are hunting insects that come down to hover over the pool.

I wait for a while, with the mosquitoes and the night and the water that never ceases to pour in two uneven streams off the top of its bed and down through sudden nothingness to arrive, plunging into the pool. The sky in the east lightens before I see the moon, and it always enspells me, watching this endless dance of water—how it flies off the cliff and tumbles downwards, of a sudden ungrounded and turned almost to another substance, a stream vertical through air rather than horizontal over ground. The way it separates out into droplets and splashes and strands of water after having been part of the flowing whole, then it all joins up again, seamless, at the bottom and heads downstream as if it had never thought of anything else. But there has been that moment of surprise when it separated, flung into air, and I think our lives are like that—flung into separateness for the length of a brief journey, miraculous and guided mainly by force and gravity before being swallowed up again at death into the whole.

When the first rays of moonlight touch over the trees into this darkened well, I see that they do not touch the surface of the pool, as I had thought, but instead strike the face of the waterfall. Part of it is picked in silver, glistening like white fire, like a doorway into something else. I move up the uneven, rocky ground, not careful now, not looking for snakes or rocks that might twist under my foot; my eyes only on falling silver, the waterfall transforming into the long hair of the Star Goddess herself as she bends to wash it in the pool. I stand in wonder in front of its glistening for ages, and then I walk behind the waterfall so that the water is between me and the moon.

This is it. Not what I thought of, but what I have discovered. At first it is insubstantial, but as the moon rises the silver sheen in front of me grows and grows, expanding, until I stand before a sheet of glistening white fire. It is the gateway into the faerie realm, surely—a gateway that conceals as much as it reveals, for I can see nothing through it. It is a veil, a veil drawn over the eyes of mortals; the veil that lies between us and the otherworld, and usually one cannot actually see it and might not even be aware of it, but I have caught it in the waterfall and moonlight and it is a real thing. I see the veil. And seeing it, knowing it, I see how everything is touched with magic, and in my eyes I am holding this knowledge, and its power shimmers and glistens through my whole being, to the ends of my fingertips, and whatever I were to reach out and touch now would be transformed.

I stand there for minutes on end—for twenty minutes, for an hour. This is what I have always longed for, believed in, sought: the magic shimmering on the face of the world, just touching; the invitation into the divine and immortal realm. The wonder does not cease. I do become tired, though, and eventually that's why I leave, aware of the journey back to the car and the drive home. When I look back at the face of the waterfall, still catching the moon's rays, it's pretty but nothing like standing behind that shimmering veil. It is a waterfall by moonlight, whereas that other was something I had always yearned for and looked for and suddenly found: the beckoning gateway into a magic far beyond my own.

Walking back is much faster, the sporadic moonlight through the trees adding to my buoyancy, my satisfaction, and the awe that has filled me with this sight I had not dreamed of. My relationship with this place in the Circle of Eight has always been strong and pragmatic, and although the many hours I have spent here have softened that a little— extended it to a place of play as I've swum under the waterfall and wonder as I've talked to the snake or felt the specialness of this rounded site, cradling water within rock, greenery all up the sides—this has added a dimension of pure, indisputable magic. I am grateful to my intuition that tempted me into coming here by night on a full moon. I leave as if wakened in a deep place, bound into the magic of the land, the earth and pool and sky, and alive to the mysteries not as something to read about but as something to gaze upon, living.

Beginning Our Circle of Eight

I placed eight cushions in a circle on the floor in the compass directions of South, South-East, East, North-East, North, North-West, West, and South-West. Because we were in the Southern Hemisphere, I thought of this circle as turning anticlockwise—the direction the sun and moon move across our skies. I thought of these positions as corresponding with the eight festivals of the Wheel of the Year, but I felt certain we would discover much more than we already knew about the festivals by this process, as well as learning about the directions and the circle itself. In the center I set a round, embossed tray for an altar, and on it I put a candle; nothing else. It felt as if I was creating the first circle, not just for this Circle of Eight but the first circle anywhere, ever, and I didn't yet know what belonged on the altar. Only the circle could tell me that, and the circle was just beginning.

On that first night there were five of us, and we each chose a direction. I sat in the North. We agreed to remain in those positions for a month, and when we next met to turn the wheel one place onwards so that I would move from the North, the Summer Solstice position, to the

North-West, the position of Lammas. Even though not all our cushions were occupied, the Circle of Eight itself seemed fully there, all eight positions represented by its cushions and directions; it was only the human component that was lacking. The second time we met, there were six people; by the fourth meeting, the cushions were filled with eight of us.

From the very beginning the Circle of Eight spoke up, letting us know it existed just fine without us—that the human element of this circle was the secondary one; the compass directions represented by the cushions were there with or without us. We might sit on those cushions or stand behind them—we might function as channels for these directions, as voices and explorers—but we were not intrinsic. This was what we learned before we even began. And as soon as we stood there, in our first positions in the Circle of Eight, looking at each other; as soon as we sat down in those places and began working magic, more and more things became clear.

Although the Circle of Eight *looked* like a circle, in fact its whole structure was based on lines. The spokes of a wheel are what hold a wheel together, as much as or more than the rim. The person sitting opposite me showed me this the minute I raised my eyes beyond the altar and saw her there. It was my friend Elvian, and in this circle she was immediately the most relevant person to me—or the South was the most relevant position to the North. It was her I looked at full in the face, and in doing so I looked straight through the center of the wheel, its hub and our altar; I looked *from* my direction but *into* her direction. My perspective was a view of the position that was directly opposite the position I held.

Elvian and I already had a strong connection; we had worked ritual and magic together for years and knew each other's strengths and flavors. And we were, in many ways, opposites; we had played on that in both magic and friendship. I was earthy; she was fiery. I preferred to work and deepen within one system over years; she liked to be always learning something new. I was immovable in my beliefs and arrangements; she preferred to flow with how she felt. Sitting in the Circle of Eight and looking across the hub of the altar at each other showed us what we had already known between ourselves, but perhaps not known to apply more broadly in magical terms: *opposite* can be closest ally.

This immediately added a depth and dimension to our rituals for the Wheel of the Year; no longer did we consider that the Spring Equinox, for example, was closest to Imbolc and Beltaine, the festivals before and after it in the Wheel of the Year. Instead, it was glaringly obvious that the festival it was most deeply related to was the Autumn Equinox, situated directly across from it. What is begun at one festival may grow and change as the wheel moves around, but at its opposite festival it is completed. There something else is begun, which is completed in turn when the starting place is returned to. So the new growth in the fields of the Spring Equinox results in the harvest of the Autumn Equinox. That harvest saves the seeds for and is the vision that inspires the work required at the next spring season.

This especially made sense to me, who had been transiting between hemispheres for years, realizing repeatedly how festivals that are celebrated at the same time on opposite sides of the world, in fact on the same day—such as the Winter and Summer Solstices or Beltaine and Samhain—have so much in common. These festivals are opposites; they lie not just across the earth but across the wheel from each other. The birth of the Year King at Winter Solstice is completed by the height of his glory at the Summer Solstice. Samhain is the time of death and Beltaine, opposite it, of fertility. They reflect and complete each other across the globe, like tossing a ball back and forth in a complex game that crosses the circle repeatedly instead of passing it tamely around the edges.

Seated in the North, the line that crossed our North-South line on the square, the East-West line, also flared in significance to my eyes, though no one sat there on that first night. Those four positions looked like they held the corners of the world, the turning of the earth; we were grounded into the solstices and equinoxes, our points and lines bright and clear and obvious. We were the four arms of a cross within a circle, and it felt solid, like the foundations of a building, the structure of a sentence, or the framework of bars of music before the notes had been written. These two lines with four positions stamped at the ends of them were the axes of the world; on them you could imagine settling the middle earth that we lived in, with the heavens propped above and the underworld supporting below; the whole creating the cosmic sphere.

Between each of these quarter positions lay another quartered axis on the slant. These two lines ended in the four positions of the cross-quarters. One of those cushions was empty on the first night, but that was not the only thing that made that cross seem shadowy, hard to pin down. Those four points were in flux, held between givens, cradled between certainties. They shimmered, they hovered in and out of sight; they brimmed with potential as the meeting place between two differences, the overlap of two influences, like a tidal zone. Where the quarters of North, East, South, and West seemed absolute, predetermined, and definite, the cross-quarters appeared to be between the worlds, not quite belonging to the circle in the same way; instead questioning it, commenting on it, and offering an elusive alternative, like the sideways step it takes to enter fairyland.

Once we started turning our wheel and moving from position to position, I noticed a difference between moving into a quarter or a cross-quarter position; this got stronger as we continued. When we turned the wheel and I shifted into a cross-quarter, the whole room seemed to tilt. The patterned carpet we sat on looked suddenly crooked, the walls loomed out at me at strange angles, I felt dizzy and sickened. Trinda teased me, saying it was just that I was used to looking at the room from a certain angle. Next month when we shifted, she looked at me challengingly. *It's ordinary again*, I said. A month later when we shifted, I felt her eyes on me as I sat down, by now in the cross-quarter of the South-East. I would have fallen over if I'd still been standing; it was as if the floor of the room swiveled round to meet me. *It does look odd*, she agreed from her own cross-quarter position. *Yes*, I said, *it's the cross-quarters—the whole room's crooked*, and this time she could only nod.

It became a given. When we moved into the quarter positions, the circle steadied; the room settled and seemed as obvious as it had ever been. When we moved into the cross-quarters the world tipped; we were off the square and into the realms of mystery. We tried putting the carpet on a slant, oriented to the cross-quarters, to see what difference that made; it made none at all. We had to learn to accommodate a slight dizziness in the cross-quarters, as we looked at the circle differently. It was as if we crossed the barriers into the *other* realm with every cross-quarter. One of the most fascinating things about this was it implied the otherworld—the shadowy, magical one—did not lie *over there* somewhere but was contained within where we were, in-between, somehow, the more standard realities. Each shift around the circle alternated stepping into or out of ordinary and extraordinary realities.

It confirmed what is written into the accepted celebrations of the festivals: that the cross-quarters of Beltaine, Samhain, Lammas, and Imbolc are more significant magically than the quarters of the solstices and equinoxes. But this does not seem to be enlarged on elsewhere, in magical or ritual understandings and ceremony. Why, for example, when we cast a circle into four directions, do we choose the quarters and not the cross-quarters if they are so potent? How did this come to be unquestioned, when the quarter festivals are not assigned greater significance than the cross-quarters? And further, why do we emphasize the fixed instead of the moving in magic, dedicating each direction to one element and doing everything the same each time? Having understood the potency and intrinsic magic of the cross-quarters, why do we not embody that in everything we do?

Discovering the nature of the cross-quarters changed how we cast a circle, how we celebrated the festivals, and how we understood the wheel. We felt it in our bodies, as was typical of our discoveries in the Circle of Eight. The circle spoke to us, spoke through us; and in our dialogue with the Circle of Eight, we could see glimpses of, catch whispers of the great Wheel that it echoed—that pattern of stars that spun around us, that Wheel of the Year we danced through blithely, thinking we knew it, thinking of it as a descriptor of seasons' passing scenery rather than the great teacher, the endless depths of all the known and unknown realms. That physical unease, the almost-sickness I met again and again transitioning into a cross-quarter, brought me up short every time, reminding me I knew next to nothing and had placed myself bodily into the place of my unknowing.

The circle made patterns all by itself and irrelevant of who was sitting in which direction. They were structural patterns. There was the strength of opposites, a clear call and support, as if that magnetic tension of looking towards each other and yet almost pulling backwards to stay apart was what held my place on the circle. There was the bracing of those sitting on the cross to either side of me—as opposed to those sitting actually next to me—that felt like the bracing of the circle, whether we collectively held the quarters or the cross-quarters. The steadiness of this was helped by the fact that it was always the same people at the same angles wherever we were on the turning Wheel, because although we moved every time we met, we moved only around the perimeter of the circle, maintaining our positional relationships to each other.

The carpet might tip under you, the walls tilt about, and everything look shadowy and partly underwater, but the same faces looked back at you. The context is different, the surrounds; one time I see the wall behind Elvian, the next time the windows, but it is always Elvian there, like a complex dance where you swirl about the floor but look into the eyes of your partner, and that and knowing the steps of the dance is what brings steadiness, rather than the dizzying surrounds. Magically, this was our constant; the circle itself and our relationships to each other brought steadiness and resilience into the unknown, ever-changing whirl of directions.

The Circle of Eight has no hierarchical structure, and its emphases are always changing—with the time of the year or particular people or combinations of people in certain directions. I had longed for a magical group based in equality, shared leadership, and each person representing a dynamic force, not all following along after the loudest speaker or the most insistent personality. In the Circle of Eight I felt we were all working together; not so much because everyone took on leadership or was equally committed, vocal, or participative, but because the circle itself insisted on that equality. Of the eight positions, none could be called the lead position. Every direction was part of our working and essential to the circle. Even if a direction had no one sitting in it, no one representing it at that moment, it was still there, part of our magic and working.

Every new moon we came together, and each time we met we shared what we had learned in the previous month. We talked about the direction we had been holding—how it had felt and how we had sensed it. If the group was following some particular enquiry about elements or a myth, we gave feedback on that. But each of us also spoke of what was happening in our work, relationships, and physical and spiritual lives. We listened, and it was as if those words, those stories, were pouring through a filter of that direction. Looking and listening to someone sitting in the West, we were looking West to where they sat, and we were hearing West in what they spoke. Next month, when a different person spoke from the West, that also filtered through West, and so we gradually built cumulative pictures of each direction.

After we'd done our magic or working for the night, we turned the wheel. Turning the wheel was a ritual that evolved, gaining more and more magnetism as we continued to do it. We each stood in our place and stripped ourselves energetically of the direction we had been holding, imagining it spilling down onto the cushion as if it were a cloak we were shedding. Then, stepping free of its influence, almost hovering above it, we began to sing, each time the same simple song. We tuned our voices to each other's, singing louder and clearer until we vibrated with sound. We put our left hands into the center of the circle, creating the hub of the wheel, and half-turned so we were facing the direction we would move in. Slowly, slowly we began to pace, taking maybe a whole minute to move the few steps from one direction to the next, each person turning through only one-eighth of the wheel each time. We turned our Wheel anticlockwise, the direction the moon and sun move through the sky in the Southern Hemisphere.

This turning of the wheel became a thing of great beauty for me, so much so that often I would have tears in my eyes as I felt the dance of the stars move through me, felt the moon setting below us, felt the year turn into its next season. I would look up and see the delicacy, the severity, of this slow turning; catch a glimpse of someone's eyes or the turn of their head as together we became the wheel and I was cradled in it, carried by it and astounded at their grace. Sometimes I held my right hand out as well into the empty space around our circle, and it felt like I skimmed the stars with that hand, caressed the black night, or stroked the living sunlight into being.

We stepped outside time for that turning, but then as we arrived in our new places there would be a shiver through the space, as if we had floated free for a moment of the structures of gravity and time but now connected again, to a different energy than the one we had left. We lowered our hands and turned to face the center, seeing—again, still—whoever stood across from us, but in a different part of the room with a different orientation. Sitting down in our new places, we were silent a moment and then spoke, each only two or three words, the very first impression of what we had come into. *It's all bright. The room's on a tilt. Quiet, still. Opening.* If we had planning to do, practical things for our next meeting or ritual, we did it then from our new places. Finally we released the circle, grounding the energy back into its eight directions but each person continuing to carry the connection with their new direction.

Throughout the month, between our meetings, I would be in constant dialogue with my direction, meditating on it, opening to its learnings. I would ask myself what the North had to say about my relationships, what North characteristics I already held or could learn from, in what way the North was special or unique and how I could embrace it more fully. If one of the festivals occurred during that month, each of us would bring the energy of our own direction to that ritual. Doing this, it felt as if the directions themselves were meeting to hold the ritual through us, rather than us holding the ritual within their space. We were spokes of a wheel, holding it together, and even though each of us brought our own interpretation of each direction, that was merely an added flavor and not as strong as the direction itself.

The circle had its own imperative. At the beginning I felt I was anchored within it, overwhelmed in my position, saturated by it and unable to see or feel anything else. Everything I experienced came filtered through that lens—everything through eyes of East, if that was where I was, or everything through the eyes of South. I was completely immersed in that place. To shift positions at the end of the month was a wrench that felt either like a great release or deep mourning, leaving behind some place I had loved or loathed and heading into the unknown once again. I could *see* the rest of the circle—the other people in it, the other positions and other festivals—but they were like foreign countries, distant and not commensurate with any experience I was having.

After we had been around the whole circle a few times—and each circuit took eight months—I began to feel lighter in my journeying, as if I did not, each time, arrive in a completely new place with a different landscape than where I had been before, but instead traveled on a continuum; although the experiences and the scenery changed, they were changing in degree rather than utterly. I felt as if I trod more gently, not that I was ripped from one position and plonked into the next, but as if I walked delicately and continually around the wheel the whole time, shifting like a minute hand, which is only noticed each time it falls onto one of the marks set around the face of the clock but really is moving all the time.

And I became aware of the Great Wheel—the spiral of the universe, perhaps—this infinitely bright, fiercely sparking, living white starfire-light, spitting and electrified, gloriously celestial but also immensely present, a thought of it, an echo of it, here held between the eight of us, our eight cushions and our little circle, turning with the wheel on every new moon. It was not a smooth, sculptured wheel I felt in the vast background but more like endless thousands of sparklers bound together in an infinite circle and we—our little human lives, our circling—threaded through and amongst this. It was so vast that the sparklers were like stars in the sky, although they seem so close together, although this sparkler-light seemed dense and everywhere and everything, like the spaces within atoms they were also far distant from each other so that lives and planets and seasons fell in quite simply along the pathway and were not burnt to oblivion by their nearness to the fabric of the wheel.

One of the dynamics of our circle was the cycle of the moon. Because we met and turned the wheel on the new moon (when a crescent could be seen in the western sky), each position we were in followed the same development. We started in a new position on the new moon and gradually settled into it as the moon waxed. At the full moon it felt as if we were peaking at the height or depth of that position, then as the moon waned we gradually integrated our understandings and arrived at some resolution. We traveled through the dark moon and emerged again, now more familiar with that direction and its part in our lives, ready to release and be released by it as we moved on.

The yearly cycle of the seasons, of the festivals, and the year came through less regularly. The pattern was much harder to see of how the eight solar festivals interacted with our twelve or thirteen moon-based shifts each year. There was an energy—an almost tidal energy—to do with which part of the year we were in, as if whoever happened to be holding that place of the season or festival we were up to had a spotlight shining on them; that position momentarily had more weight and lent gravity to our whole circle. So when I was in the Samhain position and it happened to be Samhain, it was as if those energies increased for me not exactly in weight but more like in density—because not only was I energetically and magically in that place in our circle, but the whole year was there too, so I was doubly there, like a king tide. Whereas if I were in the Samhain position at the Spring Equinox, I held Samhain more closely to me, more personally, while the world around me—and I, to a certain extent—experienced the Spring Equinox. And so I learned the flavor of the Spring Equinox when viewed from a position of Samhain—and all the commentaries that all of these positions have on each other; all degrees of difference and similarity, all the ways one can highlight or accent each of the others.

There came to be a mysterious synchronicity and force as we ran this magic. In the very first meeting I sat in the North, the direction of fire and the Summer Solstice. It was not my favorite direction or festival, far from it; fire was the element I had always been least comfortable with. But that was where I felt determined to sit, as if the circle itself needed me there. Some years later, I turned forty. The direction I was holding at the time was the North. It was as if by entering into and doing this work with the Circle of Eight I had grown into my power; sitting originally in the North had signalled that and then when I turned forty the circle reflected that back to me.

Did some part of my subconscious calculate that? It seems unlikely, since I don't have a particularly mathematical brain and of course hadn't known our circle would even last that long or that it would become so meaningful to me. Was it coincidence? And yet it had so much meaning for me, and this type of incident occurred so often—with everyone, not just me—and seemed to resonate so deeply. We felt we merged with this circle, this magical system, and it spoke through our lives with authority and inspiration; we were in tune with it, and it with us; we co-created this magic. I couldn't exactly say the wheel or the Circle of Eight was dictating the minutiae of our lives, but it seemed as if our lives responded to these patterns as again and again each of us created new things in the Imbolc and Spring Equinox positions, had successes or major challenges in the Summer Solstice position, and retreated and released on our way to the Winter Solstice place.

As we circled and circled through these eight places, we deepened our knowing of them. Over months and years this information distilled. When I knew not only this current experience of East, but all my previous experiences of East as well, I could begin to see some essential grains of how it was for me in the East—what all those times had in common—and that became more central to my understanding of East than just a single occurrence. And because I heard everyone else's reports of the East as well, I began to differentiate what was mine when I was in the East from what was Cathryn's or Glenn's in the East, from what was common or seemed universal in the East.

Passing through these positions many times I went into deeper and deeper aspects of each direction; what each time I sat there had in common was often an understanding I would not have arrived at without this experience. Sometimes, for example, I approached my favorite position of the South-West with dread and sometimes with eagerness. Each time I left it I saw that regardless of my attitude or what had occurred during the month, my experience in that direction was always one of deepening. I heard each other person's variations on each direction every time they traveled through it, and this built and built until I saw the layers far more clearly of which pieces belonged to the direction and which to the person and which to just this instance of that person in that direction.

I loved the journey of moving in this way; it was like being planets in the sky with a relentless, slow dance swinging about our center, visiting and revisiting places over years and so understanding how the energy shifted and changed from position to position, not just in me but in the circle itself. I loved the variations and the patterns. Sitting in the dark half and looking across at the light half of the circle, I would hear and hear again in those voices the brightness, while around and within me I felt the deepening, and I knew they were heading here and I there. I knew that we were all one thing, yet at different moments, holding different aspects of it. And it was ever turning, and relentless.

When we began the Circle of Eight, I had positions I favored—ones I felt were easy, familiar, or filled with gifts—and others I was wary of, reluctant to enter, or even dreaded. Approaching the direction of Lammas always made me anxious, not knowing what sacrifices would be called for but aware that whatever fullness I had built up over the previous four months must begin to shift and change while I held that position.

I was afraid of the power of it and yet it was indisputable. Each position flavored not just what roles I took in a ritual and where I sat, but the whole tenor and content of my life. It was not as simple as the East bringing new beginnings; it might well be that the East highlighted my longing for the new or my exhaustion or illness. Rather than a series of gifts, it was more like being put under a microscope. Each position challenged me, strongly, to prove myself in that place—to examine that part of my life, sort it out; some parts I found harder than others. Everyone had these dreads and wariness about certain positions, peculiar to each one of us. Each of us also had positions we looked forward to: places to catch our breath that felt familiar to us, nonthreatening.

The people in our Circle of Eight changed from time to time. We would make a commitment to a cycle of eight months, after which we'd reassess it, each person choosing to recommit or leave. People also left when they moved away from the area, when their relationships broke up, or as they decided to explore different spiritual paths. Most people stayed for years. We didn't always have eight people in the Circle of Eight, though we always had eight directions and eight cushions. All of this compounded the sense that *people* weren't the vital elements in this structure, the positions were. When someone was sitting opposite me in the circle, I would see myself reflected back in what they were saying, what they were experiencing in that direction—the differences and the samenesses—and when no one was there, when I was looking at an empty cushion, it was like a mirror to see and remember myself in that position a few months earlier. It was as if there were eight of each of us in that circle: eight different selves, and we could see them overlaid on each position.

As we circled round and round, as I came to see the beauty of the whole rather than the parts, gradually I lost this resistance, this preferencing. Gradually I came to feel that I held the whole inside me, and wherever I was on the edge of it was simply an indicator of a moment, not a singular truth I was wedded to. I began to feel the circle dancing through me, much as I danced around it. Each position—every position—arrived with the same feeling of wonder and recognition as I grew more and more into knowing how each held a part of the whole and how therefore neither the Summer Solstice nor the Autumn Equinox could even exist without Lammas, and how Lammas was in some ways a twin of Samhain, my favorite; how every position was its twin, all contained part of its flavor, as it contained all of them.

How to Set Up
Your Circle of Eight

The Circle of Eight is simple to set up. It requires a compass, a meeting place, up to eight people, and a basic knowledge of the Wheel of the Year or the local seasonal changes as related to the equinoxes and solstices. You can also work the Circle of Eight on your own.

The Circle of Eight retains the very broad structure of the relationship between the sun and the earth that is found in the Wheel of the Year. Beyond that, it focuses on the local and immediate rather than theoretical, abstracted, or general notions of what belongs or occurs in each of its eight positions. Every Circle of Eight is an experiment, discovering through observation and experience how the eight points of the circle exist in *this* place and time for *these* people. It is relational, learned through the process of inhabiting the eight positions, and it develops as you develop your understanding and practices.

The Circle of Eight is ideal for groups or individuals whose surrounds do not match what is written in the books. This applied to us in the Southern Hemisphere, where even if you reverse everything and turn the wheel the opposite direction, still the seasons and resonances are all different. In Australia, for example, the summer sun is not the beneficent, welcomed delight that it is in England; it's a ferocious energy that brings drought, bushfire, and skin cancer. In other places, also, the climate and terrain don't match what is assumed for the directions or the Wheel of the Year. In Switzerland winter lasts well past Imbolc; in Malaysia, practically on the equator, there is almost no discernible difference between the seasons.

Even in a temperate, well-ordered climate that echoes the expectations set down in books, the Circle of Eight will teach local magic. It may be harvest time, but what is being harvested? Avocados, wheat, mushrooms, coffee? Harvest may not be at the Autumn Equinox at all but spread throughout the year or at several times of the year for different crops. The Circle of Eight localizes magic and ritual, placing it within the context where it occurs. This strengthens the magic; Paganism draws on earth energies.

The same necessities exist for the Circle of Eight as for any other group: to choose how often to meet and where; if the group is open or closed, and, if it requires a commitment, for how long the commitment lasts; to decide the content and organization of meetings. The nature of this work lends itself to a more committed group, exploring in depth. Having everyone there every time enhances this, rather than always explaining it to newcomers; however, it may take a while for your group to settle or to find eight people, and during this time you may choose to leave your circle open for people to come and go. For solo practitioners a minimum length of time to explore this system is eight months if you change position every month, but ideally you would stay with it over several years to drop into the deeper levels of the work.

You may choose to meet with your circle outside or in a different place each time. You may choose to celebrate the festivals as well as meet as a Circle of Eight, or your Circle of Eight meetings may be combined with the festivals. If you do choose this—meet eight times a year—be aware that in your circle people will always be in the same relationship to the Wheel of the Year. That is, the person who is in the

East at the Spring Equinox—and so "on" the festival—will turn with the wheel to Beltaine and so be on the festival again, continually. Someone else will be just ahead of the festival every time, another just behind it, and another always opposite it. Meeting and turning the wheel sixteen times a year would provide more variety, but it would result in a similar outcome, a regular pattern.

We tied our circle meetings into a phase of the moon (the new moon), but you could meet on full or dark moons or any other phase. You could meet every two, three, or five weeks in order to meet more frequently than the festivals and thus provide a more random and changing selection of experiences for those in the circle.

Your group may choose to work with the Circle of Eight simply to explore the eight directions and the nature of the Wheel of the Year in your location and deepen your magical relationship to these things. It may be that you are already a group that meets together—a discussion group, ritual or magical group, women's or men's group, or support group. It may be that you are seeking a container within which to create magic, celebrate the seasons of the year, or do other work, such as mythic, dream, or magical work, or personal development. The Circle of Eight can encompass all of these things. Essentially it is an empty structure—a powerful, vital structure, but an empty one—allowing you to bring your learning, enquiry, and celebrations into it, and in turn teaching you about itself.

How to Begin Working with Your Circle of Eight

Time: 2–3 hours

You will need:
- up to eight people
- eight cushions or chairs
- a compass
- music to move to

Optional:
- an altar in the center
- markers for the eight directions, with their names
- instruments to play

Set out your cushions or chairs according to the compass directions. Place the markers for directions, if you have them, in front of the chairs or cushions. If you have a simple altar, put it in the center.

1. Introductions

To begin with, people can sit anywhere at all or you may choose to have the preliminary discussion somewhere else and then approach the circle. Spend some time introducing the ideas behind the Circle of Eight and explaining why you are interested in it and what you think its benefits might be. Even if you have spoken with everyone individually before, it is great to have a detailed explanation given to the whole group so everyone knows they are starting together and is reminded of the purpose of the meeting.

If the group is new, have everyone introduce themselves in some depth, saying a little about themselves and why they have chosen to be a part of this. It's best to begin yourself; in doing this, you let others know how long to talk for and what to include. If the group doesn't know each other at all, you can also ask them to briefly share their previous magical or ritual experience. If you do know each other, you might ask people to speak about their current interests, passions, or learnings in ritual and magic.

2. Orientation

Briefly, using a few sentences for each one, introduce each of the eight positions of the circle. Call them by their compass direction (the North-East, the East) and mention which festival each is aligned to. The diagrams for this are on page 12. Adding some local geographic features is helpful; for example, that the sea lies to the East or the river gorge to the South-East. You can also align the positions with the phases of the moon.

Ask for any questions or comments, and then ask the group to stand and move together to one of the positions, gathering around it. Since no one is sitting or standing in the position at this moment, it's a great time to talk about how each position exists independent of people; how the people will circulate while the position remains the same. Ask everyone to feel into the position you are standing around, and after a minute or so of silence, ask for their impressions. People will report this in different ways: some may report on physical sensations, colors, or emotions, others will list correspondences for the direction or their prior experiences. Allow these impressions to build upon each other and coexist, discouraging any debate of right or wrong. Try to sum up in a few phrases what the contributions have been.

Move onto the next position, moving sunwise around the circle. In the Northern Hemisphere you will be moving clockwise; in the Southern Hemisphere it will be anticlockwise. Repeat the exercise with each position: a moment's silence, brief sharings from all, and then a summation. After all eight have been explored you can ask for general comments and observations, stressing again that there are no right or wrong answers and this is a learning experience. Keep this section brief; it is mainly to allow people to consolidate their own impressions and understandings rather than to begin discussing or overly defining concepts.

3. Choosing Positions

Put music on and ask everyone to spend some time moving or dancing around the circle. They should take the time to move into each of the eight positions, feeling their body responses and noting how they feel in each place and where they are drawn. Mention how long the music is—ten to fifteen minutes is a good length of time—and that at the end of the music each person will be asked to move into a position, which is the position they will hold until you meet again.

It's worth trusting this process. You may be worried that people will choose the position closest to the fire or next to someone they like rather than because of the energetics of the Circle of Eight, and you might even mention this to the group. There is no right or wrong reason for choosing a particular place, and by the peculiar grace of the circle, it will work out more perfectly than it ever could have if you masterminded it. People get what they ask for—that seat next to the fire may turn out to be uncomfortably hot in more than one way or that lovely friend they wanted to sit next to might become grating after one or two or three rounds of the circle... However it works out will be fine. Essentially this is people's first interaction with the Circle of Eight; let them do it how they like.

Once people have settled into a position, spend a few moments in silence, allowing impressions and sensations to gather. Ask each person to share how they chose their position and how it feels now that they are there. People may also comment on how the circle looks or feels from their position—on who they are opposite and what that reflects, on whether their position is what and where they expected, and what it feels like to step into the circle and claim a place within it.

4. Casting a Circle

Casting a circle is always a magical act, but casting a circle for your Circle of Eight is particularly so. It involves discovering a different way to cast a circle, which does not rely on anything you have learned in a tradition, read in a book, or been taught about the correct way to do it. It may take your group many times of doing this to feel comfortable with this method, which relies not on memory or a recitation of particular qualities, deities, or even elements, but upon emptying your mind, breathing into your body and the position you hold in the circle, and allowing it to speak through you.

There is a section in the appendix about casting a circle, but on your first meeting it is enough to stand facing outwards from the circle and greet the directions, one by one. If you wish to speak a few words to or from your direction, then do so; otherwise, simply call to the direction by name and ask that it present itself in the circle and in your life.

5. Ritual, Magic, or Process

Having set up your Circle of Eight and cast a circle, now is the time for whatever ritual, magic, or process you have planned. It will probably be a shorter, simpler ceremony than in other meetings, as a lot of your time will have gone into setting up the circle. You may have something already planned or you could do one or more of the following. These activities are also suitable for solo practitioners.

- Celebrate the phase of the moon, conducting a ceremony as appropriate. If it is the new moon, each person can speak about the beginnings currently in their life, and you could each draw a Tarot card or other divinatory card and speak about what that card offers you. If it is on or near a full moon, you can celebrate the richness of your lives, sharing your adventures in work, love, and personal journeys and together make a collage, build an altar, or blend oils into a magical potion. If it is on or near a dark moon, you can spend time silently journeying within, perhaps with a drumbeat and an intention you've chosen. When you emerge, share your journeyings and your glimpses of your deepest selves. For any of these activities, encourage people to also comment on any contribution they feel the direction they are now holding may bring into their lives.

- Spend some time creating music together, using drums, rattles, voice, and any other instruments you have. Teach and share chants you know, or allow your voices to blend and sound in a wordless song. If you wish, you can offer this music into the eight directions, allowing it to change as it shifts around the circle.

- Work with a guided visualization led by one or more people that reflects the time of year you are in. You can use this meditation to conduct spirit journeys out across the land, speaking to the elements and the living creatures who share this geographical space with you, asking them for their wisdom or ways of understanding this piece of land and time of year. Afterwards, share your individual journeys with the others.

6. Conclusion

At the end of your time together, decide when you are meeting again and make plans for that meeting. You may wish to each bring something for the altar, representing your direction, for example. One or more people may take responsibility for that meeting, or each person can bring a piece or an activity to contribute. Discuss how people intend to explore their direction during the intervening time; this may be individual or you might agree to an activity everyone will undertake.

Casting a Circle

This little beach is full of surprises.

The access is down a steep, rocky pathway, but the path is well made, wide and steady. It's more a cove than a beach, shaped in a gentle arc and small, with high rocky headlands at either end. The first time we came here as a group we made a ritual offering, as we often did, out of whatever we found—a small round altar divided into eight segments with markers at each point corresponding to their directions. A seaweed circle with sticks, shells, feathers, and white cuttlefish standing in the different directions. The beach slopes gently to the sea; the waves were breaking a little way out and just sighing up to the sand.

Suddenly the next wave swept in and came right up to us, through our circle; it ate half our offering in one bite. We leapt back, laughing, with half of us wet as the wave curled back to the sea, and we looked out, amazed to see the tide still some distance away and not seeming to encroach on us at all. It was talking to us, interacting; hungry or eager, we couldn't tell. Our offering was swept about over the sand, with parts of it missing and only the westerly curve holding its original form. We started singing to this South-East place that correlates with Imbolc and signals the new, the incoming, the shift in the wind. When another surprise wave swept in, we were ready for it and allowed it to devour the rest of our small offering; we stood around with half of us in and half of us out of the sea and called to the directions and cast our circle. We felt welcomed and kept on our toes.

One time I came here at night. The moon was shining onto the sea; I could see that from the road. I imagined that little beach as a fairytale playground with silver on the waves; I could almost taste it. I started off down the track, through the rainforest part and down the first steps, bottlebrush and rough native grasses until I got to the turn where the track switchbacks to descend towards the beach. There's a clear view from here, and what I saw was nothing I'd thought to expect.

There was no beach at all. It was gone. The waves were right up to the foot of the cliffs; the path, which had always before led to the beach, led that night to a realm of water. If you stepped off the bottom step, it would be straight into the waves. It wasn't a fairyland that night, more a place of mermaids and sea dragons; a shifted universe, the kind you usually only catch a glimpse of in a mirror behind you or when you open an unread book in the middle and an image leaps out at you, which never reads the same way again when you read the book properly from the beginning. Our small beach had been transported under the moonlight, and I didn't go down but marveled, from a height, at its secret self.

To cast a circle is to step into the mysteries, and this little beach teaches that again and again. Casting is interactive, dynamic; it courts the unexpected. In this place I never feel that I am laying a predetermined circle onto passive ground; rather, that I am dancing with the boundaries of sea and land, magic and ordinary. The changeability of this piece of our circle reminds me how—although I might be the one casting and naming things—the nature of the event is not determined by me but by the place itself.

Discovering Directions

When we first set up the Circle of Eight, we stood in our eight places on my vast living room floor, our backs to each other, and faced outwards into the directions. We had our eyes open and called to them, welcoming whatever winds, whatever feelings, and whatever images came to us. I had a sense of the circle stretching out from the room and then wavering, uncertain of how far it extended. After all, if you call the East, East goes on forever. Yet my intent with the Circle of Eight had been to work local magic, relevant to this land we lived on.

The main room of my house was itself a container; the east and west walls nearly sixteen meters or fifty feet apart, the ceiling maybe nine meters or thirty feet above us, the concrete floor resting solid on the earth. Through high windows we saw a gorge, cliffs, trees, and greenery or, at night, spacious sky with stars and the new moon setting in the west. Those were boundaries; yet I had not meant for the circle to be quite so local, not just what we could see from this house. I wanted it to have a sense of geography, relatedness to the whole, much as those

European stone circles had; a sense not just of exactly where they were, but also of the land and people they were a part of.

I could imagine parties of surveyors measuring out distances and sight lines, hammering in small wooden posts that would rot in the rains or be eaten by white ants, but that was nothing like what I yearned for. I longed for that mythic sense of the land relating to us, of understanding the sight lines that already existed, of human magic stepping into and within the magic of the land. Of the landscape revealing itself to our senses, of being able to call not just vaguely *east*, but precisely and exactly East; to an eastern place that was specific and held the outpost of our circle—a place of power; one that recognized us and worked with us.

Our local area is particular in many ways. Geographically part of a vast caldera formed when the mountain exploded twenty-three million years ago, the earth is rich and fertile and the rains heavy enough to create their own small wet season most years. The green pasture cultivated after the forest was felled makes ideal dairy farming country, and dairy farms need roads; unlike other farms that can survive cut off for weeks or months, they need to get the milk out every day. This complex network of roads carving among the hills meant the land was opened up past its logging and dairy history and into the next invasive wave, housing. The reasons our little area is so wonderful to live in and so accessible to settlers and small properties stemmed from its history of volcanic eruption, rainforest, clear-felling, and small-scale dairy farming.

Politically, our shire is distinctive. Large numbers of retreating city dwellers running small businesses from home, seeking alternative lifestyles and spiritualities and a small, friendly community to raise their kids in mean our local government has a strong contingent of the political left and Green. One of the alternative centers of Australia, undisputed in terms of a New Age lifestyle, people arrive here seeking healthier ways to live, inner peace, and active community. Distinct from the city councils to the south, north, and west, our shire has a very particular political, social, and cultural identity.

The borders of the shire made sense as a boundary for our circle, the extent to which its influence would extend. But I didn't just want a line drawn on a map to guide and hold our magic; I wanted actual places, eight distinct markers, like standing stones. Instead of standing stones, or anything like them—anything that had been carted there by humans or told what function it would perform—I wanted to discover places already existing, holding their own magic, and ask if they would extend their briefs to include holding one corner of our eight-cornered circle.

We looked at maps. Water was the first and most obvious thing we saw. East of us was the sea. In fact, the sea was not just east, it was also south-east and north-east. There was a lot of sea. When we looked west on the map we saw all the streams and rivers; the larger area our shire is part of is called the Northern Rivers. There was a lot of fresh water; those rivers are so enormous that, seeing them, I am always astounded we can ever experience drought or water shortages. When we looked at the map of Australia we saw that the Great Artesian Basin lay directly west of us. This vast underground water supply, surely sacred to the continent of Australia, is to my mind the best and most magical sort of water to have in Australia: fresh water hidden and contained under the earth. In this hot, dry land, water has to be held, protected; this whisper of secret water carving its own passages through the land unseen seemed incredibly potent.

There was something else we saw on the map that first time we looked. The extinct volcano that had created this land and still dominated all the landscape around lay to our north-west. It was not strictly inside the boundaries of the shire, yet it had created the shire. The edges of its caldera swept around us; we received its rains now as the land had received its fire earlier, before humans were here. To our north lay the equator and the hot midday sun; it should be the high point of the circle, the place of the most obvious blazing power, and yet somehow it never had been. Without us planning or asking for it—and rather to my perplexedness and slight annoyance—again and again North-West came through more strongly than North whenever we cast a circle and nearly regardless of whoever was calling to the direction. Looking at the map, for the first time we saw why.

Our land was shaped by the energies of this volcano. If you listened to the land, if you called to what you felt and saw and heard, that was what you called to. The volcano—and therefore the North-West—was the origin of our land; it was naturally the orientation of our circle. We came to see it also as a guardian—one not significantly noticed by us before, but that now, within the Circle of Eight, was accorded its rightful place in our understanding of this particular land's magic.

Small Beach

. . . .

Memoir

For years, Ross was part of the Circle of Eight. We discovered the South-East point together; that day on the twisting dirt road it had been us tumbling down the track to discover a perfect beach, the cave, fresh air blowing in. We went back there many times for a half day; swimming and resting and talking. I associated that place with him—not just because we found it together, but also it seemed to represent him—and in some ways it was like him. That sense of surprise, of unreliability, but also the sudden best revealed; of daring and embrace. And I thought of it as holding a reflection of our relationship, of the ways we had been good together: exploring, discovering outposts, and creating new forms.

Before he joined the Circle of Eight I barely knew him, but as soon as he was there he took a strong, dynamic part, not just encouraging and supporting me in whatever I dreamed up but urging me forward and deeper and out to the edges of my visions. He poured focus, enthusiasm, and willingness into everything he was involved with. We worked magic together strongly, immediately, simply. His commitment to this group entranced me, and as the Circle of Eight unfolded we conducted an unsettled but highly charged relationship. Any stability we had came from the circle itself; not long after we broke up he left the Circle of Eight.

When he joined the circle I was still sitting across from my friend, who was opposite me in so many ways. I had loved having her in that position; her laughter and quickness and our familiarity in ritual had made us a strong combination. I could rely on her to match me, to pick up what I left undone, to catch and meet me. The circle had been held with her there; I felt if we stretched our arms out wide, they would meet, energetically, around the sides. Ross was on my left, but when my friend left the circle it seemed obvious that he should move to sit opposite me.

He made the move one night as we were turning the Wheel. We sang our song, left arms stretched into the hub, touching fingertips as we turned, and he moved like a cog within the wheel, in the same direction but faster than us, taking three steps to our one and ducking under people's arms, a speeded-up partial rotation, until he reached his new place. We all stopped, let the singing die away, dropped our arms, and turned to face each other in our new configuration.

As he moved I felt the magnetism of poles shifting through my body. I met his gaze across the circle as a solid thing, holding the two of us as fixed points, about which the rest of the wheel whirled and turned. He had moved from being part of the cross that was shadow to mine—the people who were in the quarters when I was in a cross-quarter or in the cross-quarters when I held a quarter position—and from coming after me in rotation to being directly opposite me. The one I leaned on and pulled away from. The direction he held was the direction I faced; whatever place I sat in was where he gazed.

The South-East place of our circle was a perfect metaphor for our relationship: sudden, dynamic, and filled with change. Perhaps it left us both short of the depth we wanted, a relationship right at the beginning of the cycle. Afterwards he moved completely out of my life, and I found that when he wasn't sitting across from me I hardly knew who he was. He changed everything about himself: his looks and clothes, his interests and activities. Once I saw him in the street and literally didn't recognize him. It made me wonder about that tremendous enthusiasm of his that enabled him to adapt so fully to his surrounds. I wondered what the truth of him was.

Another five, six, seven years passed, and then I heard that he was ill. I had moved away but was visiting; imagining, as I did each time I came back, the Circle of Eight places there as they always have been, not waiting for us exactly but alert along those lines of magic, able to come into play with each other in that particular combination when called upon. Ordinarily I don't think of him much. It seems a little unbelievable that we were ever together; I cannot recognize myself in him at all. And yet I do remember the force of that joined gaze; I do remember being welded into the strength of that line across the circle, and however much he reflected me, it was not solely me but also him, even if his was the power to support and amplify.

I ask for reports of his illness and it sounds very bad, though we are only middle-aged. I have had no contact with him for years, but I get up early one day and go to that small beach. The pot-holed road is worse under the wheels of the hire car, with wide cracked and treacherous gutters running across it, forcing the car to one or other side of the hairpin bends. The beach seems to get more distant as the road unfurls and unfurls; surely it wasn't this far? But eventually it is there, only one car pulled over, and I park and walk down. There's a couple sun-bathing and surfing down one end of the beach. At one time they might have been us.

I felt quite removed from everyday life and as if I could be in any time, any year in my history or even the history of this beach. As if I had stepped out of my own concerns to come here, to build a ritual and offer what I can to the man I found this place with. I draw an eight-segmented circle in the sand, something I have done most times I've come here. I walk about the beach collecting; I want only beautiful things. A feather the salt water hadn't got to yet; some fragments of rock from where the cliff is dissolving into the sea; a few shells; those seed pods that wash up from who-knows-where, and the ubiquitous cuttlefish, in this case small, perfect, white ones. I place them in my circle in various directions, and I smooth the sand within the spokes and around the edge. I add what I've brought: a piece of fruit and some pretty leaves I picked up on the path down.

I sit beside this small circle for a long time, thinking about the strangeness of relationships that come and go, like the tides washing in and out, and how the beach changes under them, but not really; the essential person stays the same. He is still the same person who came here with me that day years ago; I am still the same person. Whereas before I had not really been able to contemplate his death—my mind glancing off that possibility, sheering away in refusal and not knowing and not understanding—here it seems that any of our deaths are simple, timeless, and a return into the elements.

In that moment I know how to give him into the South-East, yes; as I had not been willing to give him over, even in my mind, to hospitals and pain and deterioration. Here I will be able to set him free onto the waves, send him into the wind; here I can settle him into the cave and rocks, the bones of this place. I stand up and turn to face each of the directions, calling to them strongly through the wind and emptiness. Into the South, the grounding of everything; the South-East and this beach where I stand; to the East with its winds of freedom; the North-East with that tidal flux of sex, life, and death; to the North with the height from which to see clearly; the North-West that birthed all of us from churning chaos and red lava; West that we long for, promising calm and rest; and the South-West, entrance to the mysteries. I call to Above and the stars that birthed us; to Below and the earth we hold sacred, that holds us sacred.

I cast the circle.

I want to send him my blessing; not just *my* blessing, the blessing of the circle. From this place it comes with a particular flavor, almost as if it is birth I am heralding here rather than death. I understand people putting their dead on boats or rafts and sending them out to sea; I understand them burning the bodies on pyres. To gift the loved one to the endless power of the elements, to see their life not just lost but consumed, taken into the primitive realms of earth and water, fire and air—to gift what remains of them to this—yes, I can feel it.

I start singing, dredging the song up out of memory. It's a song another friend wrote and shared with me in ritual. Another man who stands opposite me in circle, holding my gaze and working magic, and the incoming waves blur their distinctions of age and time and place. I sing of how we are brothers and sisters to each other, how we are all lovers, all family. The song comes back to me as I sing it, the tune prompting the words, and once I have begun singing I fall deeper and deeper into the spell of the song. I don't want to stop singing; it's as if I have just now found the thread between him and me, the thread that holds us both to the wheel, to the same place, the place of the living, and so I keep singing. I am singing to him, not as he was then or as he is now, but to the entire tide of his life, the spell of him, the story of his living and dying, and my singing is a little weaving of the places we have met and of the truth of him.

I sing the song for maybe half an hour and its words begin to shape not just the cadences of my breathing and thought, but my whole understanding of patterns and how this little beach is tied up with the lifelines of the people who've woven their magic through here, whether it be the Circle of Eight, the Aboriginal people, the dolphins and seahawks, or the couple who now lie sleeping on their towels. When the song finally stops it is not because I thought to end it or grew tired of it; its words had become whole worlds of fascination for me but because all of itself it whispers to a close. Perhaps death is like that. Still the words circle round and round in my head, and I believe they are somewhere nearby, piercing through the layers of time and place like ripples moving out from this place, this beginning place.

I leave the altar there, on the beach, as a gift.

Mapping Our Geographic Circle

As soon as we addressed ourselves to the concept of a geographic Circle of Eight, three of our directions were obvious: such dramatic landmarks in our small world that any map must feature them. There was the North-West, where the ex-volcano lay; North-East, where the river mouth met the sea; and the East point, Cape Byron.

A thin, rocky point balancing out into the ocean, this tip of land is not just the easternmost part of Byron Shire, but the easternmost point of the whole of Australia. It's famous for whale watching and, earlier in its history, for whale hunting and slaughtering; because it sticks out to sea farther than the rest of the coast, whales pass by comparatively closely. It's easy to see dolphins from there; they surf on the east in the swells coming in to meet the rocky cliff face. Beaches on either side of the point are sweeping expanses, and along the low, rocky point itself fishermen sometimes balance, hoping the waves won't knock them over. The lighthouse perches above, overseeing that whole expanse of land and water: a beacon, a tourist destination, and a continuous reminder of the concept of east, as it brings light in relentlessly.

Standing on the point—either up high near the lighthouse or down on the rocks near the fishermen—air sweeps across the sea to meet you. Fresh air, absolutely fresh. There's no land to the east until South America—7,000 miles away on the other side of the South Pacific Ocean. This clean, bright air is, for me, indicative of the East of our circle; lungfuls of the stuff to sing and speak and breathe, air like the first breath the land takes upon waking.

Cape Byron is in a state conservation area adjoining Arakwal National Park, and you can get there easily walking east from Byron Bay's Main Beach or by parking nearby and walking along a boardwalk through rainforest or by paying to park at the lighthouse. This accessibility made something really obvious to me: I didn't want parts of the Circle of Eight to be on private land, shut away or only available when someone decided we could go there. I added it as a criteria for all the other locations we had yet to find: that they must be on or near the borders of the shire or with reference to the shire; they must agree to hold these points, to be one of the outward markers of our circle; and they must be on public land.

This agreement from a place—a magical agreement, a contract between us and the place—was sometimes easy to determine and sometimes not. At Cape Byron I felt a broad delight, a bright expansiveness of all the meanings this place already held for so many and had for so long, certainly including its traditional owners. It was almost as if, with the obviousness of its rocky point pinning the land into the sea, the cape couldn't help but hold our eastern point for us; it was already doing so and must do so, and in its airy generosity it accepted most things asked of it: weddings and whale watchers, photographs and tours; certainly our request was one among many, not unimportant but unremarkable.

Our North-West mountain was different. It also is on public land, part of another national park overseen by the New South Wales National Parks and Wildlife Service, but the Aboriginal people, who are its traditional custodians, have a standing request that the mountain, and especially the peak itself, not be climbed. Every year about sixty thousand people ignore this request and clamber to the top of the incline, the last part of which is practically vertical, up ladders and chains, for the view and the achievement of it. But obviously we could not have the top of the mountain as our ritual point, through respect and because we were seeking a willingness from the eight places, the very reverse of the attitude it takes to go around plonking one's structures in places you've been requested not to go.

Where the climb starts, however—and this is not exactly at the base of the mountain but at the end of the road, which has already wound up a long way from sea level—there is a small rainforest trail that does not scale the mountain but crosses a creek and wanders a little way among the tall trees of the forest. We understood that this place was acceptable to the current guardians to visit and walk in, and so we went and sat among the trees and asked. It feels small to be a human there, on the slope of a retired volcano, the highest peak in the area and in among tall, straight eucalypts. We felt as if we were just another type of forest animal moving around the undergrowth; and on those terms we had our answer. If we just came and sat quietly, if we did not disturb or disrupt or seek to change or conquer, then our magic would be folded into the seams of that place as gently as all the other times had been—times of hot lava and cooling crust, times of raw earth, of growing and undisturbed forest, the time now of a managed park and all the diversity of life that lived there.

The North-East was the other point that looked obvious: the heads, where the river meets the sea. This direction is aligned with our Beltaine, and the wonderful imagery of a tidal river flowing out through the heads into the sea, then to turn and draw the sea up between banks of the land, felt potently sexual. Watching boats come down the river for fishing or pleasure, you see them fighting through the heads to get out to sea, tossed around by the churning in-and-out of the water at that point, that salt-meeting-fresh crash and thrust.

The south head of this place is close by the little town, next to the most peopled beach, and it is constantly thronged by walkers, swimmers, and sightseers. There are parks on that bank of the river with picnic tables, barbeques, and children's play equipment, and every so often a market, festival, or fair. You can buy a cappuccino or fish and chips, rent a canoe, or wade in the river's shallows. The north head is a bit of a drive along a slow dirt road with the canal on the inland side and on the other side a ribbon of coastal bush, hiding the nearby—and nearly deserted—beach. People go there to fish, and surfers visit when the waves are right. There's a small river beach tucked away from the seaside through the bush that sometimes has quiet picnickers, families with children, or a small group, but you can't buy a cappuccino and there's no sense of the hum and social life of the opposite bank, even though it's all there, only just across the water.

It was here we felt there was space for our circle to be held, at the beginning of the long beach that stretches north away from the breakwaters; it's an empty, open place. We had often come here to greet the Winter Solstice sunrise; it already had layers of our rituals on it. I felt that it knew us. The other side of the river was frantic with activity and obviously the popular, successful side; this side, then, would be magical. This clean sweep of beach would welcome our rituals, dropping them into its emptiness and openness as it did seagulls and surfers and the echidnas that sometimes wandered out of the bush onto its expanse.

That was three points; we needed five more. Returning to the map, we looked to the west. Far, far west of us lay the Great Artesian Basin, but we needed something much closer than that—one of the rivers or creeks, I thought; something with water. Even though the sea lay all to the east of us, I was wedded to the idea of honoring water in the west; perhaps simply because that was my familiarity, my understanding, of the balance of a circle. If you drew a straight line—we placed a ruler on the map—due west of Cape Byron lay a huge, human-made dam. It was a water catchment for a neighboring shire, but the creeks and rivers that fed it ran through our shire. Those creeks were beautiful in themselves—we had all been there on hot summer days—but they were mostly quite inaccessible, and there was no clear ground beside them to do rituals or bring groups of people.

When we went to the dam, it was perfect. Even the long drive seemed to fit; in Celtic mythology, the west is an impossibly distant location, lying somewhere over the seas and through the mists and barely ever attainable, even in a story. The west holds the setting sun, journeys, and the beckoning of dreams and the impossible; to have to drive a long way for it was appropriate. And once we were there, the place itself won us over. It has been there long enough—built sixty years ago now—that it appears natural. It sits gently in the land.

More than a dam, it is a huge lake with water lilies, black swans, and flocks of other birds. Forest comes right down on the far edge of it. It has sculpted lawns near the car park, and when you walk across the causeway there's a parklike section with glades and patches of bush, all native Australian, and the water itself is pristine; no boats, swimming, or fishing are allowed because it's destined to become drinking water. I loved it. When we made a little offering of an altar in the shape of our eight-segmented circle, the place felt wide open, as if it had always known welcoming us would be part of its job. And that no one could actually go on or into this water fascinated me: sacred water, held at a distance from human beings. Sanctified.

For the South-East position, we knew it had to be on the coast. All three of the eastern positions of our circle are held on the coast, this long waving border of our shire where much of the industry, population, and attraction centers on the sea and its beaches. Ross and I had driven south, along the back beach dirt road, and pulled off the road at every beach we came to. We were looking for a particular energy, that half-emergence of Imbolc, the idea of something in the process of becoming. All the major beaches seemed too obvious for that, however beautiful they were.

The first beach off that back road had its small pull-over jammed with cars; surfers. We didn't even stop. The next beach had potential; we parked and walked down, but it didn't sing to us, didn't call out to be a part of our magic. We drove on. You have to go slowly on the sharply twisting, dusty, and deeply ridged track. At the next beach we were higher up on the road and there weren't any cars in the pull-over. When we got out of the car, we could see a vista of sea over the tops of the squat coastal trees before we went down the pathway. Entering that pathway is like stepping into a story that opens suddenly through a painting or a door in a wall that wasn't there before. My ears felt pricked up; the air was alive.

We took the turn in the path—the one where the beach below is dramatically revealed—and it was as if it had prepared for our arrival. A crescent of sand, rocky cliffs at either end, waves rolling neatly in. We went down, excited, and raced about as if discovering a new land. The cliffs at the north end provided some shade on the firm-packed sand. At the south end were two small caves: one inaccessible due to powerful waves breaking into the mouth of it and rocky protrusions through the sand all around, and the other a small, cone-shaped retreat, like a dragon's cave—just a small dragon.

It was beautiful, and it was ours; no one else was there. We tried to judge the angle we were facing and thought you could probably see the sunrise from the beach, even on its southernmost rise. We went in the water; it was a playful beach, splashing and curving in waves. We knew we had found our South-East.

Unlike the simplicity of that, both the North and South involved a lot of discussion and several excursions. For the South we had the idea it should be rainforest, and we visited a few patches of rainforest in a southerly direction but couldn't settle on any of them. The one that had looked most promising on the map was literally packed with tourists on a small circular walk that was mosquito-filled and felt as if you couldn't stop for a minute. It was not unfriendly exactly, but busy with other things, and it didn't feel like there was any space for our magic. When I finally remembered the waterfall that descended into a round pool, some of us set off to find it; it had been many years since I had been there.

The roads came back to me as I traveled down them, and we parked in a small cul-de-sac down a dead end. Then we started wandering along paths, hunting for the falls. We heard them before we saw them and made our way through the weeds to peer onto the stream, following along the edge as it became rockier until we were looking down to a steep-sided paradise. A round pool with two streams of water falling straight down, fringed by trees and embraced by cliffs. We climbed through a fence and walked along; I remembered there would be a way down eventually, even though the stream was now hidden from us.

We clambered down the path with some difficulty, as the children had brought their swimming boards and we had packed a picnic, as well as towels and various pieces of clothing. Then we started traipsing back in the direction we had come, but now on a level with the water. The waterfall arcs out a little from the cliff, and behind it is a cave. The pool itself is round and the whole place seems guarded, safely held by those rock walls. It's not what I had thought of when I imagined the South—I had thought of deep forest and here instead was a pool and waterfall—but the circularity of it, the cave, and the surrounding bush and cliffs were enough to convince me, not to mention how it welcomed us, embracing us into the circle it made with the rock and trees and pool.

The North caused us more problems. We felt it should be somewhere high, possibly the highest place in the shire, especially because our North-West point was over a thousand meters high. Nothing could compete with that, but of course if it were closer to us it would look high. There was an obvious peak in the north of the shire: a gorgeous, iconic cone. It was prominent in the local landscape, admired from every direction, and looked on as a locator for working out where you were. But it lay on private land, and the walk there was about half an hour. I thought it was not enough to have a beautiful North; it also had to be accessible.

The lookout in the North was perhaps the last point we settled on. We had visited it many times in various combinations to debate its worth; it was unpopular because it was not high enough. It won out in the end because we didn't find anything better and also because it had sweeping views: from there we could see most of the shire and nearly all the other points of our circle. Its view of the old volcano was spectacular, clear and adulatory. It didn't compete, it flattered. It also felt to us delighted—even excited—to be a part of our circle. After all, it was dedicated to community use, set aside from the housing development all around it. It was local and accessible, friendly and open, and we finally decided that was enough to hold this point of our circle.

The place I had the biggest expectations of was the South-West, our Samhain position. I wanted it to hold mystery. We looked at maps, we drove around back roads, we debated. Finally I remembered an Aboriginal ceremonial site, a bora ring, which I had been to many years ago. It did lie to the south-west of us. It was well out of our shire, but I thought it was worth a trip if we could find it—and if we could establish whether this place, dedicated to a magic and tradition other than ours and far older, was available at all to be a part of our circle.

I found it quite easily on a map, and we went out there as a group one weekend afternoon. We drove and drove—it felt like a long way—but of course Samhain, the night of spirits, with its doorway into the spirit realms, *is* a long way—a long way into the depths, a long reach from the rest of the festivals. Driving along one of those country roads that carves through from one place to another, we'd rounded a bend and driven straight past it; we saw the sign flash by. We had to stop, turn around, and go back more cautiously. I liked already that its entry was easy to miss.

When we pulled over into the rutted driveway, we saw an extraordinary thing. I had not remembered it consciously. There was a cemetery—a Christian cemetery—that lay between the road and the bora ring; you had to drive or walk along a rough track with graves to either side. To get to the bora ring, the place we hoped would hold the point for our place of mystery, you had to pass through the land of the dead. Literally.

We were silenced by it and silenced still when we arrived there. A bora ring is a ceremonial place, not that obvious to the naked eye. This one is a patch of ground with a slight depression in a circle and a deeper round depression in the center. There's a stand of young gum trees to the north and a low log fence carefully demarking the bora ring itself, not closed in but with an entryway outlined. This entry was jammed into the corner of the nearby paddock wire fence line, not near the direction we approached from. The sign we stood in front of marked it as a bora ring, stating that the entryway lay in the south-west and that a further bora ring lay to the south-west of this one, in the neighboring paddock.

The south-west, the south-west, the south-west. We had come look-ing for that and found it written down for us, in the land and on the engraved plate. We did not go inside the bora ring but walked around it. These places are sacred land and we believed this one was dedicated to men's gatherings, so we only stood at the edges. The bora ring sat on top of a ridge line, the highest one around. It had distant views beyond the trees, of paddocks and roads; it gazed back towards our shire, towards the rest of our circle, and it seemed an outpost, a far-flung ref-erence to a memory of the time when all the land was known as sacred and of the mysteries.

I visited many times, and each time I sat on the land, wondering what it would mean to hold this place as part of our circle, I felt what I can only describe as a gentle amusement—the kind of attention you might give to a toddler when you are engaged in other things. I felt that we were leaves dropped to the ground to blow away or fall to dust; a slight, passing tremor across this place that held vast time in its know-ing. Yes, it was open to us, as it was to the kookaburras in the trees or to the breeze that blew through or the sightseers who regularly visited—getting out of their cars but leaving the music blaring, asking each other *Is this it? Is this it? What are we looking at?* before leaving, usually within five minutes. Even the way the cemetery guarded its doorstep seemed to allow our presence in the way they lay next to each other, calmly and alone on this hill top; companionable, as if one piece of sacred ground recognized another.

I felt the bora ring, or the land surrounding it, accepted us but not as any great thing. We were a few seconds of its history. It could easily—almost without noticing—fulfill what we asked of it, and perhaps that brought a glint of pleasure to it, a passing nod to its own magic. That old magic, silent maybe in recent years—that period of rest was also nothing much: to this place a short afternoon sleep, maybe, in the tens of thousands of years of Aboriginal history. Of all our places in our Circle of Eight, this relationship was the most delicate. It is still signifi-cant and known to local Aboriginal people, and so we sought only to rest at the edges of it, only to speak to and recognize it.

Our final completion of our Circle of Eight was the center. I had wanted a hub, a place where the spokes joined and the magic flowed in and out. We went back to the map. In what is very nearly the center of the shire, there is, amazingly, a labyrinth. It's not on public land, but it is open to the public. It lies in beautiful sculptured gardens. There was no debate about there being a better center to be found; how could you do better than a labyrinth? I liked that there were others there, engaged in their own rituals: seated next to it in meditation, walking solemnly along its paths, or gazing in wonder at it and its walkers. I liked how children were part of it, dashing madly round and round, skipping over inconvenient places and shouting when they got to the center. The very image of a labyrinth—entering more and more fully through layers into the center of a circle—was a wonderful image for the center of our own circle, and when we did ritual there it felt like the admiration was mutual; that it welcomed us and our piece of focused ritual amongst its more general chaos.

So with the labyrinth at the center, we had our entire geographic circle: the waterfall in the South, the small beach in the South-East, the cape in the East, the tidal-river-meeting-sea in the North-East, the lookout in the North, the mountain to the North-West, the lake in the West, and the bora ring in the South-West. Standing together in my living room suddenly the walls fell away—our borders reached out magically and imaginally and we felt the expanse of it; the energies from each of those directions flowed into us and our ritual. We didn't just call to those places, we felt them as energetic anchors in the landscape but also as flavors, present to inform, support, and guide us as we worked.

How to Cast a
Geographic Circle of Eight

The emphasis in the Circle of Eight is on locality, wherever you happen to be. An understanding of your particular circle and its greater structure is gathered through a combination of several things. There's the experiences and understandings wrought by your developing relationship with local conditions; the internal understandings reached by holding each direction; and the external aspects of the festivals, the elements, and the directions themselves, including places you associate with the directions.

These places do not necessarily appear overnight. It may take you six months to a year to locate, choose, and then establish relationships with places connected with your Circle of Eight. When we began this work we had just a couple of places we knew had to be a part of it. We were close to—and felt intimately connected to—the easternmost point of Australia, a place iconic to our whole area and recognized worldwide. The mountain to our north-west not only dominates the landscape visually but is also the source, in its volcanic era, of our rich soil, the caldera of our valleys and hills.

The whole concept of "north" or "a place to the north" is a vague one; after all, how far north? There are, presumably, hundreds of places to the north. Criteria and guidelines are excellent; as are some good maps, possibly survey or topographical maps as well as the more standard variety. The criteria for each Circle of Eight will be different. You might want places that are all within walking or biking distance; you might be searching for relatively private places or for places very obviously associated with themes of their direction, such as a good place to view the sunrise for the east.

Our starting criteria were that the places should be on public land and accessible; that they should be either part of, on the borders of, or referential to our shire; and that they must feel responsive to our ritual and willing to hold a place in our Circle of Eight. Of those three criteria the only one we stuck to rigorously and absolutely was the final one, having made an exception for the labyrinth being on private land and an exception for the bora ring's distance from the shire. We felt each of our eventual nine places wanted to work with us and be part of our circle and were, in some way, already a part of it; that they had just been waiting for us to find them.

How to Set Up a Geographic Circle of Eight

These steps may take weeks or months to complete. I have placed them in a particular order, but you might need or choose to change this to make the process work for you. All are suggestions only.

1. Discussion and Brainstorming

As a group, talk about how your geographic Circle of Eight might look. Cover the following discussion points:

- Are there any general or essential criteria that should apply to these places? (For example: access, distance, landmark features, relationship to each other.)

- Are there any specific criteria that ideally will apply to particular places, such as elemental correspondences or types of energies?
- How do people imagine the whole circle looking and feeling? Does it need to look circular when placed on a map?

2. Short-Listing Possible Places

Using maps and memory, compile lists of possible places for the directions of your Circle of Eight. Sometimes you can only target an area on a map, not knowing its details, and have to go there physically to explore.

3. Visit Your Potential Places

Start visiting your places. We went out singly and in pairs, looking for places and reporting back when we thought we had a possibility. We didn't definitively choose any place until we had been there as a group, done a ritual there, and felt, all together, that it was a place that belonged in our Circle of Eight. Even the two places that seemed already chosen for us we visited as a group and did questioning rituals to see if the places would accept us and the role we had planned for them.

4. Further Research

When determining if a particular place should be part of your Circle of Eight:

- Explore the general area, preferably on foot. Notice different parts of this place or nearby that you might not have known about before.
- Spend several hours there and let a sense of the place sink into you. Is it different than the initial impression you receive? Does it seem welcoming to you? How comfortable are you there? What moods does it evoke? Is it possible to do ritual there? What type of activities does this place invite? Are they activities that add something to your sense of what happens in that direction?

- Visit the place at several different times of day and possibly in different seasons. Continue gathering your impressions. Do you sense a relationship developing between you and the place?

- Bring or make an offering. This could be a small altar you construct on the site with what you find there, such as shells or colored leaves, stones or flowers, or something that you bring with you, such as water, flowers, or another environmentally appropriate offering.

- Do a ritual there. This could be alone or with any number of you. Keep the initial ritual very simple. Cast a circle, then speak to the place of your intentions and wishes. Spend some time in silence—perhaps twenty minutes—while you open your thoughts and feelings deeply to the place, then share the impressions you each receive. If you are alone, write or draw them. If you feel the place has been generally receptive, you might like to sing or do some other simple activity. Then release your circle, thanking the place for whatever answer you have felt from it.

5. Choosing Places

Some questions to ask when determining if a particular place is part of your Circle of Eight:

- Does the place fit or creatively challenge your initial criteria? For example, we had always thought our South would be an earthy forest, but it turned out to be a pool with a waterfall. Held within rock walls, trees all round, and with a cave, it still felt close to the essence of south, even though it was different than how we had pictured it.

- When you are there, what is the mood of the place? Does this mood fit with your feelings of this direction?

- What is the activity level of the place? Will you be able to spend time there at different times of the day, week, or year? Will you be able to do ritual there, either alone or in a group? There was one place I liked on a map, but when we got there it was in constant, ceaseless activity. We could never have done ritual there quietly or uninterrupted.

- When placed on a map with your other places, does it roughly fit into your circle?
- How does it relate to the places on either side of it and the place of its opposite direction?

Elements

Standing at the edge of the cape, the wind blows straight up the cliffs from the sea. The air is fresh; it's a long, long way until land in that direction. I think of that wind blowing across the ocean's surface, across the vast emptiness of the globe until it reaches landfall, which in this moment includes me, standing here. Once I flew in a hang glider, a tandem flight over these cliffs at the edge of sea-and-land, gliding down onto the long beach south of the point. Up there it is silent; that's the most surprising thing. We were moving with the wind, utterly and not against it, so there's no sound of rushing air; we're part of the planet's breath. We climbed and turned into the updrafts, and that soaring, venturing into air as if it were stairs beneath our feet, as if we were birds, was dizzying. This is the air of the East.

From this point you can watch the full moon rising out of the sea. If you turn and look west you will see the sun setting onto the land, sinking behind hills. Silver light can wash you from one direction, gold from the other. It's a place of passion; rocks piercing out into the sea, waves smashing up against them; I've had moonlit trysts here, and I've made promises of kisses and vows and I've stood here at midday and felt the sun sear me even as the breeze and sea did their best to offer coolness. There is fire—gold and silver—in the East.

Dolphins play in the surf below the cliffs, and there's a tiny beach tucked in north of the point. So many rituals I have been part of there; by myself, with children, with lovers, friends, and women's groups. We've swum naked in the night; we've built circles marked out in stone with the smooth rocks that lie piled up on the beach; we've crafted a sea-diving mermaid from sand and shells; I've sat on the cliff holding the moon in one hand and the sun in the other. Once I stood on the beach with my four-year-old son and two dolphins cavorted in front of us—so close it seemed we could wade out and touch them in their paired leaping and passing, their bodies wholly out of the water again and again. I had to physically restrain him from rushing out to them. Water resides in the East.

It's the limits of land, the easternmost point of the continent, and it's rocky, as many of these end-points are. I offered my wedding garland to the sea here, leaning out over the edge of the earth. Even though the boundaries are so sharply drawn between land and sea, it seems a place where one could be mistaken for the other—where we could venture off along the spike of the point and just keep going. Once I saw the moonlight begin a silver road far out to sea, an impossible path, and then as the moon rose further the path shimmered closer and closer to me, where I stood on the stretch of rock, waves near my feet. The moon rose higher, and the path—promising adventure, the otherworld, the place beyond fairy tales—widened and grew until I, not having taken a step, was standing on it. It came for me swiftly, embraced me, and I laughed, already on the path and tempted to take that next step.

Local Elements

In Australia, as in many other parts of the world, the elements are up for constant questioning.

For a start, they're nothing like how they are described in European Pagan and Wiccan books. Fire is not a warm, friendly thing that can be merrily celebrated at the Summer Solstice; during that time we're in a period of total fire bans with the very real threat of bushfire and the constant presence of drought. In a fire ban, no naked or enclosed flame is allowed outdoors for any reason, with large fines and prison sentences attached. The burning sun through our ozone-deprived skies threatens dehydration, skin cancer, and heat exhaustion. It dries up creeks and rivers, burns vegetation, and makes outside an unpleasant place to be over much of the country throughout much of the summer.

Water is another element substantially different from how it is often described. We have the crashing beauty and grandeur of the oceans surrounding us, but pure water—water for drinking and bathing, irrigating crops and watering livestock—is precious, hoarded, bought and fought over. Excess freely running, clean natural water exists only in small pockets of our country; water for the fish and rivers, water that hasn't been polluted by stock or the runoff from fertilized crops and that hasn't been siphoned away by all the upriver farms until nothing is left for the river itself but a muddy trickle.

Sometimes referred to as the oldest continent, the earth in Australia is thin. It's impoverished in minerals compared to other continents because of erosion and also a lack of any geologically recent volcanic or tectonic activity, both of which bring rock and minerals up from deep below the earth's surface. One ritual practice often recommended is mixing salt into water to bless, purify, or to help create sacred space, salt representing the essence or purity of earth that dissolves in water. In Australia, salinity is one of our foremost ecological problems. This is where groundwater levels, which have been raised through agricultural irrigation, contain high concentrations of salts that were previously part of the soil. These higher and now overly salty groundwaters then poison the land and whatever's growing on it.

Mixing salt into water amounts to magical pollution here, and sprinkling it on the ground would be desecration. I even have a problem with pouring it down the drain; surely magical actions are symbolic ones, so whatever we mix into our water to create blessings with shouldn't be salt. Scrunched-up gum leaves from the most iconic of Australian trees release some of their oil into water; I've used those. A small amount of soil from a special place mixed into the water; I've used that. Or—swapping the proportions of water and earth—a small amount of water mixed into earth, creating mud or clay; I've used that for blessings and cleansings.

Air. We have that in common with the rest of the world; we all breathe the same air. In Australia we have a variety of airs. We have thick, humid air of the rainforests and swamps; this is air that's more like breathing water and which suspends insects in it in plague proportions. We have scorched-dry desert air, the type that dries out the inside of your mouth and leaves your eyes and skin coated in a thin layer of dust; air that seems so thin sometimes it's surprising there's enough of it to keep breathing. We have air that's fan-forced by forest fires; the air of cyclones, whipped into destructive whirls that eat up whatever's in front of them; as well as the fresh air off the ocean.

Compared with the gentle descriptions in many books, our elements seem ferocious in their raw form and absolutely indifferent to human survival or wishes—as destructive as they are beneficial. We don't take them for granted. We don't call on fire without specifying exactly what fire we're talking about: where and how big and how much. When we call on water or earth, we also tend to specify location, nature, amount. Calling elements into our circles is a matter of careful judgment, respect, and never making assumptions. If we call on the rains to end a drought, we're as likely to get a flood as anything. The elements are most often extreme, and their relationship to our magic has to be weighed, negotiated, and measured.

Aether, or spirit, often called the fifth element, is different in these surroundings, too. The sum of all the elements added together—the center point of the circle, where they meet and blend, contained and emerging—surely this fifth element is primarily responsive to the makeup of the other four. Aether therefore speaks not just of the insubstantial, as its name implies, but also of the very essence of the land in which it dwells. It brings the essence of All into a particular locality and time: *this* circle that's being cast in *this* place.

The nature of the elements is not the only complication we experience in Australia, a complication that is shared with other places of extreme weather (or weather different to the UK, where this generic Celtic-based Paganism emerges from), including much of the United States, Northern Europe, and the tropics. We also have a hemispheric complication; the sun and moon move through a different part of the sky and in a different direction. Widdershins is a word that means "against the sun" (turning in the opposite direction to that of the sun as it moves through the sky), but it has come to be understood generally as meaning "anticlockwise," as in the Northern Hemisphere the sun moves through the sky in a clockwise direction. Widdershins magic is variously mentioned as being magic for undoing, negative magic, or black magic. Our widdershins is exactly opposite from what's generally understood by that term; to move backwards around our circles is to move clockwise.

It doesn't stop there. In Celtic-influenced practices, the assignment of elements to directions is also influenced by this movement of the sun across the sky. Thus the element of fire is placed in the south: the place of greatest heat and the highest part of the sky the sun reaches, as well as the direction of the equator. The element of earth is placed opposite it, in the north: the place of least heat, the part of the sky that remains unvisited by the sun, and the direction of the North Pole and the Arctic. Air is placed in the east, along with the sunrise and the new breath of each day, and the element of water is in the west, accompanying the idea of the sun sinking into the ocean at evening.

Placing fire in the south of our circles seems like a non sequitur. That's not where the heat comes from, and it's not the part of the sky that the sun or the full moon swing through. But there's more. Having had to question so much of what is written and taught just to make sense of where we find ourselves, Australians generally keep asking questions. People living on the east coast of Australia ask why they shouldn't call water into the east, and, while they're at it, what about calling earth into the west, where all the land of this continent lies, stretching away from them? So that's what some of them do. Casting circles recently in mountainous rainforest, we entirely discarded the notion of calling elements into directions, instead calling them all from and into the center. We called to earth in the ring of mountains all around us; to water in the clouds that dwelt in the valley; to fire that lay deep beneath our feet in the sleeping, ancient volcano; and to air in the winds that blew through the trees.

The elements are everywhere, of course. Air does not keep to one quarter of the circle; fire lives in the heart of the planet, over our heads in the sky, and anywhere we light a candle. Earth and water are what our bodies are composed of, what we consume in food and drink; we cannot move a step away from earth or go more than a very short while without water. We are bound to these elements, composed of them and reliant on them, and we are acknowledging this wherever and however we call to them in a circle. But beyond that, their characters do change from place to place, and in a Circle of Eight the exploration of the elements and their nature, both general and local, plays a part and feeds through into our magics.

The Cape

. . . .

Memoir

It was early evening, still light as we clustered at the foot of the wooden walkway. Women chatting and laughing and greeting each other, about ten of us ready to walk through to the little beach for our ritual. Up the stairs, on the walkway, two young women stopped, turned around, and watched us. They waited as we started climbing, and when we reached them they said hello. *Where are you going?* they wanted to know. *Can we come, as well?*

A women's ritual, we said; *a Goddess ritual down at the beach. Yes, you can come; why not?* They were bright and excited, reflecting our own energy; it was as if we had drawn them to us.

We walked through the trees above the coastal scrub and round the point, then down to the tiny and, at this hour, deserted beach—the one that's just the right size for holding a ritual. It nestles beside the point, huddled in next to Cape Byron. This group met every week, and always one or two women volunteered to lead the next meeting. It was different all the time, but this week we had dedicated to the Maiden, and just by finding these two young women it was magical already.

We got to the beach and cast a circle. We were an informal lot; whoever happened to be standing in that direction called to it, whatever way they liked. We decided to sculpt a mermaid in the wet sand near the sea's edge. We made her diving seawards, arms stretched above her to call the waves in, tail S-bended on the sand behind her. I marked out the scales with a twig, pressing the lines in, while others worked on her hair, her breasts and body, the fins at the end of her tail. She was astoundingly beautiful, and it was easy to believe she would come to life once we had left and swim off oceanwards, into the east.

We sat in a circle then and talked about maidenhood, how it had been to be a girl growing up and about the parts of us that were still maidens, though many of us were mothers and some felt they were crones by now. We went around the circle and each woman told a story of her first bleeding. Two main stories were repeated, again and again.

Some of us told a story of shame and confusion. Our mothers had never told us—we didn't know what had happened—it happened to us at school or when we were wearing a pretty dress at a party—we didn't know what it was. We thought we were sick, injured, or even dying. Some of us were too ashamed to tell anyone. Some of us were laughed at, teased by other girls, or told the bleeding was dirty, nasty, and smelly; something we would have to hide and pretend never happened. We didn't understand, though we were told it meant we would have to stop playing with boys and be more careful now; we couldn't climb trees or run round or wrestle. Some of us hated this sign that we had become women.

Others spoke a story of clinical information. We had been told what would happen by our mothers or at school. We knew about reproduction, the menstrual cycle; we knew all women had it, and it didn't mean anything special. We were told it was easy to deal with, a natural part of being a woman, and no reason to skip games or activities. No big deal. No one told us about the cramps or the tears. We'd seen diagrams, been given pads beforehand. We knew what to do with them, what to do with the blood; we just didn't know what to do with our feelings. No one had mentioned there would be feelings.

A slow depression started to build; the weight of coming into womanhood through this bleeding process that now we regarded as sacred, the source of life, but at the time had been an awkwardness, shame, fear, pain, struggle, rage, confusion. The night darkened. Finally one of the young women we'd picked up on the path spoke.

She'd lived part of her growing up somewhere utterly different, on a small island in the Pacific, and her family was still there when she started bleeding. The native women had come for her. They had bathed her and dressed her hair, they had given her flowers to wear and danced, all together, and made a fuss of her, welcomed her among them. She'd felt special and alive and as if something miraculous was happening; she'd been loved and held and told stories. Ever afterwards she remembered it, that special feeling that was part of being a woman.

We were silenced. I thought maybe that story was why we had met these women on the path, invited them to come along. This story of difference. It changed the energy. Some of us were mothers of daughters, and we spoke with reinspired voices about ceremonies, how to acknowledge and honor them when they started to bleed. How can we bring some of that sacredness into our modern lives; how can we let the girls feel at home with their bodies and their bleeding instead of attaching the general social shame and disgust? How can we get through their resistance to offer them something of the sacred?

Then we turned to each other, to the women either side of us in the circle, and offered them blessings. *I bless your bleeding, I bless your blood, I bless your sacred women's body.* These quiet moments in the near dark went some way towards meeting our envy around that experience we didn't have, our longing to be recognized and held and honored just for this, for being women. For our maiden's journey, which when we took it was confused and hidden and dismissed.

Afterwards some of us went swimming. We took our clothes off and followed the direction of our diving mermaid into the waves. The water is silky and cool. It's a sheltered little beach, and the water comes in gentle swells rather than breakers. The soft, dark air meets the water;

being a mermaid at night would be wonderful with the whole wide ocean to play in. I lie on my back for a while and let the swell of it carry me, as if I was held in the hand of the Goddess, cradled. I can feel her heartbeat in the waves rocking under me, washing me gently to the side, and I can feel her breath in the air that blows across my face.

I let the blessings absorb into me while I am rocked in the sea, the blessings of my body, this creature of earth that I am. This body, fluid in the sea and the night, which has sheltered and born a child; this woman's body, with its softness and strength, that can dance and swim and make love. This body that grants me the gift of life on this planet, with all its limbs resting here on the ocean, hands and feet that move enough to keep me afloat, its fingers and toes that wriggle and separate, that can point and hold on and direct. My back, holding me up on the water; my neck, supporting my head; and all those wonderful, intricate, incomprehensible inner organs and cells and bacteria. The element *earth* as we know it most intimately, in our own living and dying bodies.

I am not so different from a mermaid, after all; not so different from a maiden. The ocean always seems to hold the promise of washing clean, of removing history, pain, and awkwardness. Here I can be stripped back to essence, my clothes and daytime self left on the beach and I in a place inhabited by dolphins and mermaids. I turn on my front and see a couple of other women still in the sea, treading water and talking quietly together. Their bodies look luminous in the blanketing night, as if all the light left in the air is pulled to them.

I take a deep breath of the night sky. *Air*, I am blessed with air. Here, I've always believed the air special; coming to me over acres of ocean, land so far away it has forgotten what land's like. This is salt air, filled with the freedom of waves and open spaces, with rushing currents and idling stills, nothing for it to come up against, to tangle in or be slowed by. This air that I breathe and breathe is the air of emptiness; wild air, elemental air. And when I breathe I take in a little of that, changing it, transforming it, but still partaking of freedom and emptiness, tasting that existence far out to sea, in the furthest sector of the east where only mystery dwells, before the first light, in a dark, darkened place like this beginning of the night.

The sun has set, the new moon slipped down under the horizon as well, and for fire there are only a few stars showing, along with the sweeping lighthouse that is not far away but whose beam spans out far away above us, sending a message of the land into the sea; it does not concern itself with small life huddled down at the base of the rocks it stands on. But I am warm with life, I carry fire within me in my beating heart, my life that's infinitesimal compared with those other fires and yet still blazes, for me. The blessing of *fire* I claim for myself.

I take a breath and roll under the surface so the water streams all around me, caressing and washing my hair to and fro; lifting and dropping me. Salt water, buoyant and slightly alien, sustaining its own life. A place to play rather than to dwell, since I'm not a mermaid, in the end. *Water*, this flow and release that brings the promise of healing and the reminder of our origins; this oneness that surrounds our planet; the waters we were born from, the great seas that birthed life onto the earth. All the mysteries of the deep oceans—the beauty of the night sea, the depths of the unknown—I receive and acknowledge as blessings.

There's the hugeness of sky and ocean, this edge of the continent we're at, then the tininess of our mermaid offering and our own bodies. *Spirit* lies in here somewhere in this mix, this crossover between the vast and personal, this moment of the mermaid meeting the sea or women returning to their maiden selves for a night, of washing clean in the ocean and listening to each other's stories and giving blessings. Earth, air, fire, water, and spirit; I meet and hold all of them.

Discovering Elements
in the Circle of Eight

Working with elemental energies and recognizing them as the sacred foundations of all life and the earth itself are fundamental cornerstones of contemporary Paganism. The word *elements* refers to two things. Firstly, elements are considered as the named elements of earth, air, fire, water, and the fifth element, known as aether or spirit. Secondly, elements refers to a broad set of fundamental understandings and magical practices. Elements become both the stuff without which we would not be here and, in concordance with that, the stuff without which we could not create magic.

The Circle of Eight felt immediately elemental in both senses of the word. Because we had gone right back to basics, assuming nothing but instead setting out to discover what we found in each of the eight directions, it seemed we were right down with the elements of magic—the smallest pieces that go to make up ritual and magical workings. As we questioned everything, elements were one of the first things that came into play in discovering what was part of our circle and how it operated.

The Circle of Eight also felt elemental in that it was a land-based circle. We were placing this circle onto a particular piece of land: our fertile, semi-rainforest land with cliffs and waterways, trees and rocks and birds. This land was immediately and continually referenced to the sea our rivers flowed to and that formed a long border for our local area. Many of our weekly activities took place by or in the sea; people went to the beach for walks, surfing, swimming, and yoga. We went to seaside cafés for coffee and early breakfasts; we went to the cape or the river heads to view sun- and moonrises. The beauty of our area was created by these two things: sea and rainforest. Very elemental. Our rich volcanic soil, drenching wet seasons, and sunny, mild winters were famous throughout the country.

When you stand still and look around, the elements are present in all directions. For example, when we stood in my garden and looked around we saw earth in the form of a deep river valley backed by a cliff to the south. To the north and west was a clifflike ridge line; to the east a valley dipping in folds through trees. Air, of course, came from all directions; those warm northern breezes, the sudden change of wind or a storm blowing up from the south-east; the dense wet breath of a rainforest remnant in the west. Water was more temperamental; there was the river somewhere to the south, heading east; there was the spring to the west; a little stream that ran in heavy rain all down the west side of the garden; and there were water tanks to the east and north. The ground beneath our feet was often wet; unable to take in any more rain, it would squelch as you walked across it.

Fire and spirit were no simpler. Of course the sun rose in the east, but it set in the west, and the western view through the windows was what we saw as we cast our circle: the colors of sunset in the west and the new moon etched in the sky. The fireplace was on the northern wall of the main room, where we held our circles; candles could be anywhere but most often were in the middle to help us see. Aether, or spirit, seemed to have the best and clearest position. By being in the center, it implied that it was everywhere—that it could not be contained or confined in a particular quarter. Yet it also had no home—did not belong to any of the eight directions—and so was liable to get left out, tacked onto the end of a calling, with no one in particular dedicated to it.

Furthermore, there were four—or five—elements, and we were a circle of eight directions. If we did assign the four elements to four of the directions, what would happen in the other four directions? Would they be element-less? Would those four just partake of Spirit in a general way, indistinct, while the four cardinal directions were individualized, each with their own element? As well, we didn't want to be sitting inside a room blindly assigning elements to the directions; that seemed as irrelevant as getting them out of a book. No, if we were going to work with elements, we would have to discover them. We would have to look in our directions, all eight of them, and see what happened; find out what was there and discover how we felt when we held those directions.

The first and most obvious alignment for us was that of fire. You can't live in Australia and not know where the sun is. Houses are built with their north-facing eaves low enough to cut out the midday sun in summer but high enough to let in the winter sun. It's an essential design feature for an energy-conscious house, to make it cooler in summer and warmer in winter. The sun blazes through the sky. We don't live in a place shrouded in mists or blanketed by clouds or with just a warm, pleasant presence that's occasionally there. Once I spent a week in Beijing with my son. On about the fifth day we noticed a muted disc-like shape shining dully from behind the persistently grey sky. I thought maybe it was the moon—I tried to work out what phase it was in to be seen in that position of the sky—until I realized it was the sun. That was the sun in Beijing. It was the only time we saw it all week.

In Australia the further north you go, the hotter it gets. Not just mildly hotter, not just a few degrees warmer; it gets much, much hotter. From Hobart in the south to Darwin in the north there's an enormous difference in temperature and humidity at any time of the year. We are a continent ruled in summer by the ever-present threats of both drought and bushfire. Some of our native trees and shrubs can't propagate except through fire; the scorching heat of a bushfire cracks open their seedcases like something out of myth; phoenix trees, burning up to regenerate. If you live rurally, each summer you'll be reminded to review your Bushfire Survival Plans: clear the ground around the house, clean the gutters, trim back growth near the house, and have decided what to do in the event of a fire—to stay and fight or get out.

Sitting in the North in the Circle of Eight looked like you were on top of the circle. It felt strong and a little wild, powerful and headed outward, away from the wheel. Flaring and inspirational; that reminder that when you're at the top, there's only one way to go—downwards—so now's the moment. Seize the day, speak up, be bold, get out there. It's the blaze of glory, somewhat heedless of past or future. In elemental terms, we thought it had to be fire. But that fire energy also…leaked. It wasn't confined strictly to the very top of the circle, to that Summer Solstice position. Summer doesn't just arrive out of nowhere, certainly not in Australia, and it doesn't leave very quickly, either; the solstice is just the beginning of the really hot weather. Our heat stretches on and on—until everyone's praying for it to end—well into the next festival, Lammas.

In this region, by Lammas everyone's longing for rain. We may have had a few heavy summer storms but usually we're drying out, waiting and waiting for the summer wet. This can be almost monsoonal, sweeping down on towns and rivers, flooding with day after day of drenching, straight-down rain—the kind that lets up only for half an hour here and there over days. The tanks fill up, gutters overflow, roofs and windows spring leaks, driveways and parts of roads wash away, bridges and causeways and low-lying roads go under, and paddocks drown. This can happen any time up until the Autumn Equinox. Sometimes it lasts, on and off, for most of three months.

Where we live fire and water are ferocious, the most obvious elements. Heat and rain. As it happens, our whole region—its fertile soil resulting in lush growth and therefore eventually prime farming country—was carved out, created by volcanic eruptions, twenty-three million years ago. The broken peak of this extinct volcano remains, half its original height but still looming over the valleys surrounding it, visible for miles and commanding, so it's said, the very first view of the winter sunrise from mainland Australia. That's if you happen to be up there on a clear morning, and that's harder than it sounds, for this peak nearly always has a cloud clinging to it. Sometimes the very top of it hooks out above, over the cloud; other times it vanishes in the white shroud. Even when there's no clouds anywhere else in the sky, there's often a cloud here, caught by the mountain.

The mountain lies to our north-west, our direction of Lammas. Right in the calendric place of our ferocious, flooding summer storms; fire and rain. It's like the overlap of the cross-quarter itself, caught up in a tempestuous battle between fire and water energies. People holding this direction, the North-West, are uneasily invaded by conflicting forces; they shout out in rituals much louder than was planned and often say surprising things. They invoke gods we hadn't planned on, call fire forth from the sky, and, unless they are aware of this beforehand, can bring a disruptive energy into the ritual. Sitting in that position myself, I generally feel an unsettling mix of urgency, unrest, and doomed grandeur.

Fire, by itself, when we placed it in the North, felt bright and clean. Water, when we let it settle in the West, felt deep and secretive; those rivers filled up after all that rain, brimming dams and the cool, past summer's heat. Placing our precious water in the West aligns it with the Autumn Equinox, traditionally a time of store housing, of harvest. Sitting in the West always came to me as a relief after all that heat and turbulence; as if I'd arrived somewhere I could rest, sink within, feel the deeper patterns. Not like the surf—tossed about and crashed down on—and not really like our rivers either, running rapid or slow through twists and turns in the hills, over rocks, into sudden pools, and on and on relentlessly. More like a pool of water, a lake; somewhere below the surface, deep. The water drinkable but vast, not subject to temperamental variations of local weather. In the West I felt held.

Between the North and West lies the North-West. When we allowed our elemental concepts to expand, they mixed and met in the North-West; fire and water. It began to look like steam or something cooking, coming to the boil; perfectly depicting our brooding ex-volcano and that time of the year that's torn between oppressive heat and flooding wet.

This explained so many things: why our Lammas rituals always had an unexpected edge to them, struggling with death rather than surrendering; why the person calling North-West always mysteriously called louder than the person calling to the North; even why I dreaded to hold that direction, of them all.

That volcano taught us a lot of things. It showed us how the cross-quarters can catch energies from the quarters on each side of them; how they transmute them into something different: no longer a single, pure element but something mixed, dynamic, changeable, and potent. This led to the cross-quarters looking more true to real life than the quarters, where traditionally single—pure—elements are placed, unmixing, with each other, whereas earth, water, fire, and air are all really mixed together. In a surf you have the sea mixing with air and crashing against sand; in a volcano there's rock becoming molten fire; in a bushfire wind and flame combine to burn wood; a rainbow is composed of water and air.

We looked at the other cross-quarters to see what mixtures they might hold. If we left air in the East and let earth hold the South, we would be left with a more or less traditional arrangement of the elements and then could focus our gaze on what was becoming more interesting: the mixing of elements in the in-between spaces. It was not hard to leave air in the East. A fresh wind blew in from the sea; all the coastal places were cooler for it, while the settlements tucked between hills sweltered away in a summer steam bath several degrees hotter. Of course air moves around constantly, but there is a definite relationship between the line of the coast and air, with warmer and cooler air meeting there, creating coastal weather patterns and updrafts.

The East, like the West, was often a relief. Not unlike a breath of fresh air, the darkness and uncertainty had bled away by then, and arriving in a solid quarter where light and dark were balanced seemed settling, a precursor to greater things. It was as if our eyes could look up, out of the mire of the inner worlds the dark half of the circle is more attuned to, and take in the world again. Air—with its promises of boundlessness, of distances and possibility, of the new potential with each breath like the new hope of each sunrise—sat happily in the East.

In the most general sense, to the south of us lay great farmlands—not the vast acreage of cattle stations in the north of the country but the green fertile places where sheep were raised and fruit and vegetables were grown, apple crops and peaches and wheat. Our own area still had some dairy, avocados, bananas, and a few specialty crops like macadamias and coffee; earth energy was all around us. When we placed earth opposite fire, we were resting our circle on foundations already established, even though in other ways we leapt away from tradition.

The South position in the Southern Hemisphere feels and looks like the bottom of the wheel. When I was there, I felt as if I was underneath everything—at the lowest point and yet also supporting the whole circle. There's something solidly satisfying in it, like being at the base of a mountain or in among the roots of a tree. You know how the whole thing is supported down there—you can see the structure of it, and it's not mysterious or ethereal, it's obvious. It doesn't seem to matter that it's in the middle of the dark half of the circle because when you look out you see the light, just like the Winter Solstice. It's the darkest time of the year, but that doesn't matter so much because it's also the turning point where light starts to return.

For me, sitting in the South was the position where I felt I had the clearest view of the whole of the circle. The North looks up and out, carried away by its own greatness. East and West seem to gaze across the circle at each other in their endless commentary of sunrise-sunset; both in the half-dark, half-light, like gazing in a mirror where everything is the same, except opposite. But the South looks into the wheel—cradles it in arms held wide, braces the strength of it. It's as earthy as you can get, and not especially the human-related aspects of earth: body and food and shelter. This is more the earth of rock and field and forest: the flesh and bones of earth. Sitting there, each time, I felt immovable. Alert, growing, quivering with life but utterly stable, locked in.

So then, between these quarters and fixed elements lay the cross-quarters, the blending. Apart from the fire and water mixture of Lammas, our North-West volcano, this system left us with a mixture of earth and air in the South-East (Imbolc for us); air and fire in the North-East (Beltaine), and water and earth in the South-West (Samhain).

Immediately these positions looked much more chaotic than the quarters, but they also felt much more chaotic than the quarters. Rituals for the cross-quarters are often more vibrant, powerful, and challenging than those of the quarters; in their highly recognizable forms of Halloween and May Day, Samhain and Beltaine in particular have a popularity that survived all the censure and disapproval of the Christian church.

Beltaine. Fire and air mixed together creates—what? A bushfire? Brushfire? Wildfire, maybe. A fire that's not harnessed to human approval, like a candle, fireplace, or even the nicely predictable movement of the sun through the heavens. This is fire that jumps and skits, that turns on you, whirls or spins; the type that leaps roads and fire breaks; it's shooting stars, fireworks, and meteors crashing unexpectedly through the earth's atmosphere. It's fire that can't be tamed, that won't light when you want it to or takes off in a raging blaze when you'd imagined a gentle, steady burn. Like the passion Beltaine is associated with, fire and air together are unpredictable, unsafe, and very attractive.

This fire and air combination goes a long way toward explaining the abrupt, surprising, and always unsettling energy of the North-East. Every time someone moved into that position and ventured to speak their hopes for deep connection with others, a warming up of their life, or a love that might blossom, we held our breath and averted our eyes. It was, out of the whole circle, the place of the unexpected. We could pretty much safely say that whatever you expected or wanted when you moved into that position, it wouldn't be like that. Moving into it myself, I had the trepidation from having watched how it had dealt with others holding it, yet I still felt the allure of the unknown—some entrancement of the possible. It was like holding your breath at the top of the Big Dipper or taking the hands of a stranger in the night. It's very immediate, this position; in contrast to the ages-old, bones-of-the-volcano feeling in our North-West, where fire mixes with water.

Air is also present in the mix of the South-East; this time with earth. That's not a standard elemental combination, and we spent a while puzzling it out. There's one phenomenon where air and earth interact, and from a human perspective, it's not a nice one: tornados, cyclones, or dust storms; times where the whole sky is darkened with traveling earth, or in a twister where there's the threat of solid objects being twirled up high into the sky, raced across the countryside, and deposited somewhere else entirely. These things are a mixture of earth and air— but does it fit at all with Imbolc, usually considered a mild and simple festival?

All the cross-quarters have their unexpected sides, the twist that comes from being on the slant, being between two known qualities and thus by definition becoming unknown; that's what makes them so intriguing, so delectable. Ask anyone whether they'd rather attend a Summer Solstice or a Beltaine party, or offer them a choice between an Autumn Equinox party and a Samhain ritual, and the answers are predictable. In spite of all that hype about our ambitions being a steady job, a reliable relationship, and a stable housing situation, offer us the edge and we're off there, racing. We love to flirt with the unknown. But does Imbolc come into that category? Isn't that a simple ritual of lambs and snowdrops, welcome and lovely in its own way but hardly exciting?

I think we've forgotten the terror of Imbolc. In our first-world luxury, we don't think of starving through winter—of not having greens or dairy foods for months. We don't know uncertainty as attached to any particular part of the year. In our consumerist world we believe any shortfall in the supermarket will be redressed soon, and every need for a product will be catered to. The Winter Solstice promises a turnaround from winter, but it's Imbolc that provides it. Imbolc is proof that summer and plenty will come again; defying the snow, those first snowdrops or lambs that are born into the traditional landscapes defy the dark and promise change. In this vision, Imbolc is the most vital of all the cross-quarters because it's the one that delivers renewal.

Sitting in the South-East (it would be the North-East in the Northern Hemisphere), I felt a sense of wonder at having survived everything the wheel could throw at me—darkness and death and the downward plunge of the cycle—to emerge. I felt fresh, as if the circle were new again; I could hardly remember this upward swing I was now engaged in, and it was wondrous. And yet there was a wrench there, as well.

That muddy place of the South-West—that's my home; the positions on either side of it also felt homelike to me, welcome and comforting. I felt they were known quantities. The South-East, on the other hand, was unknown.

I felt about the South-East as one might feel about being born: stupidly ungrateful for this chance at beauty and instead wondering what I had gotten into. From this perspective, the circle looked almost empty; open. I wondered if that was because from this position I could see almost the entire house. I could see the huge room our circle of cushions took up only a fraction of, the kitchen, and the second story above us, and I could see out the west doors, so there was a sense of spaciousness. But it was more than that. I felt released from the heaviness of that downward half of the circle and flung outwards—into nothing.

Air and earth. Like a seedling, a seed that's finally sprouted out of the dark earth and ventured up into daylight and fresh air. Like a baby, born from the womb of its mother, all flesh-enclosed until this moment and now—that first breath—lungs opening to engage this entirely new element. Earth and air. Like the springtime breezes that blow, softly, before the cold has really left, but the air suggests something else, hints at what's to come; the air brings the melting with it, the drying, the warming. Air mixed with earth can be as ordinary as a baby taking its first breath or as dramatic as a dust storm that lifts the fertile top layer of soil off the countryside and carries it into the city to cover the streets and offices and people in a layer of dirt.

Wildfires, tornadoes, volcanoes—they're a violent lot, these cross-quarter elemental combinations. And yet the most frightening cross-quarter of them all, the South-West, comes out looking tame beside them. Earth and water: mud. Of course, sometimes earth and water combine to form mudslides, or earth slips; there's also quicksand and mud pools, but more common and obvious than any of those is just simple everyday mud. Of the mud pie variety. Of clay, to form pots and plates and cups. Of ceremonial paint, differently colored clays and earths mixed with water to form colors—white and yellow and red and black—to paint on the human body, bark, or canvas.

In many creation stories, mud is what humans were formed from—a bit of earth, a bit of water, and the hands of the gods shaping us into being. This fits well with our South-West: that in the place of death and undoing, creation also resides. When I sit in this cross-quarter I experience a vast sinking backwards into the velvet night; there seems no end to it. With other positions I'm mainly aware of their forward focus towards the circle, into the hub of the wheel, a piece of pie that meets the other pieces neatly, in the center. In the South-West it's the space behind my back I'm most aware of, as if this triangle piece goes out and out forever, filled with stars and nothingness.

Those stars. Our planet is made from that, from stardust, and we are made from the components of this planet. Everything's made from the same thing really, like the eloquence of the gods making us from dirt; that's where we come from. Stardust, dirt; death and life; all parts of the same, and I like the juxtaposition of this direction of mystery corresponding with mud. Primal life, stretching our vast prehistory back to exploding stars, comets, the beginnings of the universe. That's what we're born from. I feel infinite in this position, as if it doesn't matter if I talk or not. I have the new moon setting behind me, over my shoulders; just rock circling around us, but how beautiful. As if the stars have turned to mud in this position, but that mud is the force of creation.

So we arrived, gradually and with much discussion, at our elemental circle, layering in between the conventional earth, air, fire, and water our cross-quarter elements of air with earth, air with fire, water with fire, and water with earth. Even the quarter elements are intimidating, those powers of earth, air, fire, and water being immensely out of human reach, with us humbly requiring their cooperation in matters of sustenance, shelter, and well-being. Sometimes we look at our altars and fondly imagine that water is a lovely chalice, air a pretty feather, fire this simple candle, and earth a piece of crystal. In the cross-quarters there can be no such misunderstanding; once two of those immensities are added together into mud, volcano, wildfire, and tornado, their volatility and power is irrefutable.

It's in the very center of the circle, the hub of the wheel, that the opposite elements finally meet: earth with fire, water with air. These are the combinations that don't exist in the cross-quarters, since they sit across the circle from each other rather than next door. They come together in the center, four absolutes meeting again; rather like those color wheels that, when they aren't moving, contain a rainbow of pie slices, but as soon as they move whirl into white. The center, the hub; the place where all differences meet, blend, and reflect back oneness. All the reds-oranges-yellows of fire; those blues and greens of water; the blacks, browns, ochres of earth; the invisibility of air—all meeting and spun by the turning of the wheel itself: time. The center place. The beginning of the universe, the big bang, the birth of something from nothing; the vastness that holds everything. Spirit is the element that is all of them, none of them; irreducible and untouchable.

How to Incorporate Elements in Your Circle of Eight

Elements are central to some groups; in others, they have less significance. This may be influenced by where you meet, the magical backgrounds of your participants, and the type of work you plan to do in your Circle of Eight. When people are new to magic and ritual, the elements can offer immediate, tangible relationship to different aspects of magic and ways of understanding energies. A circle that meets in a high-rise building may have very different relationships with the elements than one that meets in someone's backyard or another that meets in a country dwelling. The importance and relative strength of different elements will vary, depending upon your landscape.

You may choose to combine the elemental work with casting a geographic circle, heading out into the directions and seeing what you find or searching on a map for obvious land features and elemental influences. You could import the elements into the directions, then seek out locations that support these associations, or you could work the other way, beginning with what you find and building up your elemental associations from that. You may choose to have several variants of each element—salt water and fresh water, for example—to cover all eight positions, or you may choose to stick with four elements in four directions, allowing them to spill into the cross-quarters on either side.

What follows is a set of suggestions. You may already be used to calling to certain elements in particular directions and not wish to change at this stage. I certainly know of groups of people who have quite differing views of which elements should be called in which directions. Some settle on a particular pattern, agreed upon simply for the purposes of that group but not expected to be kept in personal or other magical workings; some call the elements into different directions each time, depending on what the ritual is or who's in charge of that working.

For a Circle of Eight, it works well to have the elements in directions that make sense to the group and the location. The Circle of Eight is local magic, so what your Circle of Eight will have in common with all other Circles of Eight—or Pagan and many other types of magical circle—will be that they acknowledge the elements. What might be different in your circle is the places in which you acknowledge the elements and the variations on the elements you may be working with. This is already different between hemispheres and I think can be different from locality to locality with no loss of power or overall magical impact. We are all revering life and the elements that compose everything we know; that they occur slightly differently—in different forms and directions and intensities—from place to place should be no surprise to us. Certainly it is no surprise to our planet, which encompasses winter and summer simultaneously and a wealth of seas, jungles, deserts, forests, farmlands, mountains, and every other type of terrain. In one place storms come in from the east, in another it's from the north; one place has a river to the west, another the sea in the south. You are located in among these global and local influences, and orienting your circle to them is the essence of this magic.

How to Find Elemental Associations for the Circle of Eight

These steps are best taken over a period of weeks or months. You might change the order from how they appear here to make the process work for you. The steps should be taken as suggestions rather than a rigid procedure.

1. Open Discussion

Begin this process with an open discussion, where everyone gets a chance to talk about the elements. Points you might like to cover in this discussion include:

- each person's relationship to the elements, magically and literally
- each person's previous magical and ritual practice (if any) with locating the elements in particular directions, and the level of their commitment to those pairings
- a brainstorm of possible elemental associations with directions for your particular location

2. Exploration within the Circle

Place three or four expressions of each element in the center of the circle. For example, you might include a wand, a feather, and a scent infuser for air; a candle, burning incense, and a box of matches for fire; a chalice, a seashell, and a spritzer with scented water for water, and a rock, a crystal, and a flower for earth.

Ask each person, seated in their direction, to pick up and handle the different objects, noting their reaction to them. You might like to do this work in a light trance. Afterwards, share your feelings.

You can also ask people to pick up different objects and move around the circle with them into various directions, feeling their responses to this. Again, share your experiences afterwards.

3. Exploration into the Directions

Travel to locations you feel are associated with the directions of your circle. If you have already set up a geographic Circle of Eight, travel to those places. When you are there, look around you. Notice the ways the elements are represented in each place. If you don't have a geographic circle set up, visit places such as a nearby river or local mountain, park, or monument that lie in the directions around your circle. Again, notice the presence of the elements at each place, their strengths and characters. Be aware these might change during the course of a year, from season to season.

4. Focused Discussion

Bring all your thoughts and learnings into one discussion. This time, explore the areas where your understandings differ from each other or from the standard arrangement of elements, remembering that what you arrive at might not be modeled anywhere else.

Some parts of this process might be:

- Think about and discuss your group's priorities in assigning elements to directions. Is it to stay true to your locality, no matter what? It is to match up to standard Pagan elemental designations? Is it to create something completely original? Once you know this, it will assist you with the rest of the process.

- Find out where the overlaps are—what everyone agrees on—and begin with that. If everyone agrees, for example, that water must be in the west—whatever the reasons—then you have one clear marker to begin with. Or everyone may agree to assign elements only to the quarters and not the cross-quarters, or to seek unique elemental representations in each direction—elements with names such as mountain, storm, river, and sunrise.

- Create a map of your Circle of Eight on a large piece of paper, maybe on top of a literal map of your area or otherwise just with the eight directions and characteristics or places your group already associates with the different directions. Make some colored elemental symbols on separate pieces of paper (a blue wave, a red flame, a depiction of wind, a tree or mountain) and try moving them into the different directions like pieces on a game board. If you are thinking of having two directions for each element or two elements in some of the directions, have several of each of your elemental symbols.

- Undertake a trance journey as a group into the etheric level of your Circle of Eight. Visit each direction in turn, asking for further information. While it is most likely each person will receive different information, it may fit together; one person may receive sensations of wetness, another of coolness, and another of uncertainty or strong emotion, but all of these may be aspects of water.

5. Test Your Correspondences

Even if it is imperfect, start testing your model out. Set a time for this testing, such as two or three months, and revisit the discussion after that time. Some things remain imperfect and others come to make sense as we work with and adapt to them.

Elemental Work in the Circle of Eight

Usually, in any circle, the person standing in or holding a particular direction calls to the element associated with that direction when the circle is cast and thanks it at the end, when the circle is released. You can also work with the elements in many other ways. In the Circle of Eight, people do not get to choose the element they are holding at any particular time; it is part of the sequential movement of the wheel, and over time everyone gets to experience each of them.

Here are some suggestions:

- During a ritual, the people holding the directions of the elements can contribute that part of the ritual—for example, in a dark moon ritual, the person in the air direction can direct the visioning trance, the person holding water can create a ritual of release and renewal, fire can lead the energy raising, and earth can be in charge of both the grounding and the sharing at the end. Or during a Spring Equinox festival, the air quarter could be responsible for the chants and music, the earth quarter for coordinating the decoration of spring eggs, the water person for blessings of each other, and the fire person for a spring dance.

- You can work with the elements to explore a theme or magical working more closely, each person viewing with the eyes of (and speaking with the voice of) their elemental association. For example, if you are creating a ritual for the Summer Solstice, each person holding an elemental direction can bring that understanding into the ritual; what is the fire experience of the Summer Solstice; the air experience; the water and earth experiences? If you are working with a myth, you can explore it through elemental understandings; where is water in this myth; air, fire, earth? What are they telling us about this story and how to work with it?

- Use the elements for inner work. During the time you are in a direction associated with a particular element, delve deeply into your relationship with that element—the favorable aspects and the more challenging. If you are holding fire, you might discover that although you value your creativity and your passion, you have an issue with anger and have never felt able to express or listen to it properly. Working with fire as an ally, devote yourself to exploring this in ways you can support. You can do this ritually through personal or group process, or literally by working with the element directly; you might choose to make candles, to learn to lay and light a fire, or to take part in a fire-walking experience.

Invocation

Where the river meets the sea is an endless, changing drama. The river is tidal, rising and swelling twice a day with inundations and releases of water. With fresh water coming out and sea water coming in, the heads are always in turmoil. Boats on their way out to sea for fishing or sight-seeing tip and plummet up and down on the wash, thrusting their way through the top of it. People fish off the rocks into this meeting of waters, balanced precariously on the sharp, black, slippery rocks, bucket wedged next to them.

It's a study in contrasts. Turn and face inland, and there's an idyllic scene: gentle waterways, an inlet leading to a harbor, the sloping hills behind; a pastoral, humanized landscape. But the other way—out to sea—there is wilderness and nothing. The slopes of waves, heaving away to the far distance, a vast greyness or blueness, an enormity of unchanging seascape barely touched by human forms; maybe a small boat floating at the horizon line or a couple of surfers in the foreground.

I come here at night, running from my safe human house, my unset-tling human relationship. It's a long way in the middle of the night, but there's hardly any cars and it's a timeless experience driving dark, familiar roads to the unfolding of the beach. It's so different here from the secretive hills with tall trees leaning over everything, the rustlings and creakings and murmurings of forest. Here instead there is space and breeze, an openness that offers me air after the cloistered hills, the closed house. It's midnight, we're in a dark moon, and the universe stretches out around and before me.

I stand on the cold sand, the breeze blowing around me gently. I think I could stand here for a long time, hours, and it wouldn't be counted as hours because it's night, because time stretches away over the ocean, and stars count in millennia. I feel my desperation, my aloneness and sharpness as I reach out to the sky and sea and air, just breathing and not knowing what to call in, what to ask for, when a sparkle speeds across my vision, towards the sea. I look up and see a second, then a third; shooting stars. I've never seen them before, not really. Sometimes after other people cried out I looked up and caught an afterimage or the very tail, but I never saw this before: a long burning arc across the map of sky, an anarchist trajectory etching a vision onto the night.

It's brighter, stronger, more powerful and directed than I imagined; there are dozens of them, and I see them long, long after they have passed; inside my eyes, inside my thoughts. I could be the only one who sees this, sees it so exactly, was waiting, so ready. And the dark, staid jeweled universe has given me this, brief burning life against the arc of atmosphere. I don't know if I invoked this or not; it's more like it has invoked me, and I've come to life again now that I've seen this. I'm reminded of brilliance, of the burning worth of a moment's beauty, of the uncounted brilliances scattered indifferently across the world in art, in nature, in human kindness. I hold it as long as I can, then finally I turn and go back to the car and drive back, now, to the house; filled up. Reminded of stellar visions, of startling essence, reminded to ask and open my eyes and let them fill with falling stars.

Invoking the Living Land

In the Circle of Eight we wanted to call not just to a direction—the east, if we stood in the east—but to the actual *place* of east as it existed for our circle. Not some concept—a castle in the clouds, for example, or a temple of purple and gold or the home of the four winds—but an actual place that lay to the east of us. The place you would discover if you went east, a place that was the magical anchor of the eastern point of our circle. We would not just be standing in the east of our circle, calling eastwards to this place—so stretching a direct line of energy out to it—but we would also be invoking the place into our circle, calling for some of its energy to return down that line we had thrown out and thus be present itself.

This would mean that whenever we cast our circle we would have not just the idea, but the energy and presence of the eight places that lay around it as part of our magic and ritual. Our ritual landscape would be eightfold; by traveling its perimeter—which might appear to be only twenty paces or so inside a living room or out on the lawn—we would actually be transiting through these eight physical places, geographically far distant from each other and ourselves but brought into presence by our calling. The invocation would be a web that stretched, point to point, around our circle, as well as around the shire, linking the places to each other and also to our circle.

To do this, we stood in our directions and faced outwards into the direction itself. We imagined before us the landscape of that direction as we had last seen it or as we had seen it many different times and different ways. We allowed things to inform us—the time of day, the time of year, the weather, our intuition—and this resolved into a particular set of feelings, a vision, a memory, or a sense of what was most important in that moment. Then we called out to that place, imagining our voice traveling not just behind us, to the rest of the circle, but also forwards, on a line bound straight for that place. We imagined our voice arriving there as we spoke what we saw and felt, and then returning to us, like a line we were drawing in with the flavor of that place on this day, to presence it within the circle.

This invocation was based in relationship: a relationship with that place and with all the places that we built up over time. Although we were invoking these places in the etheric realm, our knowledge and relationship—and thus our ability to invoke in this way—did not rest within the etheric but within the real. We went to these places; not once but again and again. We went with offerings, we went to observe, we went to do ritual. We went at dawn and dusk, moonrise, midday, and sometimes midnight; we went at every season, and we stayed there; sometimes for half an hour and sometimes for half a day. We went there by ourselves, with friends and family, with another person from the circle or the whole circle. We had picnics, went swimming, or did ritual; we built altars, sang songs, meditated, and talked. We did this in every one of our directions many times.

In Pagan belief and practice, the land—all land—is sacred already. There's nothing extra to be done to make it sacred; it is sacred all by itself. We recognize it as sacred, and we honor it for giving birth to us and all life, for supporting life, and for receiving our bodies back again when we have finished with them. We honor the land for its animals, plants, and birds, for its insects, microbes, and all the things that are a part of it. We honor different parts of land for their own attributes; we honor the swamp for being a swamp, the mountain for being a mountain, the forest for being a forest. We honor the particulars of that piece of land: *this is the swamp the water birds call home, this is where the mangroves grow, these are the reed beds. This is the mountain of the red rocks, which crumble into clay we paint with and whose soil is rich and fertile when it is washed into our valleys. This is the forest the bats shelter in by day; the forest with the giant fig trees, with the small creek.*

As we come to know the place more and more intimately in its different moods and seasons, we create deeper relationship with it and may even begin to feel it is speaking to us. So that when we visit our South-East direction to discover the tide is way out, therefore letting us visit the second cave whose entrance is usually filled with smashing waves, we feel we are being let into a secret, shown a new piece of this small place. We might even wonder what new parts of ourselves are being born or revealed just now. When we visit our South-West and see it smoothed in a thin shell of green, new grass, we realize the impact of the recent rains and feel grateful, asking if we might refresh also the place of mystery within ourselves.

In the Circle of Eight, the richness of our relationship with place builds layer on layer into rituals and understandings. We don't seek to impose our beliefs onto this land and these places but to relate to what is there. Thus that second, secret cave in the South-East might not be incorporated into general callings to that direction. It would be a secret, just as it is at the beach; something glimpsed but hardly ever entered. On one occasion, perhaps, feeling a sudden need for the new, I might sense it rising up in me as I stood in that direction, and I might mention it then, as the revealing of a secret. If the weather was dry—and it's much drier in our South-West than in our own shire—I would not imagine or call to that flush of green I once saw after rain, but I would hold it within me as the shimmering potential of that direction.

Having seen and known that place, at least a little, we allow its presence to well up within us and begin to inform us more and more not just about itself, and even about ourselves as we inhabit that direction, but also about the circle. We do not just invoke the known but also the unknown, thus we call to the essence of that place and expect it to be vibrantly present. Calling North-East, we feel more and more of the push and pull of the North-East; the in and out of the river with the sea, informing us not just of the North-East's obvious sexuality and fertility but of the tugging, teasing undercurrents; of need and compulsion and sometimes repulsion; of the endless activity and interaction that this direction is involved in.

The more we invoke the mountain that anchors our North-West position, the more aware of its presence we become, not just in the direction it happens to lie in but looming over and orienting our whole circle. It brings the dominance of heat and rains that our whole region is finely balanced between; the beautiful sunny weather that tourists endlessly arrive for and our drenching rains that renew and replenish our green landscape. Our invocations are like phoning up someone we know, someone we may even be coming to know quite well. But what is said in that phone call—exactly what we will say and most certainly what the other person—the place—will say, is unknown until it happens. What they have to say is revealed only by asking and listening, and what we hear is sometimes more than we knew before.

Journey Through the Circle

. . . .

Memoir

I feel like I am falling apart in deep loneliness, but there's always the circle to save me. It's the Summer Solstice, and I'm holding the South-West, an odd combination of down-into-the-darkness married with the height of the year, so that I feel mixed tides of strength and release, hope and despair. It's the midst of our holiday season—Summer Solstice is followed a few days later by Christmas, then New Year and my son Damon's birthday—so there is a swirl of social and ritual activity I am committed to. And I have reinjured my ankle, triggered an old weakness; I have it strapped but am hobbling; it's swollen and sore. Altogether I am struggling, hardly knowing how to be with myself or where to turn. It's also the last quarter of the waning moon, and I feel a determination to turn with it, to go down into the night and release and let go and rise again somewhere different.

I want to clear myself of the old, sweep clean all those past relationships, and make space for something real. I know what I want but feel overwhelmed, unsure of how I would get from this part of my life to a time of meeting joy and love again. On December 23 I take a hold of myself and drive to the labyrinth, the center of our Circle of Eight. The weather is hot, too hot, but the labyrinth is shaded by trees and there's some breeze. I stand at the entrance and don't know if I can do it. I'm planning to visit my eight directions over the next eight days, and at this point it seems an absurd plan: to fit all that in among these celebrations and holidays with my ankle how it is; standing here I don't even know if I'll be able to walk the labyrinth.

I decide to take it step by step. I got here—that's the first step—now I'm going to step onto the path. The narrow path, the one that twists and turns so measuredly, that flirts with itself, passing and turning and doubling back, that unwinds, dancing, eventually into the center, only arriving after the center itself has been forgotten in the movements of the dance. I still feel the tides of the solstice, and in the freedom of the labyrinth I clothe myself in its energy. I walk forward as the Summer Queen and imagine walking forward into the embrace of my beloved. I feel energy dancing, an invisible cloak that flares and wraps around me and lends me lightness, conviction through uncertainty. I walk slowly but supported by what awaits me in the center; I feel threads of it already.

Time blurs for me, and even though I am walking slowly I arrive at the center smoothly, as if the complications in my life did not exist. As if I were meant to be here. It's like a secret is being passed to me, so secret I don't know what it is yet; if it's knowledge or love, the new year or the deep healing and stripping away of the past I associate with my direction of the South-West. But I feel something definite inside me when I reach the center: resolution and trust and the call of the unknown. I walk out of the labyrinth to a small chant that seems to be breathing its way out of me; my ankle is still bearing my weight, and I bring that hope and trust out with me for the next day.

It's Christmas Eve, and I drive with Damon, who is thirteen, to the South-East, even as the year and the moon are nearing the close of their cycles. Everything is going down, but we journey to the place of beginnings. And we discover a low tide, so the cave can be entered; I crawl in, right to the narrow back of it where there's a bed of smooth stones, and lie down on them, salted wet rock walls above me and to each side. It's cramped and humid, but I close my eyes and begin to breathe deeply. Perhaps if I can sink deeply enough into myself in this place, I can emerge into a different piece of my life.

When I rise to come out of the cave, I begin singing; I am singing my offering to the circle, to the beach, and at the entrance to the cave I am almost assaulted with sudden light and air, the hugeness of this small beach compared to the rocky, moist closeness of the cave, and I call forth my emergence, my offerings, my desires towards life and love and joy, and I walk into the waves. I haven't been aware of other people, at all, through this ritual; I left Damon back at the other end of the beach, but as we go to leave, begin climbing up the rocky steps to the road, I look back and see a naked man walking into the sea. It seems promising, as if the direction itself is promising something.

On Christmas Day we drive, Damon and his father and I, to the East, the cape, and it's a lovely day to be doing it. All the people we see are having picnics and parties. My ankle is improving. I can walk to the cliff edge, where we gaze downwards into a dolphin festival of waves and their sleek, surfing bodies daring the strong surges of water near the base of the cliffs. I almost imagine myself into their presence, down there in the water diving and rolling, twisting free of the force of the wave and then giving myself to it again, surrounded by other tumbling, smooth shapes. The East has me in its grip, and I feel both vulnerable and powerful; given over to the ritual three days now and gathering strength, and the waves meet inside me as if all the directions arrived here, headed to this point and converged suddenly and dramatically. I turn to them one by one, thanking them, acknowledging them, but they are singing inside me, alive and magnificent; I am trembling with the power of them.

The next day I am pleased I don't have to drive too far. I don't know how I will get through the rest of the circle; all the far-flung places are yet to come, and I hesitate in doubt before deciding not to think about that but just to focus on the North-East. Of all directions, this one most symbolizes what I am calling in: love and sensuality. I go there on my own. There's no one there: no fishers, no surfers. I take all my clothes off in the hot sun of the beach and walk into the cool waves. I feel impelled. Each place has been intensifying; alive; waiting, almost, to join into my circling nine-part ritual.

The waves play with me, coming in to lift my feet off the sand, setting me down; incoming, they caress my breasts again and again until I am laughing with it; lighter among the froth and crests and swells and then a wave comes for me and I am just the wrong height for it, I have to grab my breath and dive under or be crashed by it, and so I do, feeling its power sweep me and then push me beachwards. I am more cautious afterwards, more wary, but I still feel I belong here, as if the ocean is doing the ritual with me. It's just that there's a warning or two, a few difficult places with the waves as well as lovers; I have to stay alert and can't lose myself entirely to the timelessness and buoyancy. But I'm immersed in the ritual.

On day five I go to the lookout. The North is the direction I sat in when we began the Circle of Eight, and for me it is both the beginning and the height. I contain it, and from me it flows forth. I look down to that beach where I swam yesterday, over to that mountain I'm telling myself I'll get to tomorrow, across west and south to all the hidden places I can't see but know are there and then to those sea places of a few days ago, the cape that I can see clearly and the blur beyond it that I know holds the small beach with the cave. Here at the pinnacle I hold the threads of those places and feel them humming; all the lines of power flow through me as I sing to them. It feels high and free and also simple to be part of this turning wheel of days, this spinning circle of places and magic.

It's a long drive out to the mountain on the sixth day. I take it slowly, driving myself towards the peace of forest, of my temple. This is the place of genesis for this land, and I feel its vibrancy through the hot air, its potency in the rich soil. The circle is bringing me back to life as I traipse, place by place and day by day, out to these directions. I drive through the shadow of the black cockatoos, hearing their screeches resounding as if through the temple, feeling their shadows imprint onto me the knowledge of endings and beginnings. Once on the slope of the mountain, I am quiet; I feel almost asleep in the depth of it, but eventually my song comes to me, the song I have been singing in increments since the labyrinth, and it winds out of me, casting in whispers into the forest and the land, weaving my threads in here as well.

The next day is the West; the beauty of lake and bird and deep water. It doesn't matter about the driving anymore; my ankle is coping, my mind is on hold. I am caught into the strength of the ritual, and things arrange themselves around me; I can no longer imagine not completing it. At the lake I meet again its serenity, vastness. The endless grace of water, of sky. I feel soothed, stilled by it; offered ease and assistance. There's quiet here, patience and depth that doesn't change; the West holds itself and offers that to anyone who comes here. My song is simple, clear, almost silent in the bigness of the place.

Day eight, the second-last day of the year and the second-last place: the bora ring. I go early, and it's hot. That smell of dry earth; the Australian summer. Being at this place feels essential, stripped back, no glamour in the wavering gum trees, the faded cemetery, the busy ants. There are magpies and kookaburras, and life seems brief between the cemetery and the ancient lineage of the bora ring, but the now is with me, and I do not feel less by all this timelessness. I feel the fullness of myself, of body, flesh, bones; watching the process of life out of death and back again, that endless spiral. There's nothing here, and it's all here; if I spend a moment or an hour or a day, it will all be the same to this place.

On the final day, December 31, I go to the waterfall. South. It's the eve of Damon's birthday; fourteen years ago I was in labor. My ankle is tricky on that descending dirt path, on the sharp rocks leading up to the pool. There's no one there when I arrive; other people are caught up in preparations for New Year's Eve and not thinking of bush walks and water holes, so I go in naked. I remember suddenly, in the water, that I am the Summer Solstice Goddess, that at the labyrinth I invoked that, and in the round, lapping pool I feel the satisfying weight of that. I have not had a lover for a year, over a year; no one has kissed me or touched my skin, but here I feel alive again, almost excited with the fullness that's coming to me, birthed from me, met in this completion of the circle, of the eight directions. I sing in the water and feel filled with joy.

Correspondences and Totems in the Circle of Eight

Tables of correspondences have always irked me. I see the attraction of wanting a symbol, a reference point, a simple emblem of a large magical construct, but to say, for example, that yellow is the color for east—well, what if your east is pink, searing white, or dusk-deepened blue, depending on the time of day? Tables advise herbs or flowers as related to a particular direction, element, or festival, but what if those aren't native to where you live? What if they don't even exist there, or they're invasive weeds? The whole correspondence table reads to me like a suspect marketing plan; why would I buy a quartz crystal for the east when I could pick up a perfectly good shell actually from the east (my east) or assign a piece of obsidian to my earth direction when what I actually find in that direction is sticky, crumbly red rock?

I felt certain that the directions themselves would provide their own totems and correspondences and that recognizing and working with *these* correspondences would strengthen our bonds with the direction.

We all had different ways of deepening our relationships with the directions, and this was one of mine.

There's a wonderful place called Damanhur in northern Italy, a magical-socialist miniature city-state carving out a small revolution in occult magic, social and economic experiment, and visioning for a new world. The people there, its citizens, take on new names when they become Damanhurians. They each take an animal name and a plant name to align their human selves more closely with the rest of the planet. It can take several years to discover one's names. They work with the animal name before the plant because they say we are closer to animals, so it comes more easily to identify with them. I followed this advice in working with totems or correspondences for the Circle of Eight and began by looking at the animals and birds.

Every time we go to the cape we look for dolphins because they are so often there. They like to surf in the waves breaking onto the rocks from the east, although sometimes they mix with human surfers on the northern side of the point, in the longer, rolling waves. Sometimes they're farther out and harder to spot, but if I stay there long enough I've nearly always seen them.

Whales pass the cape between winter and spring, migrating north to their breeding grounds and then later returning south, and populous whale-watching parties cluster the headland with their binoculars, picnics, and cameras. As the easternmost point of the mainland it sticks out a long way, and since the whales' water road doesn't take this into account, they come quite close. In the past this meant it was an ideal whale-hunting station; now it's ideal for whale watching. But that's only twice a year; they don't stay—we're just one station on a long trip, and not even that; to them, we're passing scenery. The dolphins, on the other hand, are locals, or at least very frequent visitors. So for me it's always been dolphins for our east place in the Circle of Eight.

Just down the coast is the little curved beach with the caves. It's scooped between cliffs that back it quite closely, and often I've looked up or lain on my back and seen ospreys, locally known as seahawks, fluttering or gliding there. I imagine those cliffs, that coastal scrub, and the relative peace and quiet from humans in this not-so-frequented spot give them safety, supplies, and a good launching place. They're not as big as eagles, not as dramatic, but they have a swerve and lift and lightness I appreciate. So I thought it was seahawks who belonged to the South-East.

I went to a talk by a Bundjalung woman working for National Parks. The cape is adjacent to Arakwal National Park, co-managed by National Parks and Wildlife and the Arakwal people, who are part of Bundjalung Nation and whose land it traditionally is. This was the first agreement made in Australia to come under the Indigenous Land Use Agreement as a result of a formal Native title claim and seven years of complex negotiations. The woman spoke eloquently of her mother and aunties, their growing up and their relationship to the beaches and ti-tree lakes, the birds and animals. She talked about the different local areas, the cape being more masculine and how it had dolphin energy, whereas just a little farther south (where our South-East point lay) was feminine, and its animal was the seahawk. I felt as if my ears were leaping out of my head to catch every nuance of every word.

Dolphins. Seahawks. I knew I was doing something right, looking at what was there. I was seeing. It created great faith in me, this simple lecture aimed as much to the school holiday children as to the few adults who'd come to hear what she had to say. I approached her afterwards and asked what she thought about the issue of doing Celtic-based, imported magic on Australian land. She didn't give too much away; she asked me questions and nodded her head. She said that, generation by generation, Aboriginal thinking was changing, and she had shared things with us her parents' and grandparents' generations never would have, but she and others thought it was imperative that we had to care and had to know in order to build our own relationships with the sacred and come to understand this land we lived on.

I took it as encouragement. Seahawks, dolphins; I had found the same totems not by coincidence and not by any special magic but simply the same way as others did long before me: by looking at what was there. I was drawing a different map, that was true; one designed not by Dreamings or song lines but by an eight-pointed circle based quite arbitrarily in my house in the hills and subscribing to shire boundaries marked on a map. But I can never have that heritage of being born and raised one of the Bundjalung; I cannot know this land that way. I must know it my way or not at all, and the small miracle is that there are overlaps between our ways of knowing. Dolphins; seahawks.

A few other animal totems for our directions were obvious. In the North-East there are always pelicans. Pelicans hang out in the river near the bridge. Perched on oyster racks and in the small harbor, they seem to live permanently on the tops of the poles, a strategic position next to the boats and close to the fish shop. They look like sculptures balanced there, often four or five of them apparently asleep, each on their own pole. They fly low, skimming over the waterways that twist between the mangroves, networking their way through to the sea, flapping strongly to skim down low or rise, slowly, to bank and turn and fly along the coast to other favored spots. They're an icon here. I was happy to acknowledge them as the sacred animal for this direction.

In the South place of the waterfall and round pool I met a green, yellow-bellied grass snake, not on grass at all but on rocks, near the base of a tree. The next time I came I looked for it again and saw it—or another, similar one—twisted in the trunk of a tree near where I'd seen it the first time. When I spoke to it and reached out to touch it, it glided slowly down the slim tree trunk towards me, twisting around a bit to keep its purchase. It seemed guardianlike. Another time I came to the top of the falls and, curled up there in the sun, inconspicuous in spite of its coloring, was a green and gold tree snake, possibly the same one; unlike me, it could probably directly travel the cliff face between the top and bottom of the falls. Or maybe there's a family of them there—a clan, a colony; I don't know how snakes work in that regard. None I had seen were small; slender, yes, but longer than my arm. And not unfriendly. Grass snakes in the South.

In the West, many water birds browse and cruise, rest and snack on the lake. But the kings and queens of them—the boldest, grandest, and most imperious looking—are the black swans. They're often there, two or three of them gliding or sometimes a dozen or so in a drift looking like property managers surveying their holdings as they tour around; unlike the ducks, they stand out, heads well above the water and red beaks showing off their gleaming black plumage. They are such an Australian bird, the shocking inverse to white swans; looking like someone had made a mistake when they were first seen by Europeans, I'm sure—like they came from the bottom of the world. But to me they look like the imprint, the original that somehow faded out to white in those colder climates. Black swans, then, in the West.

I did notice how many birds I had and how few mammals. I went to places and waited; I listened and looked. In the daytime I saw nothing especially noticeable, and in the night heard only scuttled rustlings and rearrangings of the undergrowth; I never came across any gorgeous possums or little native mice. Of course they're not keen on people, even quiet, well-behaved people. They didn't appear, and so I had to assume that although of course they were there, part of the magic and life of these places I was so attached to, they weren't putting themselves forward to be the animal face of the place, the totems. There were bats—a great swathe of bats passed through the shire nightly on their way to feed—they just didn't seem to belong to any of the places in the Circle of Eight. They were travelers, part of the landscape but not dedicated to any one of our directions. Mainly birds were what I was seeing. There are a lot of very beautiful, colorful, and noticeable birds in Australia.

We have kookaburras, rosellas, honey eaters, blue wrens, and hundreds, at least, of small bush and grassland birds, along with many water and sea birds. We have parrots, as well: cockatoos and corellas and galahs. I love them all with an anguished kind of affection; my most especial favorites are the sulphur-crested white cockatoos, partly because they make a quite horrible screeching cry with great glee, loudly, and pass it back and forth between themselves as if it was the best sound ever. I think of it as the sound that ripped the world open to let in the light back in the beginning times, and I think of them like the birth of the universe: white feathered coats and a sunrise headdress.

Even though I was looking for them, it was their cousins I found, the more stylish black cockatoos.

I was driving the twists and turns it took to get to the mountain in the North-West. It was a bright, warm day and I had the windows open as I drove along the final road that ends at the foot of the walks to the summit and into the forest. I heard them first: they have a cry more fluting at the end than the white cockatoos; it trails off suggestively, as if something else is going to follow. It's the kind of thing that could happen without one noticing, except this day I was noticing. Maybe I was thinking about animals in the directions anyway, maybe I was just driving cautiously on the narrow country road, maybe I was in the right mood for it, or maybe they called to me and I heard.

They flew over the road right in front of me, low and so close I didn't actually see them—what I saw was their shadows on the road. Black, like them. Three black flying shadows on the road, in the air in front of me, as their cries sounded out. And as I drove through those bird shadows they seemed to fill the air, shadow feathers flying inside the car and into my lungs, and I felt they were inhabiting me as I swallowed, claiming space, and still I heard them calling out, that wavering end to their cry as if asking for an answer. So I called back to them that yes, I'd seen, I had them now, I knew what they wanted: to lay claim to me and this place, to stamp their shadows onto the North-West.

The yellow-tailed black cockatoos are majestic, powerful birds with a wingspan of nearly a meter, magnified in shadow-form. Like other cockatoos, they are known for their destructive capacities; originally put to the purpose of ripping dead bark off trees and rotting logs to get at the insects burrowed in there, they appear equally happy ripping off pieces of windowsill and veranda railing. In a forest setting they hurry up the decomposition cycle of dead wood. For this direction, it's entirely appropriate: the beginning of the downward fall, the slow descent that culminates in midwinter and the South at the bottom of the cycle. Black cockatoos have another association as harbingers of rain. When they descend in threes or fours into the bowl of the valley that holds my house, circling low with their floating cries to settle momentarily in a tall tree before taking off again with another circle or two, we start looking for rain. And this mountain in the North-West is an attractor for rains; it gathers to it the mists and fine precipitation and molten downpours that are typical of this region.

Black cockatoo shadows, just as this mountain overshadows our whole area with its scarred, hooked peak. Geologically it's the force behind the volcanic formation of this land, and energetically it's the dynamic focus of our circle. Black cockatoos are perfect, bringing the rain of the region's cloud catcher to the coast and farmlands; black cockatoos that hurry death along. Black cockatoos with that flash of yellow, sunrise after a black night, like the sunrise that's sometimes seen from the top of the mountain.

I spent a lot of time in the South-West, partly because it's a long drive, so once I got there I tended to stay a few hours, half a day, wandering around or just sitting, listening, and reading or doing ritual in my favorite place. I looked for animals other than the occasional cattle in the paddock next door. There were magpies in the young gum trees to the north of the bora ring; they weren't always there, but often enough. They sang their warbling songs in the dry heat, and they are a beautiful bird, those liquid sounds, but they didn't seem to call to me or to the circle particularly. They didn't make a big show of ownership, more a pleasant background offering. I waited for snakes, possums, bats—anything that I would associate with the darker parts of the circle, the underworld and the mysteries.

Each time I came to the bora ring I brought an offering. I did that for all the directions, but for this direction it was particular. I always brought some water, either spring water from my land or rain water since it was such a dry place and I thought the land must be thirsty. I didn't enter the bora ring to give this offering; I knelt or crouched down near the entrance and poured it onto the earth. It would pool there, puddle, or start to run in dark ribbons before the soil suddenly received it, sucking it in. And I brought honey; half a jar of honey, which I would tip onto the earth near the water. I can't even remember why I first took honey there, perhaps it was to offer not just the necessity of water but something sweet, as well. It felt right, and I kept doing it.

One day, still face down to the ground having given my offerings, I noticed the ants. It had always been a big place for ants, the bora ring; they're the first into any picnic you have there, and sitting on the ground you have to continually pick them off you. I suppose they like the light, dry soil of the place. There are different kinds, but especially noticeable are mid-sized, very black ants, industrious and organized; they don't set out to bite, but they will if you're careless. Now they were busy organizing my honey, turning it into their honey.

Ants. They are certainly the most numerous creature at that place, prominent and continual, and now I see they are the groundskeepers. They take honey when they can get it, but more obviously, they eat the dead. They clear up a carcass left lying on the ground—snake, bird, mammal; they're not fussy. They take it all and recycle it into ant industry and ant breeding. Given that when I lift my eyes from the bora ring just slightly I see the cemetery it shares its land with, this imagery of cleaning up the dead is perfect. Ants. I feel embarrassed I didn't really notice them before; well, I noticed them in that irritant kind of way, but not in the sacred way. Now that I look properly—and I get down to ant level to try to do that—I see they run the whole place.

Ants are travelers between worlds; between the living and the dead, between the cemetery and the bora ring. Ants aren't glamorous; it's hard to imagine someone claiming Ant proudly as their totem, but they carry a lot of symbolism. They're so organized, regimented even; just like the relentless sweep of death and endings that greets us at the end of every cycle. No room for individualism; each of us ages and dies just like everyone else. They're the absolute of the mundane; insects which are neither glamorous nor dangerous and yet here they are on the borders of reality, inhabiting the bora ring with its thousands-year-old history, cleaning up and recycling the dead.

There's one direction left that I haven't been able to find an animal for: the North; the lookout. There are also magpies here in the trees near the car park, but again they don't seem iconic or especially representative of the place or its direction. There are a lot of dogs on leashes, being walked up the hill and down again, attached to their owners more than to the place. Once when I was here a pelican flew over, shockingly low because of the sudden height of this hill. I'm sure it was quite high up in the sky until it skimmed over this place; I felt if I reached my hand up I'd be touching its belly. But it was gone in a few seconds, and they so belong to the river mouth down below that I couldn't think of asking them to hold some other place.

Damon pointed it out to me eventually, the sign that no one reads. Lions Lookout. *It's lions,* he insisted, *this place belongs to lions!* There are no lions in Australia and there never were. They're almost a mythical animal in this context; magnificent, but they don't belong. He argued that a mythical animal was even better; why had I been so mundane in my choices, with birds and ants and snakes? And especially for this position, corresponding with the Summer Solstice; surely that should have a mythical animal, if any direction should. And they were golden, like the sun, and kings of their domain; they'd love a lookout! Especially one named for them... How could I refute this logic? I was never entirely comfortable with it and left it open in the back of my mind, but no other animal ever showed up to contradict it, and so it gradually and quietly became, as named, the lions' lookout.

These were some of my own journeys and discoveries of these eight places, but we all made journeys and discoveries. We created relationship with these places, we studied them, we made offerings and visits and then, when we stood in circle together and called to our outlying Circle of Eight, we knew what we were calling to. When I stood and called to the mountain, when I invoked its spirit to hold a place in our circle and ritual, I wasn't just calling to ancient volcanic forces, to long-ago mountain lava. I wasn't just calling to that iconic shape that sticks up out of the landscape to hold clouds captive and call forth the rains, to that place caught in the tides between fire and water. I was calling to the tall trees, the clayed earth, and the little stream; I was calling to glimpses of black cockatoos, to their shadows and presence felt and swallowed even if not seen.

This energy flooded through me into the circle, in my words and presence, in what I spoke and how I spoke it, my voice reverent for the mountain, somber for fire and flood, filled with surprise at those sweep-ing black calling shadows and stilled with the hush of forest. If I called to it in summer—well, I knew it in summer, the air hot and dense. If I called to it in winter, I had been there then, too; the snap of air, the claggy soil, bright sun in the shorter day cut to cold by afternoon. At night I had been there; at dawn. I had been there sheltered on the forest floor, soft with shed leaves and bark, in tiny groves formed by close-grown trees towering above me. I had been once to the top; shrouded in a mist so severe I could not see even a few arm-lengths ahead of me. I knew what it looked like from all directions. I knew what it felt like to sleep a night on its slopes. When I stood in circle, facing North-West to invoke the mountain I took a breath and gave my voice over to it, and through me roared its exploding rock from long ago, and it called also like the black cockatoos, sounds and feathers floating on the wind.

If I called to the West, invoking that still lake, my voice was taken by the depths, by the swans swimming across it, by the cool breeze it gave on a hot day. In the South-West my voice whispered, carrying a long way out, speaking secrets to the other realms and inviting them, through my voice and vision, into our circle. My voice held the secrets of the ants, their uncounted numbers busy about the life-and-death pro-cess; my voice held dry soil and the memory of a place sacred long, long before white people thought of coming here. In the South my voice might carry downwards with the water to fall and spill into the pool awaiting it, contained in its rock walls and greenery. In the South-East my voice was breathy with discovery—cliff path, small beach, hidden caves—the winds of change coming in, beckoning to the incoming tides, releasing with a sigh the outgoing. In the East when I breathed that fresh sea air and saw dolphins playing, the direction laughed with me for the novelty of land after so much sea and played with the dan-gers of cliffs, smashing waves, and strong winds. Invoking the North-East, I gave myself over to the conflict—the thrust and shove of river and sea; opposites meeting, surrendering, and conquering, each in turn; a primal dance. And in the North I felt the sweep of the whole circle behind me, around me; I surveyed the land and spoke its beauty.

How to Work with Invocation in Your Circle of Eight

Invocations are usually made near the start of a ceremony. In an invocation, you call out to an energy, being, or characteristic that you wish to be present for the ritual or working. In this way, elements can be invoked, gods and goddesses, spirits or energies, or even places or other people who are not physically present. I prefer not to invoke the elements, reasoning that they are already present; an acknowledgment works better, especially an acknowledgment of how the element appears on this occasion. The word *invocation* implies bringing something present that wasn't there originally.

Viewed this way, invocation becomes a more complex subject, and perhaps what we are really talking about is always acknowledgment: bringing our awareness to different aspects of deity and energy that are always present everywhere, but when they receive our attention and honoring they come into the forefront of our minds and thus take a stronger part in our ritual. Invocation, however, is the commonly used term and the one I am using here.

Invocations and acknowledgments are usually made aloud, although not always. They can be done silently using movement, dance, or inner focus, and they can be done with music: drum, other instrument, or voice. They can be made by one person, several people, or by the whole group. Usually different invocations are carried out by different people, so if you were invoking the ancestors, the Goddess, and the God, three different people or different sets of people would make those invocations. You can invoke from the perimeter of the circle—this is commonly done for elements and directions—or from the center.

I experience invocations as powerful when they rise up through the person and express themselves spontaneously through movement, words, and sound. I like to see the Horned Lord in the scraping of someone's feet, their shifting shoulders and lift of the head, and hear something of his power in their voice. Invocations that are prewritten, in verse, or read off a piece of paper don't do it for me. I have heard powerful invocations in ceremonial magic that were committed to memory and recited; the difference being, I think, that those people had deeply related to and worked with the words and concepts, so the invocations still arrived through the vehicle of their own emotions and experience as they called out the words.

In a geographic Circle of Eight, the places themselves may be invoked—called to—in ritual, to presence them at wherever the ritual is taking place. This is usually done facing outwards, into the direction, sending an energetic thread from the ritual to the place. Depending on the working, there also may be other invocations. The essence of any invocation is communication. The person invoking is communicating on an internal and bodily level with what they are invoking, as well as with the other people present, to convey to them a living sense of what is being invoked. They are a medium, a channel, and their focus, intention, and embodiment will make the difference between an effective invocation and one that doesn't quite convince or convey a sense of what is being called to.

How to Work with Invocations

There are both technical and energetic considerations to take into account when invoking. Practicing invocations before the ritual begins can be useful to adjust things such as the volume of people's voices and the length of the invocations. Devoting part of one circle meeting purely to practicing and working with invocations is a great way of focusing everyone's attention on this part of creating magic and means your group will learn to work well together and pass seamlessly from one to another when making a series of invocations. This also helps when everyone is facing outwards to invoke the eight directions and so is not able to easily see each other, relying instead on vocal cues for when one person has finished and it's the next person's turn.

Technical Considerations

- *Volume.* About half the invocations I've ever witnessed in ritual can't be heard by most of the people there. Some people may need a lot of encouragement to raise their voices to the volume where they can be easily heard by the entire group. Vocal, singing, and breath exercises can all offer support for everyone to learn to use their voice effectively. Speaking loudly enough when your back is to the group is particularly challenging.

- *Length.* Keeping all the invocations roughly similar in length adds to the cohesion of the overall ritual. Invocations can be too brief to get a sense of what's being called to and, more often, can be so long that the energy dies out of them and is lost. Having a clear agreement of how long invocations should be—for example, about three sentences—will help with consistency.

- *Content.* It's certainly possible to call to the Goddess and list a hundred or so of her attributes, but is it relevant to the ritual you're about to do? Prior to the ritual, think carefully about the invocations and the point of inviting or presencing each thing you are calling to. What is their function in this ritual? Tailor your invocations towards that.

- *Relevance.* Some people like to invoke the ancestors. Some the fey. Some Kali, or Hermes; fire or undying spirit. Of course they are all wonderful things and beings to invoke and be aware of; but do they have a part in your ritual? If they don't, they're probably better left for a different time. It could be like asking someone to a tea party and then sticking them in a corner and forgetting to serve them anything or introduce them to anyone. If you're lucky, they'll just feel ignored…

Energetic Considerations

- *Style.* Calling to fire in the same voice that you would use for water, or calling to the East in the same voice as you'd use for West, is not effective. The style and manner in which each invocation is made should represent what is being called to. Thus the fire invocation could be sparking or a ferocious roar, it could be glowing with warmth or leaping up and down, but it should not be dripping, pouring, or monotonal.

- *Embodiment.* Sometimes this is shown purely through hand movements; other times, the whole body is involved. All levels can be used to embody an invocation: on or near the ground, the mid-range we usually interact at, and above the head, arms reaching up and head thrown back. Let your invocation into your body—let yourself dance with air or stamp the ground with earth.

- *Intention.* Spending some time before the invocation—at least half an hour but preferably a few days—knowing this is the invocation you will be making allows you to drop more deeply into the feel of what you will be invoking and how to do this. You may choose to acknowledge what you will be invoking on your own altar, in your journal, or another way. It's like introducing yourself to a guest before introducing them to the whole party; it's polite, and it gives you some material to work with.

- *Intuition.* However carefully prepared you are, the real invocation is the one that happens in the ritual. Be open to how it feels in the moment; if you feel an impulse to lower your voice, sweep your arms around, or change some of the words you thought you'd say, trust this intuition. You can experiment—maybe as a group—responding to these intuitions, and see what difference it makes.

How to Invoke Geographic Directions in the Circle of Eight

Note: Detailed instructions on casting a circle, releasing a circle, and turning the wheel in a Circle of Eight are in the appendix.

1. Stand in the direction and anchor yourself there. Feel its resonance through your feet and entire body.

2. Turn to face the direction, so your back is to the center of the circle, and take some deep breaths. You can imagine that these breaths are bringing the air of your directional place into your body.

3. Name the place or the direction aloud—whatever has been decided by the group earlier. Then begin speaking in a voice you are channeling through the direction—so it is literally using your breath but coming from that geographic place in your Circle of Eight—and speak either of its qualities that you are presencing for the ritual or of the place as you see, imagine, and remember it, bringing it to life for those listening.

4. Finish with your agreed words or signal; it works best if this is the same for each invocation as a clear punctuation between one invocation and the next. This could be a drum beat, a simple sentence such as *To the South-West I call!* or an honoring: *We thank the South-West for its presence.*

5. Remain facing in that direction until all remaining directions have been called.

6. Turn together, all at once, and face the center. Now is the time to invoke Above, Below, and Center if you are going to do so. It's particularly effective if you all turn in the same direction—anticlockwise in the Southern Hemisphere and clockwise in the Northern Hemisphere.

Ritual

I've been to the lookout many times. It's an easy drive, no trekking involved. You leave the highway and wind through a couple of smooth suburban streets between neat blocked houses, take a switchback turn up a short, steep incline, and you're already there, at the top. Tourists visit, briefly; locals pass through jogging and walking dogs; couples come here occasionally and tradesmen with their lunch or a beer and a little time to kill. From the car park, you walk along a path worn in the grass past a few rubbish bins, picnic tables, and eucalypts, then the path dips and passes under an avenue of trees. Their branches meet overhead; it's the only part of the lookout where you can't see out all around you. I've always imagined it as a place for a wedding, to be walking through the trees and emerging onto the small, rounded hilltop, with the 180-degree sweep of ocean straight ahead of you and a geological survey pillar to mark where you are.

Most people only stay here ten minutes; half an hour at the most. I stay for hours and watch the passing traffic. A lot of people pass through over time; it's a brief respite from the ordered suburb below. It's not the highest point in the landscape, but it's got clear space all around it; you can see a lot. You can see most of our circle; the East and South-East, the North-East and North-West are all landmarks from up here. There are hints of the other places—the South-East is part of that coastline blur, the West and South-West are out behind those smudges of trees, tucked in behind distant ridges. Here the world is laid out below, half land and half sea, with the coastline dividing them and changing at every wave.

Once I watched the sun settle on the tip of the old volcano, our North-West, and then slowly slide down the slope on its nightward journey. I didn't want to breathe, didn't want to take my eyes away for a second, so I watched it in slow motion, delicate and perfect. I never saw that again; every time I was there at sunset, the sun was either wildly north or south of the mountain, so I could hardly imagine it had ever happened. Once, gazing the other way, I waited for the full moon to rise over the sea; about twenty people gathered, haphazardly arriving in pairs or singly to stand around, watching for the moon. One woman unpacked a basket with a tea set as if we were at a prearranged ritual, miniscule Japanese tea cups, and she poured green tea, offering it to strangers, and we all drank a mouthful or two in turns. We didn't speak much; after the moon had risen we drifted off in our ones and twos down the hill or back to the car park.

Circles Within Circles

One of my ideas is to bring the Circle of Eight into the rituals we held for the Wheel of the Year, or to bring those rituals into the circle. The festivals are already circular, of course; they progress continuously, and when we draw them in a diagram, we don't put them in a straight line but in the endlessly turning circle of the earth around the sun. It's a conceptual difference, maybe; that I want to experience them not so much as stations we happen to arrive at in the course of a year but more as an evolving revelation, each one unfolding in turn from the very center and essence of the wheel like endless layers of petals opening out, each offering a particular flavor. To experience that each festival is only one aspect of the endlessness and that they are more true to each other than they are to their individuality, the way we have come to understand the Circle of Eight.

I love complex layering. With each layer the model seems to grow in integrity, coming closer and closer to what it seeks to describe. So in our heads we carry a diagram of the Wheel of the Year, adjusted for the Southern Hemisphere and overlaid onto the compass directions. Each

of them are a Circle of Eight. Then we have our own small arrangement of eight cushions in my living room. Moving around that we have
ourselves, the human element, each holding one of the eight places but
each also, over time, holding all places. And we have layered in the local
level: eight places—nine, including the center—that act as an expansive
link for our own Circle of Eight and a concrete localization of the larger
levels of the wheel.

As well, I wanted to bring the children further in.

Lots of children come to the festivals, from babies to teenagers, and
some of them come again and again over a year or many years. At some
point I thought there were enough of them to form their own group,
and so we began a children's magic group that ran one afternoon a
week for eight weeks and then, after a break, for another eight weeks.
They named it the Phoenix Circle. Some of them were very familiar
with the Circle of Eight, having attended festivals since they were young
and been part of the seemingly endless visiting of directions with us.
They knew ritual and magic from the inside, but apart from Damon
they hadn't ever been formally taught.

I layered the Phoenix Circle into the Circle of Eight. They were on a
very fast circuit, changing directions every week, so I energetically
placed their circle inside our circle, nested within it on the fastest rotation. They were the Mercury of our system. There were six of them,
three girls and three boys, and their ages ranged from ten to sixteen. I
was the only adult in the Phoenix Circle, and I sat opposite the empty
cushion so they were all paired. Ostensibly I was the teacher, but of
course I learned as much as they did. Some of what I learned was about
their yearnings and griefs, their personalities and struggles both magically and in the world, but what delighted me even more was what I
learned about the circle.

I learned how fast the Circle of Eight can be. With only one week in
each direction, there's no time for procrastination or for energies and
projects to get distilled between meetings. In the Phoenix Circle, we
conduct ritual and discussion and go out armed with a spell to create
and bring back from one week to the next. Whether we're working

with dreams, intentions, shadows, or invocations, problem solving or attraction magic to bring what we need, we've got one week only—seven days, seven nights—to make it happen. And they make it happen. They set up spells on their bedside tables, they work on changing their relationships with their parents or solving problems at school or examining a secret part of themselves, and they do it within a week.

I learn how deeply a group of children is willing to go with each other—at least as deeply as a group of adults. The level of vulnerability seems far greater as they experiment with speaking their feelings and trying out ritual together and with the steps they take into self-knowledge. I feel like I am witnessing their very first excursions into group trust. They have an almost impatience with the directions themselves—as if they've known all that already, for ages, and don't need to dwell on it. They are more fascinated by the elements, and we do a lot of elemental magic. They like making things, so we make masks and spells and pictures and songs.

One time we sit there and each pick someone in the circle who reminds us in some way of ourselves and talk about how it is to see a piece of ourselves reflected back in this other person. We also choose someone to talk about whom we admire; it is deeply moving. I remember being admired for traits that are not usually commented on in my adult world, and it meant more to me than most recognitions. At the conclusion of our sharing, we each choose one trait we want to strengthen in ourselves, a trait we see in someone else, and we ask them for permission to borrow it for a week so we can test it out and discover how to encourage it in ourselves. The next week we returned it to them and reflected on how we had developed it and what we would do now to support that trait.

The Phoenix Circle went straight to a deep level; they were willing to believe that everything was held within the circle—that they could find and access everything. Their weekly reporting back did not have the level of insight or analysis of the adults, but it had a rawness, an undiluted whack of that direction. For me, watching and participating, it held a validation that the circle structure itself would teach, would be teacher, as well as that children could have the focus and discipline the structure asked for. Each time I would try something I thought radical—for example, making masks of our shadow parts and doing personal revealing and reclamation of these parts in a mirror, with everyone else as witness—they would claim they loved it and it was the best thing we had ever done. I learned not to hold back with them because they were children but instead to appreciate their daring and adventurousness, their willingness and honesty.

When it came to the Wheel of the Year festivals, we merged the two circles so that we stood paired in the directions, an adult with a child. And this was not organized the way we would usually expect, a parent with their own child, but organized by direction: a child and adult stood there related through the Circle of Eight as equals. Separately, but together, they held the West, the South-East, or whatever direction it happened to be.

In this way, the Phoenix Circle took a step outwards, creating and holding the circle not just among themselves but in the wider, slower Wheel of the Year, arriving as full participants. The children had always been given parts in the ritual—to lead a song or a journey, decorate altars, hide spring eggs, hold a god or goddess energy—but it was while the Phoenix Circle was operating that we saw them stepping into the festival rituals with a confidence and maturity that came from holding and working their own group. To have them participating in this way, bringing their circle into ours, taught us respect and brought a joy of working with them that we had barely touched on previously. After the formal meetings of the Phoenix Circle came to an end, they—individually and also as a group, when more than one of them were present—retained this maturity and full participation in the rituals.

The Lookout

. . . .

Memoir

My relationship is dissolving, and it's unbearable. The flat is too small; neither of us can stand the unhappiness cramped into that place and so sometimes we come here, to the lookout, and sit at a picnic table and gaze at the view. We don't talk much; he reads the paper and I try to breathe the spaciousness—air and sea and sky and forests—into me. Sometimes one of us says a few words and the other one nods.

We sit across the table from each other so he is part of my view. He's so desperately familiar I cannot imagine that space without him in it. I seem to have been rendered numb, speechless, almost without thought; I am stunned into incomprehension. I have been leaning towards the sight of him, the physical existence of him—that blond hair, sharp features, sinewy body with the confident hands; that abrupt laugh and his startling blue eyes—from the moment I first saw him across a room at a party. He arrived into my vision so completely then, he took up a space

I had never known I was searching to fill, so that I've marveled at it ever since: the living fact of him. In all our closenesses, our sometimes falling aparts, I've never thought of wanting or looking for anyone else; he burns for me, draws me in.

So he says he is leaving but he walks with me, lies beside me at night, comes and sits in this place of spaciousness up above ordinary life. You can see the river's meandering mouth here, the canals; you can see the supermarket and our flat at the edge of the rainforest; you can see the highway and the beaches and lots of sky. Perhaps we like it because we have lived so much of our time together in open spaces, not small flats; we've camped in olive groves in Italy, German forests, English fields, and the Australian bush. We've spent days and nights by beaches, country cricket pitches, narrow rushing creeks; when we've been in cities, it's been to marvel at the art, the streets, the wonder of cathedrals, and then we got out quick.

We are used to being together; we know what the other is thinking, and so this separation is half killing us, all the feelings doubled back and forth like webs binding us tighter so then I can't understand at all why he is going. Up here I can fling all that away—the air blows through me, coldly; I am chilled even though it is high summer. The wind separates out, like combing through strands of hair, all the impossibilities, all the pasts and futures, and I am thinned down to this: a small animal, sheltering on a hilltop, alive.

We discovered this place by accident. Since we've been together we haven't stopped anywhere for very long, staying in each house six or nine months before going overseas again, and so I had a recklessness when I chose a flat in this neatened suburb—this ordinary, aspirational place of ordered houses, roads all curved at predetermined arcs to make you think you're not living in a series of lined-up boxes. A developed area, town-planned; so different from the haphazard rural sprawl slowly converting to middle-class eccentrics building dream experiments that dominate most of this area. I chose a flat knowing we wouldn't stay long, converted by the price and the novelty of being on the third floor, right next to the rainforest, so the bats flew through the balcony every night on their way to dinner. I didn't calculate that we would enact our splitting-up here, trapped in what now feels like a too-small tower.

So we go out, individually and together, and walk this suburb, pacing it and stumbling across its secrets. A corner block that's never been built on and somehow has converted to a park: not an official park with notices and benches but the unofficial kind where the trees haven't been cut down, bushes have grown, and there's birds and shelter from the roads and the relentless houses that mainly seek to ooze over the sides of their allotments. A wide green culvert between two rows of the backs of houses curves like the roads do here, and maybe children come out from the houses to play, but we don't see them. A paved path that winds up the sudden steepness of a small, sharp, bushy hill; bottlebrush planted to either side of its switchback turns until you emerge at the top, the top of this place.

The lookout. It's years before it will become a part of the Circle of Eight, but this is my introduction to it. We come here and instead of looking inward like our flat insists, instead of gazing at this mess between us, we look out: to the snaking river, the wide sea, the vast domains spread below. This place will come to represent the Summer Solstice for me, the pinnacle of the year, the place from which you can see everything. My lover came back on the Summer Solstice, flying in from his five-month absence to tell me he was ending the relationship, and I saw everything then, from that viewpoint.

We had a ritual planned for the solstice; twenty or so people gathered, but my voice had vanished, I had to ask someone else to run the ritual, and my friend stepped in—the one who's always been fire to my earth, water to my air; she who eventually sits opposite me in the Circle of Eight to balance and reflect me. She sang the casting of the circle and the calling of directions as if she was gathering up the threads of me that lay scattered over the floor, blasted about by the height of this place, that view I had on the Summer Solstice that he was going to leave.

The Summer Solstice carries the irony that even though it is the best, the brightest, the crowning of the king, the victory of love and the longest day, the minute it's past we start to fall downhill. The very moment of victory signifies the downfall of the year, the long, slow turning back towards the dark, towards winter, away from the splendid heights just now attained. My relationship is like that, too. We've spent time building it, learning each other, discovering these rich, fertile places where we love and love, and now, just when we've come through our trials, our journeys, our survival and expansion, and we're back together again—now it is the end. Looking down on the world, I can see that. I can see how once you're at the top it seems there's nowhere to go but down.

Why can't I fly? Why can't I launch myself off this pinnacle and head not downwards into the mundane turn of the wheel, the year moving towards autumn and winter in its relentless way, the relationship falling apart as it seems so determined to do, but upwards, into the sky, and beyond this place? If the Summer Solstice is part of the Wheel of the Year, the zenith, I know that there is something beyond that, too. Yes, on this little earth we are bound into that pattern, those turnings, but the whole universe lies beyond that, and both the Summer Solstice and lookouts call to that possibility of extension, escape, ascension, release. If the Year King wears a crown with golden rays on his head, isn't that what he is saying? That he belongs to more than the earth; he is celestial, godlike, and so hinting of escape from this cycle.

My feet are on the earth, yes, like someone standing in the Summer Solstice position on the wheel has their feet connected to the rest of it. But all the rest of me is up above, is higher than the houses and rivers and trees, than the ordinary people with their cars on the highway and shopping trolleys in the supermarket. This damaged love I'm carrying around with me, I don't want to let it go, to fall into decay, which is the natural progression of the cycle. I want it to soar, be celestial; I want to be embraced by the gods in it, not bound down to the rot of earth.

But we cannot do it. We are, after all, human. People who come to the lookout do not gaze up into endless expanse but down into the known world that's temporarily transformed in their vision, by height. I look down into my world even while I'm grasping at the fact that he's still here, still says he loves me, and I see the inevitable crush of it; the loss and devastation, the grinding down of all that's been until nothing's left, or just a seed, waiting silent until spring. I can't welcome death but I acknowledge it, up there from the top of the world. Since I have to, I let the wind blow it all away.

And somehow these events don't stain this place. When I come here afterwards, after he has left for exotic cities and relationships I am not a part of, I feel some measure of freedom, some resonance of the blowing away and not the agony of being torn apart. It's as if not just him but his image has been blown away by these winds. It's always windy, so he is insubstantial, shadowy, one of thousands who passes through this place seeking a few moments to hover above everything, not some icon stamped here. Up here everything blows away, everything is spread out as a picture, and one can see in all directions: mountain, sea, coastal inlets, rainforest, highway.

My lover brings me here, many years later, long past that earlier lover who left. By now this lookout has become the North point in the Circle of Eight and is layered with so many rituals and magical workings that its earlier history is scarcely remembered. We walk from the car park, past the picnic tables and their ghosts and through the dipped avenue of small but solid trees, trees not immense but on a human scale, their roots veining the dirt path, branches and leaves rustling overhead. When we get to the lookout proper, the bit that perches above everything, the grassy knoll the surveyors placed their marker on, he turns to me, his face flushed, and pulls me close. He asks if I would marry him.

And I am in this place where everything blows away, even the past, and though I remember it all I am somewhere new—at the Summer Solstice of my life perhaps, having found, now, what I wanted so much, someone who wants to stand in the open air and cleave by my side, to walk down this avenue of trees and choose me when the whole world is offered. And the ring he gives me is a Summer Solstice ring, gold and silver together, a landscape of mountains, or you could see it as the rippled line of the coast with a gold serpent winding through it; the river, the tides, the striking of sun onto the outline of mountain, even as one of the ribbons of liquid light that flowed down the side of that mountain millennia ago when the land was formed, and I say *yes*.

Wheel of the Year Festivals

As we begin to fit the Wheel of the Year rituals into our Circle of Eight, everything strengthens and deepens. The rituals take on a textured, 3-D aspect when they embody the landscape of our directional places, and those places dance into life at the time of their festival, luminescent with the attention not just we but the whole year is focusing on them. Imbolc gathers to itself those fresh winds of our small South-East beach; the Spring Equinox points out into the world like the cape; Beltaine rushes in and out like the river meeting the sea. Even though we are conducting the Summer Solstice ritual in my garden in the hills, the whole energy and feel of the lookout is with us, and the ritual rises to that height and scope of vision. Lammas settles deep within the mountain, the Autumn Equinox spills onto the stilled surface of the lake, Samhain stretches out to the bora ring, and Winter Solstice drops into the pool at the base of the waterfall.

The Winter Solstice is a pivot in the Wheel of the Year, bringing the birth of light and renewing the whole turn of the wheel. The rounded aspect of our place for this direction creates the impression of being held, womblike. It's dramatic and nurturing all at once; the pool and rock walls receive the huge force of the waterfall and then send forth a stream winding seawards. For this particular Winter Solstice we call to all eight directions. Each calling references birth, each invocation comes sliding over the edge like water spilling out of the beginnings of the Winter Solstice. In the ritual we decorate candles, inscribing them with spells for the new year: love and peace and happiness. Then we go out into the darkness of the cold night and stand in a circle around our unlit fire.

Into that pool of night we pour our fears. We speak our private nightmares—the death of loved ones, loss, heartbreak, despair—and our fears for the world: disaster, war, and famine. We keep speaking until we run out of words. There is stillness. Into the dark new sounds drop—the voice of the Goddess interlaced with that of the Sun Lord. Two voices weaving and dancing together in darkness, speaking the words down line by line of stars and mysteries, the secrets of flame and bodies and souls. They speak of the life of the earth, of worship and sacrifice, song and awe and reverence, freedom and love. They offer us the bounty of the earth, to be lived with our own lives.

One candle is lit; the first light struck. Another is lit from it, and then another, until all of us hold lights; then we step forward and light the bonfire with them. We begin our songs, singing to the earth and the Lord of the Dance. We are strong and fierce on this long night; the bonfire burns bright, and we dance until we are out of breath. When we complete our ritual, we feel it still: the sheltering of the wheel, the turn and change that marks this night, and the sparks we take forward into the new cycle the same way the water flows on into the world.

The next ritual in the year is Imbolc. For us it's twinned with the little beach with the sudden tides and the wind blowing in from the South-East. It's a simple place with no amenities; not exactly hard to get to, but most people wouldn't bother. It's a direction weather arrives from; it's the scent of the new and sudden shifts into growth and difference. Imbolc can be like that: deceptively simple, easily neglected, but actually carrying the winds of change and worth the effort to seek it out.

We ask everyone to bring a seedling to give away—a native, an herb, or a bulb—in a pot. We call to the eight directions not by place names but by aspect and feeling: *breezes and the sudden tide; cliffs, dolphins, and breaking surf; river meeting sea; height and vision all around; looming, fertile depth; peace and the stretch of sacred waters; mystery and the other worlds; pool and waterfall, cave and snake.* Imbolc feels young and expansive, back in the time of sensation and immediacy and prior to concepts of naming or definition.

We hand out colored paper in the shape of leaves; we write wishes for the future on them and tie these to the seedlings. Then, imagining that we inhabited the environment of Imbolc, of our small beach looking out to nowhere, we build a collective vision of the time one hundred years in the future: *the environment is healthy and thriving; war is forgotten; the world operates on a gift economy; food, water, and shelter are rights, not commodities.* We begin singing our song, breathing life and air into our vision as if we ourselves are the winds bringing a change in the world's weather.

We move closer to our current time, drawing our vision of one hundred years with us to a time ten years in the future. Again we vision together for a time ten years ahead: *the environment is starting to heal; there are no more wars anywhere on the planet; third world debt is forgiven; we become self-responsible.* We sing and drum and dance the next line of our song, giving our seedlings to the altar and grounding our vision into the earth, growing ourselves along with them into this future.

We draw the vision back closer again, one year in the future. Now we water the seedlings, singing to them of the journey water makes from land to sea and back again; we draw the vision to us like the incoming tide. Finally we speak of the present, this turn of the wheel, and each person makes a commitment towards the visioning—what they will do to bring it to life. *I will bring environmental issues into my workplace; I will make an indigenous harvesting trail for the community; I will take up political letter writing; I will be happy; I will investigate recycling.* We light the candle on the altar and sing the whole song, igniting our vision and intent, and we each pick out one of the seedlings to plant as a symbol of our promise. We are the tides that turn and turn, we are the change of weather sweeping in, we are the fresh breeze into the new year.

The Spring Equinox is always aligned with the East; wherever you are in the world, that's where the sun rises. And our particular East is so definite: the cape and the easternmost point of Australia. We hold the sunrise position here at the pointed edge of land; we hold this balance of light and dark as the pendulum of the year swings upwards into the light. To represent this certainty, we cast our Spring Equinox circle into just four directions: East, North, West, and South.

We write wishes on pieces of colored ribbon, then we begin singing our song. We separate, still singing, and go into the garden to tie our ribbons to a tree. They flutter in the breeze as we regroup on the lawn. We've also brought decorated eggs, and now we set about the egg hunt: spying them hidden among the rocks and plants, wedged high in a tree or balanced on a windowsill. After the hunt, we gather and show off our treasures: the spiraled eggs and the ones with glitter and hearts, the universe eggs with stars or a moon, and spring eggs with flowers and ribbons. We encourage people to interpret them. If you found your egg nested in the grasses at your feet, it could mean you need to look more closely at what's right in front of you. If you had to climb into a tree to get it, then maybe the egg is telling you to reach out, stretch for what you want.

The symbols and ritual are simple like the East is simple: ribbons, wishes, eggs. Nothing that you don't see or can't find with a bit of looking, the way our East place offers itself to us every time we go there. It's simple and strong: cliffs, sea and dolphins, wind and air, water and earth.

Beltaine we see symbolized in the to and fro at the river mouth, the tidal river where salt meets fresh water. The river mouth draws in and then sends out waters; the sea advances and retreats. It's an orderly process, timed to the tides, but standing there watching it—that pull and suck and smash where they actually meet—it looks churning, chaotic, as if the balance has to be fought and found every moment and quarter moment. So it is with Beltaine, when we meet our lovers in the twisting dance of the Maypole, weaving our ribbons and creating what looks like tangled chaos only to have it emerge as beautiful patterns. We jump the fire, daring the flames not to eat us, and we throw the role of the God up into the air and watch it settle on first one, then another and another until finally it comes to rest on someone who, perhaps, we knew all along had the will and desire to draw it to themselves and hold it.

This particular Beltaine we come dressed to honor a god or goddess. We are outside and have set bamboo poles in the lawn in the cross-quarters to mark the circle. A mix of people arrive—people who've been coming to these rituals for years, some who dip in and out, and a large number who've never been before. Between the Circle of Eight and the Phoenix Circle we call into all eight directions, and the ritual feels both tightly held and also expansive; on the crest of a little hill, overlooking the house but overlooked, in turn, by the rock and tree bluff high and abrupt behind us. Everything is in between at Beltaine, the merging and push-and-pulling back and forth.

Last year's God is set free and chased by a mix of children and adults until he's run down. Then the tide turns as he's brought back to face the challenges. There are eight challenges written on colored cards, and the role of God is tossed back and forward, sometimes held for the length of a few challenges, sometimes lost immediately. Our challenges are as mixed as the season; chanting, arm wrestling, spear throwing, invocation. When the final challenge is completed, a young man has won. He's never been to our rituals before, and his wife and small children look on, bemused, as he strives for this role.

We dance around him as the Maypole; we are giving ourselves to the chaos elements of this ritual and this time of year, and our ribbons are as chaotic as anything else. There's narrow ribbons: dark green, peach, dark gold, yellow, and red bordered with gold. There's a red, mid-width ribbon that looks as if it's been cut from fabric; it's uneven and frays all along the length, but its color stands out in the weaving and another that is metallic, a sparkly gold. There are wide ribbons, too; a transparent one with solid white hearts all down its center, a deep blue ribbon bordered with gold, a multicolored cotton ribbon that looks like it's from India with a gold embossed pattern stamped on one side. After the dance, we give away some precious things: a lace dress, a book, a wall hanging, a jeweled ring. Then we feast and light the Beltaine fire.

Our Summer Solstice place is that little, busy peak in the North where most of the circle can be seen. At the solstice we're just entering the hottest time of year, with bushfires and droughts as ever-present possibilities, so we don't emphasize the fire aspects of this festival but focus on the meeting of opposites, celebration, and offerings. Just as the lookout itself isn't very grand, our Summer Solstice rituals are humble, occurring just a few days before Christmas and the end of the year when everyone is rushed with finishing school and getting ready for family celebrations and holidays.

In the garden we invoke the God as the beneficent Sun King and the Goddess as fertile Earth Mother, pouring forth flowers and fruit and greenery. Then we separate into groups to devise our ritual. When we come back together, the men present the God as a many-aspected deity, each of them contributing a part of him and each one receiving his touch. They plant themselves on the earth as if they were trees and offer us gifts from their branches. The women bring out mangos, that yellow-golden fruit of summer that blushes red. We dance with each other, then slice the fruit and offer it round, letting juice drip down our arms and feeding people with our fingers.

Then the children come into the center. They're old enough not to have needed an adult with them as they worked on their part of the ritual, so we don't know what they've planned. They put on a little play, finishing with a song and dance to honor their mothers. Then they gather themselves into a small clump and approach the men. They say they have a request of their fathers that they'd like to ask on the Summer Solstice. They ask them for more time. They stand there, so serious—eleven years old, eight, five; friends and strangers, Phoenix Circle mixed with other children—and look at the men.

I feel like crying seeing them standing there, hearing them ask this favor. It seems incredible that they know what they want, what they're missing; even in this community where fathers are around and spend lots of time with their children, it's still that: more time. The men stumble in their answers, choke, hardly know how to deal with it; to look at their own child or address them as a group; to apologize, promise, justify. Watching, I feel immensely proud of them. I don't ever discover whose idea that was or how they came to decide to do that as part of the ritual.

Afterwards we make a Summer Solstice mandala, laying out grains, fruits, and vegetables onto the dark green grass in orange, yellow, purple, blue, brown, and cream. It is all the richness of summer gathered together, like all the places and the richness of our circle gathered around our lookout. We sing and drum a disorganized chant, shouting out our desires as we circle around the mandala: *love, peace, change, growth, truth, power, acceptance, fertility.* It's all there. Then we thank the God and Goddess, leave our mandala as a gift for the birds and animals, and lie around on the grass to feast outside in the sunny evening.

By Lammas we are entirely over the heat. It's been very dry this summer, too dry, and everyone's waiting for the rain. We need it to damp down the threat of bushfire, we need it to fill our water tanks, and we need it to bring relief from the burning heat. Our Lammas place is the mountain that's sometimes known as Cloud Catcher, since it nearly always has clouds clinging to its peak. We decide this ritual is the perfect time to invoke the rains, to tempt them towards us; it's the changeover season from summer to autumn and, we hope, from dry to wet. That mountain is always so present in our circle; we write the whole ritual to please it.

We cast into the cross-quarters, honoring and reflecting the power of the mountain. We gather ourselves in groups of two and three into each of the cross-quarters for the calling, the Phoenix Circle merged in with the Circle of Eight. We hear the power gathering in the grouped voices like that feeling before rain when the pressure lowers and the air quivers. Over twenty people are here, and when we talk about our relationship to the mountain we hear how it holds a corner of everyone's map.

We're calling for rain, and we've got an elemental ritual. We break into four groups to develop the sound and energy of the elements, then we come back together and start our ritual. Each element goes into the center in turn. We have air rushing about, whistling and sighing in high voices; fire crouched on the ground and growing in strength, power, and conviction until it consumes the whole circle; water trickling and singing and pattering around the edges, only slowly converging on the center, and, finally, earth, solid and standing stable like trees, humming low and steady.

Then we add them in one by one, layering them over each other—air with its breezes and song; fire's flickering, scorching, devouring. Between them they start to dry out the land, to threaten and blow and expand and consume. Water comes in, a delicate sound we can hardly hear at first, but after a while it has an impact, raining at the edges and gradually expanding its territory, letting the wind blow it wide to damp down the fire, and it gets louder and louder; the water people drum their feet on the floor and slap their arms and legs for the sound of loud, loud rain on the roof, and the fire people huddle down in the center of the group on the floor, trying not to go out altogether, and then the earth people join in with a song about trees receiving the rain gratefully, stretching out their branches and sending moisture to their leaves; they stand in a line and welcome the rain.

We take our offerings outside to a rock altar and gift the energy we've raised to the turning of the year. The rock is embedded in the ground, one of the igneous rocks left here from the ancient volcano and now decorated with flowers, drawings, a poem, shells and fruit and vegetables. We sing our song out there, elemental and praying for rain; we hope we feel it coming into the air, pulling in some of that tide of the North-West. Perhaps it's just the dusk, but we imagine those clouds we've called to are considering visiting us, leaving their safe holding space of the mountain to venture into the valleys and towards the coast, bringing the wet season with them. We imagine the mountain might send them our way, and we thank it in advance.

Just like the Autumn Equinox, our place for the West is made up of contrasts. The festival celebrates abundance at a time of descent into the darkness; our West place is the human-made dam that has settled so gracefully into the landscape. The Autumn Equinox is a harvest feast in the face of oncoming scarcity; the dam is brim full of water like a store-house. For our ritual we call to the four cardinal directions, holding the circle steady as the year dips downwards. This ritual is one of balance: light balanced with dark for a moment; plenty balanced with scarcity.

We speak of the theme of balance in our own lives. We talk of choices: how they can run in patterns of fear and conditioning, and sometimes we resist changes we obviously should make. We have been taught to repeatedly choose light, ascension, and growth over dark, descent, and death. We know we are not in balance with these things, so we allow this time of year to teach us the value of the still, cold water far beneath as well as the brightness the swans glide across. We seek not just the beautiful flowers of the water lilies but also the depths where their roots grow—the unseen places.

We want our bodies, not just our minds, to learn this way of bal-ance, and so we divide into two groups to create a dance of chaos; pri-mordial darkness and the birth of the stars. The dark dances first—a swirling pit of nothingness, a black hole, dark energy exploding out-wards—and then the light dances in: stars born and radiant, beckoning, sweeping out to the edges of the universe. The two dances join and mingle, endings and beginnings merging together; the enveloping dark-ness, the singing light, and neither dominant. We are one; as we whirl about we sing our song for unity and spirit rejoined, and we think of the cool lake nestled in the folds of land, its dark currents as much a part of it as its glistening surface.

One of the most distinctive things about our Samhain direction in the South-West is the way the bora ring is hidden in layers. It's a long drive away, then through the cemetery, then around the outside of the bora ring, and even then one has to jam oneself between the fence and the open passage, which meet at an odd angle, to walk up to the sacred cir-cle. And, once there, women don't enter and the men only rarely. It's circuitous, to say the least, and seems to fit with Samhain.

One year we devise a journeying ritual for Samhain. It's dusk and we all wear masks, so there are elements of strangeness in vision, in knowing who's there, in staying oriented. Almost from the beginning, when we put on the masks and cast only into the cross-quarters, it's as if we've slipped through the veils. We double up for the calling, two voices into each place: South-East, North-East, North-West, South-West. I stand in the South-West, the direction I happen to be holding in the Circle of Eight; we are both wearing black crowlike masks, and we caw and echo out, imagining our cries reaching as far as the bora ring.

Two of the children lead us on a lengthy, traveling elemental journey. We start in the middle of the house with earth, naming and honoring our dead at a special altar and releasing them. Then we walk in a single file out of the house and across the property, down the driveway, back up and around the side of the house, where we are brought to a small pool that's been constructed: the Well of Mortality. One by one we kneel down and remove our masks, gazing into the water and acknowledging our life, seeing our eventual death written on our faces.

Enjoying their role as psychopomps, the children lead us up the stairs, through a few rooms, out onto a veranda, back down into the garden, around the side of the house, and onto the main veranda, where we meet a Trial by Fire. We have to call out our worthiness to continue, waiting for the children to lower their flaming torches and let us through; we call out the names of the people we love, the work we do in the world, and our hopes for the future as one by one they allow us to pass. More circling through rooms, down stairs, outside again, and now we reach a piece of flat ground and begin the song and our spiral dance to celebrate the swirling of air.

Finally even the children are tired, and one of the adults leads us on a spirit journey to meet our guides and travel deep within, into ourselves or to the other world, wherever we are called to go. After this we finally ground and release back into the cross-quarters. Standing again in the South-West I feel it there, close and also receding: the bora ring, glimmering through the veils, ever present and also deeply held by spirit rather than the real world. All that circling and journeying, reaching inwards, traveling the elements backwards—an unwinding of sorts, and now finally we take off our masks and go to our feast.

How to Integrate the Wheel of the Year Festivals into Your Circle of Eight

The Circle of Eight is ideally tailored to celebrate the festivals of the Wheel of the Year: Winter Solstice, Imbolc, Spring Equinox, Beltaine, Summer Solstice, Lammas, Autumn Equinox, and Samhain. You don't have to begin at any particular time of year; after all, the wheel turns around endlessly. It is just as valid to begin celebrating the festivals at Beltaine as at Samhain or the Winter Solstice. If you already celebrate the festivals but want to change the style of celebrations to reflect more local content, again, there is no special time of the year it is better to begin this. My first ever public ritual was for Lammas; the one after we began the Circle of Eight was Beltaine, and the first one after we'd begun working with the geographic Circle of Eight was the Summer Solstice.

Some people use older, different, or indigenous names for these festivals while still holding them at the same times of year, on the equinoxes, solstices, and cross-quarters. I don't think it matters what you call them. Just as you may need to translate the names I have called them by, so you should feel free to translate these suggestions, guidelines, and instructions. The whole point of localizing your magic and ritual is to find what works for you where you are and for the people you are with. This process of integrating your Circle of Eight into Wheel of the Year festivals is a two-way process to allow the direction to speak to the ritual and the ritual to speak to the direction. People are the translators—the vessels within which this negotiation, balancing, and recognition take place.

There are several different ways you can incorporate your Circle of Eight understandings and your geographic Circle of Eight into the Wheel of the Year. Each position in the Circle of Eight translates immediately into one of the festivals; this is shown, according to hemisphere, on page 12.

You might choose to make the celebration for each festival completely local, according to what each direction means to you. You could choose to hold the rituals at the site of your directions, actually in the place, and let that inform your ritual; a ritual on a beach or in a park will be different from one held in a forest. You may choose to allow a more conversational thread to emerge, where the direction influences the flavor of your ritual without rewriting it altogether. Perhaps you will try a variety of these methods, finding what works for you or just enjoying different approaches.

How to Incorporate Your Circle of Eight into the Wheel of the Year Festivals

1. Discussion and Brainstorming

Begin by sharing all you have learned, as you have journeyed around your Circle of Eight, about the direction that corresponds to the festival you are planning a ritual for. You can have one person taking notes or you can have a large sheet of paper and all write down your understandings in single words, short phrases, or pictures and colors.

If you have been working a geographic Circle of Eight, either continue (or begin another sheet) with your understandings, feelings towards, and relationship with the place in your Circle of Eight that corresponds with this festival.

Now examine the festival itself. You might like to discuss it thoroughly—its historical roots, its place in the wheel, the traditional activities associated with it—or just talk about what it means to you: how you have celebrated it in the past, the parts of it you feel resonate with your own life, the place where you live, the type of magic or ritual you work, as well as any aspects of the festival you would like to explore further. Continue note-taking for this section.

2. Selecting What to Work With

Look back and read through all the notes, picking out the pieces that speak most loudly to individuals and the group. Highlight or underline those that several people agree on as being important. Place these on a new page or large sheet of paper.

3. Asking Questions

Ask the group: If we were to build a ritual to celebrate this festival based on this information, what might it look like? Where would we hold it? Who would we invite? What would the major themes be? Does it represent our locality—what we have discovered so far in our Circle of Eight about the direction that corresponds with this festival and (if working with a geographic Circle of Eight) specifically the place of that direction? What activities could we have, as part of the ritual, that would emphasize these points? Is there anything else, based on our work with the Circle of Eight, that we would want to include, such as calling to eight directions rather than four, including themes of the opposite festival in the celebration of this one, or references to the geographic locations or the nature of the eight directions?

4. Crafting a Ritual

Try putting your answers together in the shape of a ritual. Check the shape and length of the ritual so that there are a variety of different activities and that people's needs are catered to. You may need to add or subtract pieces of the ritual to meet these requirements. Sometimes parts of a ritual can benefit from practice while other parts can be left to flow. Ritual by ritual, you will find what works and how to create a structure that reflects all that you want it to.

If you follow this method, you may end up with eight rituals, over a year, that look nothing like each other. One might be a silent midnight walk across the moors, another a picnic with games and festivities, another an afternoon of craft, deep sharing, and spellworking. Or your rituals may emerge looking recognizably connected to each other but entirely different than what is found in books on the festivals, or they may be entirely related to what's in the books but with a strong local and immediate flavor. After each ritual, it is invaluable for the people who created it to meet again, discussing what worked best and what they would change or improve on next time.

Myth

The side of the mountain isn't quiet at night. There are rustles and scuffles, stirrings and creakings. The stream runs louder in the night air. Unlike the day, there's no human noise except for what we make. I always marvel at this: how the most beautiful places are crowded by day but deserted at night. The beaches empty, the forests pristine, the rivers free. In this place of tall trees, uneven footing, and deep red earth layered in blankets of fallen leaves and composted bark, plant, and animal, being human seems even smaller than usual.

We have flashlights but prefer not to use them. We wait until our eyes adjust. Two of us are traveling the whole circle in two days, spending time in each direction, and it's fallen out that it's night here. The moonlight shafts through the trees, striping the ground. Looking up we see white light catching on branches, leaves, and tangling among the crowns of trees. Not every tree or branch is lit, just some of them; the rest are dimmed out to the soft sheltering of darkness. Moonlight picks and chooses differently than sunlight; what it doesn't choose can hardly be seen at all, whereas by day there's so much reflected, dazzling, bouncing light, even in a forest, that everything can be seen.

Entering this world is like stepping into a fairy tale, a magical place, a myth. I make my steps careful; the moonlight slows me down. It looks like a different forest from the one we usually visit, and it's easy to imagine this is a doorway to another realm—that just beyond here will be the orchards with trees of silver and gold; there'll be a fairy court, elves dancing, and a goblin market; the spirits of the trees will step out to bathe in the night air and the rays of the moon. Myth is alive, and magic—real, potent, here-and-now magic—is happening all around, touched with the spark of white fire in the moonbeams, as if we have already crossed through the portals of time and place. I've never been one for calling in white light; what is this peculiar obsession with the purified, the disembodied, ascension, and reaching beyond this beautiful earth? The light we have on earth, golden and pale and sometimes red, is enough for me. But now there is this light; the original white light. Things look bleached; it's their shadow selves—their spirits—I see, quivering and revealed by this pristine coolness, the translucent moonlight.

Both European fairy tales and local, indigenous stories seem equally alive and potent, equally immediate in the magic of this place by night. The mountain breathes; its Dreamings unfold. Frogs and lizards and small marsupials own this place of red earth, old volcano, tall trees. Owls and maybe bats; they're here too. And us, taking a few hesitant steps onto the edges of this realm, in this place that formed all the earth far around it, erupting as fire many years ago but now resting, given over to the enormity of life unfolding and the deepening of magic.

Stepping into Myth

I've always loved myths, from when I was a child. I drank up those fairy stories, folk tales, and Greek myths book after book; they were my gateways into magic and possibility, quite away from this world. In that place I was transformed. I was the princess questing for the golden apple, I was the third son setting out on an impossible quest, I was the beggar girl at the gates of the castle, the witch's apprentice, the child who could speak with animals. This seemed far more true to me than the prosaic reality that I was the girl who sat in the corner and read, although one created and allowed the other. I sat in the corner and read, but in the inside world I was immersed in adventures, passion, and magic.

As a writer I made it my practice to step into myth and fairy tale, to inhabit the landscape of those stories until events twisted around me and I found myself living some version of them, their motivations and understandings unlayering themselves to my imagination. Dreaming, I found myself again and again within the terrain of my own stories, or I wove the stories with fragments of dreams; dreams and myths seem to share that landscape of becoming and rewriting, of the magical imagination. There were parts of my life when, for weeks at a time, I walked through those lands of myth, dream, story, and real life as if there were no borders between them; they overlapped and commented on each other, peeling back to reveal new layers and correspondences.

In ritual, in magic, what could be better than to step into a myth? To dedicate a night to Persephone, especially if it were on the dark moon; to cast a spell with her pomegranate seeds from a real pomegranate that I could split open myself, with the red juice running down my arms and my own mouth eating those seeds? Of course entering these myths alone has certain limitations; I am with Persephone, yes, but there are other roles in this myth—Hecate, Hades, Demeter—and they remain shadowy to me while Persephone leaps into life. This has a certain allure to it—to become one with Persephone so that I see the story through her eyes, feel its dimensions with my own emotions, espy details that were barely mentioned in the story, brushed over by eyes that were not Persephone's. Ever afterwards her symbols have a doubled importance to me as her emblems but also, now, as they become mine.

For the myth, when entered into in this way, does not remain static, as it was written on the page. It leaps into life, into *my* life, and starts unfolding there like one of those storybooks with pop-up constructions, so that suddenly a whole castle or forest is erected within the open pages. Persephone's pomegranate now symbolizes—as well as her binding to the Underworld—that night when I met the Dark Goddess willingly for the first time. Even so, I walk through these landscapes of myths alone but for the characters and stories that people them. What would it be like to walk here with others, under their own volition, exploring the myth in their own lives?

One of the things we did in the Circle of Eight was to open a myth over our structure as if we had split open a fruit, and each of us took different segments of it—not all to be Persephone, but one to be Hades and one Zeus, one Demeter and one Hecate. The landscape became peopled. When we came together to create ritual, it was rich in discoveries, as complex in motivations as the interactions of a whole cast of beings, not just one in isolation. Roles that were previously given marginal importance were discovered to hold intrinsic parts of the story—

decisive underpinnings without which the whole thing would have turned out utterly differently.

Working with a myth this way, we could turn it and turn it, like a kaleidoscope, through all its different angles, not only discovering its resonances with our own lives but also discovering the hidden heart of the whole thing, the knot at the center of the paradoxes that claim any myth. In turn, this would feed our magic, our ritual, as we strove for learning, revelation, and personal transformation. We divided the roles up according to where we were sitting rather than a personal preference, so the myths were layered into the Circle of Eight itself and we transited through that landscape; if I sat in the South-East, I would be holding the dawn of a myth; in the North, the most prominent character; in the South, a subterranean aspect. So it seemed that the whole mythic landscape was something we moved within, whichever myth we happened to be exploring at any moment.

Sometimes we chose myths directly related to the season so that our rituals and festival were weighted again and again into one direction. The aspects of myth, season, and festival strengthened each other until there was a glory all bound up together and I did feel, then, that the mythos had come to life; not just me alive within it but that it was enormous and real, the whole landscape. We would take the essence of what we had learned and what we still wanted to learn and place it within the heart of the ritual. This intensive working and reworking—delving deeper and deeper within one myth—seemed offered to us by the complexity we created with our own layering; the different energies of holding the story and character privately, then bringing them together as a group, then opening them up for everyone at the ritual.

The Mountain

. . . .

Memoir

It seems I shall never have another baby, but I cannot quite let go of it. Still I have this longing, still this senseless beating in my mind of wishing for what's impossible; not just my age, though definitely that, but also my partner, his age, the age of his children… It is all just not: not going to be, not going to happen, not possible. I try to concentrate on the child I have, and I am fiercely grateful for him; I remind myself of the choices I made all through my adult life that led to this and precisely not to my having more than one child. Still each month when I am in my fertile phase, never mind that I am forty-four and would be very unlikely to conceive; still I go through this mourning and this almost anger at my body that it still longs for what it can't have.

I decide to do a ritual to honor this longing properly, yes, but also to put it to rest. It feels so repetitive and undying that I decide on a repeated ritual; I will do it every month at the full moon for three months. I am at a part of the circle that seems perfect: moving into my old nemesis, the North-West, the position I used to dread and still have a healthy respect for. If I do the ritual for three months, it will take the whole downward swing of the wheel: the North-West, West, and South-West.

I go to a toyshop, a place I haven't visited for a few years since my son grew past that age of wanting wooden animals and craft kits. For him I now visit games shops and search on the Internet for books by obscure authors, but for myself I go into a toy shop and scry along the shelves. I find them eventually in a section of plastic boxes filled with knickknacks: tiny dolls. They are cheap and naked pink plastic but there are few different ones, and I pick out three—not paying much attention to my choice because, after all, when you have a baby you don't get to choose red hair or brown, boy or girl. I buy them and put them into my pocket; I don't want them in a bag but close to me.

At home I put two of them on the altar, nestled among other things, not obvious. The third I keep with me in my bra or pocket or under my pillow at night, nearly as close to me as a real baby would be. I don't feel anything especially as I am doing all this; necessity, perhaps. As if I've got on a train and now I'm just watching the scenery go past. I don't really think of the tiny doll as a baby, even a potential baby or a missed-out-on baby, just a tiny toy I am keeping close. I don't think of it as having its own life or will or interests, though perhaps I feel it has a part of my longing with it.

The direction I'm in is one of sacrifice: to make sacred with one's gifts to the gods. Perhaps because I've been watching it so closely, even courting it, it doesn't seem to hold the unpleasant shock or level of surprise I've often had in this direction—that kind of surprise where the rug is pulled out from under your feet, the volcano explodes, or there's a devastating flood. This time I'm pulling the rug out myself and there's a kind of satisfaction that this might be equal to what the position demands. It feels clear and simple and not the kind of thing to discuss with anyone else.

I find a day when I can drive out to the direction without anyone missing me or wondering where I've gone. Since I'm holding this direction for the circle it would be normal to visit it, but I don't feel like answering questions and certainly not like having anyone else along. As I drive out to the foot of the mountain I'm in a quiet space, an inner zone that allows for recognition of the traffic laws, correct driving and navigation, but not much else. I'm not thinking; I've gone into another realm.

I've made a little bed for my doll, or I guess you could call it a coffin. It's a matchbox covered in red paper. I thought about putting fabric in there, like a real coffin, but that seemed suffocating in so small a space and not what I wanted anyway. I've folded some fern fronds into it and some tiny feathers, the colored ones from rainbow lorikeets—those birds so noisy at dusk they fill the town with an immensely loud chattering as they settle themselves for the night. Their downy feathers are tipped with red, orange, and yellow. It reminds me of those fairy tales of tiny children—Thumbelina or the Gum Nut Babies—though this baby is even smaller. It's still resting in my pocket, not yet given over to the box.

I arrive at the car park. It's always crowded, cars full of walkers determined to reach the top. Almost no one walks along the little side path over the stream and into the forest. The path doesn't go very far, and before it ends I see a setting of tall trees just above me on the slope. You could call it a grove, if a grove was big enough to hold only one person. When I'm in there, crouched down at the base of the trees— and they have tall, straight trunks with fibrous, reddish bark, with no branches for twenty feet up—I could be one of the tiny children as well, so small am I compared to them.

The trees around are holding me so close—three in front in a tight triangle I am wedged into and two more behind my back—that I almost feel I don't need to cast a circle; they have cast one for me and cast it long ago and will be holding it long after I leave. A good place to leave my little one guarded, surrounded, and buried in magic. I get out my compass and set it down. I have offerings as well, a flower from the garden and a piece of fruit. I call out silently to each direction, not to their names but to the places.

I call to the small beach with the waves that crash in; the cape with its rocks, fresh air, and dolphins; to the mouth of the river where it meets the sea; to the long beach heading north, lonely except for sea birds and fishermen; to the lookout and that height, much lower than I am now but where—unlike here—you can see everything. Here you can see nothing except itself. I whisper to this place, the one I am in, and then stretch my mind out further again to the lake with the swans, to the bora ring with its mysteries, and to the waterfall endlessly gliding into the round pool within the circle of rock walls.

I call to the center, the labyrinth, that metaphor for the inner realms, and I am in there now, in my own mythic realm. I start to sing a little song; I am making it up—I don't think about the words, they are simple and there and then gone. I shift forward, still sitting on the ground, and begin to dig a hole with my hands. The soil is soft, not even really soil; it's shredded bark and leaf mold and debris from all the moist, crumbly things that come before soil. I'm digging between two of the trees, right up close in the North-West of my tiny circle; the North-West of the North-West. I don't expect to get very far into the ground but I get a hand's depth or so, dirt packing under my fingernails and into the creases of skin, and then I'm stopped by rootlets.

I take out my matchbox and the tiny doll from my pocket. It's been traveling with me a few weeks by now, and I feel an attachment that's more to do with having cared for it, kept track of where it is, and kept it in my mind than any emotion about it or about babies I might want to have or that I'm not going to have. It does seem a little grim—not placing it in the box, where it looks like it belongs, but sliding closed the lid—I don't like to think of it staring at a piece of cardboard forever and of course its eyes are fixed open. I slide the box out from its casing again and turn the doll sideways so it is facing a piece of fern and feather instead; that seems much better. I fold the springy fern over its body and slide the box shut.

I'm still singing quietly to myself as one might sing to a baby, a baby that was nearly asleep. I wedge the box down into the hole I made and fill it in with light dirt, carcasses of leaves, and odd, hard bits of undecomposed bark or stick. The trees seem more aware of me or I am more aware of them now I have given them a task, involved them in this working, and designated them the guardians of this piece of my spell.

They are immense compared to me; compared to the size of that tiny doll, they are planetlike—immense angels, vast and unknowable.

I do think, in an abstract way, of actual babies, but they seem very distant whereas this little buried doll that won't ever come to life seems much closer. I am supposed to be burying my hopes for a baby, putting an end to them, but here in the forest they don't feel as if they have an end or particularly need one; they seem just another link on the chain of my life, and this ritual is a part of that link. I think of the doll's brother and sister waiting for me at home. I'll spend the rest of this month with no little one in my pocket or by my bed, and then when we turn the wheel again and I move into the West, I'll pick one of them up and keep it close to me for a few weeks before I take it out to the dam and leave it there with the black swans.

I can't exactly say what I feel when I leave that place. I don't release the circle I cast but leave it held by the trees or to sink gradually into the soil surrounding my sacrifice, my little doll, a thread of my life I won't be having. I am quietened, even quieter than when I drove here. The trees have given me that, with their height and the otherness of their life, with their ability to guard a piece of myself, to stay there watching over my baby who's buried at their feet among their roots. I think maybe the essence of my gift will pass into them and that little thought of an unborn soul will touch them in some way they might not have known otherwise. It feels safe as well as sacred, and I feel alone as I drive away.

Exploring Myth

Our concentrated period of working with myths came before we created our geographic circle, but it could work either way. Places in a geographic Circle of Eight may suggest myths to work with and could provide wonderful settings for enactments or rituals relating to those myths.

We began our mythic explorations by each of us invoking and working with a god or goddess during the month between our meetings, whichever one called to us or we felt belonged in that direction. In this way I worked with Isis when I was in the North, Gaia in the North-West, and Nephthys in the West. When the Circle of Eight met, we reported back on these explorations and incorporated what we could into the group, but it soon became obvious we would get a lot further if we all worked on the same myth, particularly if we all worked on different aspects of the same myth, creating a type of mythic constellation where we placed ourselves within the myth, holding the different characters, and watched what happened.

The first myth we chose was the Greek story of Persephone's descent and return, including the background story of how Hades became Lord of the Underworld. It was at the time of the Spring Equinox. We happened to have three men in the circle, holding the quarters of East, West, and South. The three brothers of Greek mythology divide the world between them, Zeus taking heaven and earth, Poseidon the seas, and Hades being left with the underworld. We gave Zeus to the East, Poseidon to the West, and Hades to the South.

Women were sitting in the South-East, the North-West, and the South-West. We gave Persephone returning to the South-East, Persephone descending to the South-West, and Demeter to the North-West, the time when the grain harvest begins. We could hardly believe how perfectly the positions divided up. The one character we hadn't assigned to anyone was Hecate, and we thought the descending aspect of Persephone contained the elder Hecate, already a mistress of the underworld.

When we met in circle a month later, we stripped the myth down to its essences and began. We played over and over again the meeting between Hades and Persephone, trying every combination of people so that we saw the story many different ways. We saw abduction and fear; seduction and play; enticement and possession; invitation and mutuality. Myths hold their ground so well because of their layered complexity. It was obvious to us that no single version of this meeting was the truth; instead, they were all concurrently true. Each one of those meetings between the underworld god and the young goddess held some of its essence. Added together, layer on layer, it began to resonate with the strength of a myth.

In this way—repeating many times with different combinations of us—we also played out Persephone's parting from Demeter; Hades' farewell of Persephone, when she leaves him to return to her mother for a season; and Persephone's eventual return to the underworld. But the most moving piece was something that's often left out of stories altogether or brushed over so lightly you would think it had barely any importance. This was right back at the beginning, before the story of Hades and Persephone even began, when the three brothers divided up the world.

Watching this play out, we saw in Zeus arrogance, grandeur, automatic self-promotion, and a belief that naturally he would get first choice and it would be the best. In Poseidon we saw the eager second brother, keen to hold his place in the order of things, to back the stronger but also to have something special for his own—an area the others could not touch. We saw his intelligence as he made these calculations at lightning speed; his swift pursuit of goals, made no less for the fact he did not speak first. We saw his creativity as he took what Zeus had not bothered with and promised silently to make it his own and spectacular. And then we saw Hades. A couple of times he tried to speak, only to be overridden by the others. His wishes were not consulted; he was not thought of as the other two divided up the world between them. He spoke last, and then only to take what had been left unwanted. We could not see what he was thinking; he held his feelings in check and barely spoke.

It was enough to make one weep, this neglect of the less powerful or outspoken, the relegation of an unwanted sphere to a disregarded brother. And in that context, when he came forward to claim Persephone—and when he farewelled her for the length of a summer—we saw his need, his longing, to be known and loved; his willingness that maybe made him a better companion than either of his brothers. We came to regard him differently. We did see his dark energy and his rage, fermented in loneliness and neglect, but also we saw his compassion and understanding as he released his bride—whom we did not doubt he loved—to return to the upper world and her mother for half the year, every year. Which of us can say we are so generous in relationships?

Another time we had only four people, and we chose the Welsh myth of Llew. Trinda held Arianrhod in the South-West; Glenn was with Gwydion the magician in the South, the hidden place; I held Blodewedd the flower maiden in the South-East; and Ross had Llew in the East. I fell in love with Blodewedd a little. She was just flowers. She had the ferocious innocence of nature: she was petals and pollen, she turned to the sun, she opened and blossomed and died without thought. She did not care for love, she did not care to be human; her blood ran through her veins as sap, cool and dense, and my mind blanked out with her. Everything seemed very simple. I did not want to think about complexities, love and motivations and betrayal. I could see why they called her cold-hearted; she did not care about their stories, she had not chosen them, and her allegiance was to something older and far more essential: the sun and the blossom and the business of offering oneself to the life force.

We invoked these four beings into our ritual and into ourselves in an aspected trance. One by one we stood into the center and let the character pour through us, let them express what they would, and then we spoke with them. Trinda was first, and Arianrhod came in raging, furious at her mistreatment. In the myth she is tricked into giving birth to Llew, then tricked again as the curses she has laid on him are sidestepped, one by one, through Gwydion's cleverness and Llew's desperation. We listened to her storm of hurt and anger, and slowly we started singing to her; we could not offer a different story but, as we soothed her with our attention and concern, she quietened. We asked her to remember her gifts of clear sight and strength, to remember her greatness as a goddess and accept that Llew was part of the world, and she agreed. It touched a raw nerve in Trinda, who was deeply aligned with the Goddess, to carry this part of a story where the feminine is so manipulated and degraded.

We invoked Llew, and he came through Ross as suffering and uncertain, not knowing where he had gone wrong. We saw the young boy needing his mother, his parents, guidance, and love. We saw Llew's innocence in this story as he is born unwanted, adopted by Gwydion, and involved in the darker strains of Gwydion's magic: first tricking Arianrhod into granting Llew a name and giving him arms, and lastly creating his great magic, the woman of flowers to be Llew's bride. We saw Llew's confusion as he was rejected, and the role reflected a part of Ross—that longing for relationship and connection and a willingness to blur the edges a little to achieve it. As he stood there in the center, seeming not to understand the story he was enmeshed in, we told him of his innocence, how he had been used by everyone and trapped by desires greater and stories older than his own. We sang to him, holding out our hands and offering him the path to initiation, and as he took our hands we felt a change came through him.

Glenn invoked Gwydion, and he came bearing burdens, talking endlessly of his tasks, responsibilities, and knowledge. It was as if each character was viewed through the lens of the person carrying them, so in this version of Gwydion we saw Glenn's preoccupation with things undone, achievements not reached, and the concern to get everything right. It was not entirely Glenn; these things were just a thread in him but came into full force when he invoked Gwydion. It was an overlay between the two of them, which highlighted an aspect of the myth for us; for the person carrying it, it brought forth an aspect of self to examine or question. In Gwydion and also Glenn we saw that tremendous gift of a restless intelligence—how it prompted learning and enquiry but did not allow for trust or rest. When we sang to him as he stood in the center, he joined in the song; he would not receive but had to be active, guiding the story, creating.

Lastly, they called to Blodewedd, and I felt coldness settle inside—a chill, icy and serene. As she came into me, I felt her huge indifference. Who cared what magicians did or about the complex relationships between mothers and sons? Who cared if men desired women or wished for brides to hold and love in the mortal realm? She did not. The flowers did not. And yet as they called she was forced into that story. When they caught and bound her in magic, shaped her into a nature not her own, she was all confusion and longing; I could feel that. But the longing was to be free, to be herself again—mindless petals—not to be claimed or married or held to faithfulness. Flowers are not faithful. Flowers are the lovers of the world. Blodewedd felt ages old, portrayed as young but actually holding a great and ancient power, nearly untranslatable but back to the oldest goddesses.

Several months later we did another mythic working, this time from a modern story. The novel *The Eye of Night* by Pauline J. Alama is set in a mythical land ruled by four gods and four seasons. Across the wheel from each other sit the Rising God of Spring and the Turning God of Autumn. Crossing their line is the line from Summer Solstice and the Bright Goddess through to Winter Solstice, held by the Hidden Goddess. The book is a journey made by a group of mismatched characters to seek out the Hidden Goddess, who holds the hinges of the death and rebirth of their world. They travel through the seasons, festivals, and realms of the three other deities to reach her. We spent our month dwelling not on the story in the book but on these aspects of deity.

When we met in ritual together, we held very still on our Circle of Eight, each in our place according to the characters, as if the slightest movement could tip it off balance. Between us we felt the enormity of it—the Wheel of Balance, the Wheel of Life, the Wheel of Becoming. We met each other's eyes; gravity and the very birth of the universe seemed contained at the center. Then we spoke in turn to each person, naming how we saw their own character corresponding with the aspect of deity that they held. We spoke of the seeming youth and uprightness of Glenn, holding the Rising God in the East; passion and softness held within both me and the Bright Goddess in the North; the offering and vulnerability we saw in the Turning God and also in Ross as he sat in the West; the terseness and depth of the Hidden Goddess that so well reflected Trinda, holding the South.

We stood and walked around the wheel halfway, until we were opposite to what we had invoked, and we spoke again, this time naming the shadow, or less immediately obvious qualities, we saw of each person. We saw and named Glenn's reluctance to engage as he stood in the place of the Turning God, as true to him as had been the Rising God's brightness and beginnings. They spoke of power as I stood with the Hidden Goddess and the cold surface that comes with that. We saw the striving, the eagerness to be accepted and approved, in Ross and the Rising God, still mixed with the vulnerability of the Turning God he had held minutes before. In Trinda we saw the personal generosity and depth of service she offered, lit like a backdrop by the Bright Goddess. Each of us felt the turning within, the different faces, aspects; these four parts that together make wholeness.

We danced and rattled and called upon these gods, who seemed to us more accessible, more married to our own wheel than any myth we had yet explored. We called on the Bright Goddess to be reborn onto the earth in the bodies of women; we called for the stability and commitment of the Turning God, he who brings the balance. We called on the potential of the Rising God, his yearning towards fulfillment, and we moved into a vast landscape, calling finally to the Hidden Goddess in her ever-presence, her mystery, her utter inevitable all. The energy twisted and turned between us as we sang and invoked and called out, rising between us and weaving stronger and stronger, not just us four but the depths of the old gods, the gods of season and turn and stillness, and we felt held by them and by the wheel, and no amount of movement, agitation, or even neglect could shake them off balance or alter their positions in relation to each other and the wheel.

Into the Autumn Equinox Festival ritual that came shortly afterwards we threaded the Hidden Goddess. She walked through the room veiled and silent as we sought to redress the balance of the world, a balance coming unstuck through wars and power struggles. A list of countries the US has bombed since the end of World War II was read out as she paced among us: *China, Korea, Guatemala, Indonesia, Cuba, Congo, Peru, Laos, Vietnam, Cambodia, Grenada, Libya, El Salvador, Nicaragua, Panama, Iraq, Sudan, Afghanistan, Yugoslavia.* She disappeared as silently as she came; a tall young girl dressed in black and with a sheer black veil, she brought with her the idea of veiled women, of young widows, of girls who don't get a childhood, and of all those touched by war, their lives altered, ruined, or compromised. And yet she held the mystery as the Hidden Goddess; hers was the power to give birth, to celebrate life, no matter the circumstances.

One time we decided to work with the Greek myth of the labyrinth and the Minotaur hidden in its depths. It's filled with questions, this myth; is the labyrinth a maze or a path? Is it simply the layout of the ancient palace of Knossos on Crete? Is it a mechanical wonder with tricks and traps or a temple with the most sacred hidden in the inner? Is the Minotaur a monster, the King, or the priest? Sacred bull, son, brother and lover to the Queen…and the queenship held by two women in this story, or is it three? Pasiphae, who gave birth to the bull-headed one, and Ariadne and Phaedra, her daughters?

We spent hours making a full head mask with cowlike horns, painted black and with a cloak of fur that fell down over the back of the wearer. It was animal and more than animal. Worn by a human, it transformed them to monster: mythical, unworldly, and deeply disturbing. It was the animal married to human, as shamans and gods had been depicted throughout the ancient worlds. Wearing that mask or seeing it on another, it wasn't hard to conjure the unbelievable weight carried by those who have access to the voices of the gods or those who are born blasted into difference and separation.

We drew a labyrinth in chalk on the floor. It was dark and cold. One by one, we entered the labyrinth as our characters. Glenn as the Minotaur went first, silent to his prison or his sanctum; watching, we could not tell which. Ross as Theseus entered the labyrinth boldly, claiming it as his own even as the Minotaur paced towards him, meeting him on a turn into the darkness. They stood and argued about fate in a passage of the labyrinth. Theseus sounded strident and determined, the Minotaur wounded, sad; everything constricted in the narrowness between the chalk lines, and Theseus turned, killing decisively before leaving a victor.

I was next to enter, as Ariadne; she sang her way in, as if she had been taught the paths from childhood. The intent, the words, the focus came through me but from somewhere else; all these layers we have accumulated over the years to explain *Ariadne*, this wounded aspect of a wounded feminine. There's a heartless exterior where things glance off her; she's battled with concepts of duty and passion, conflicted loyalties. But that's all on the surface—there are older layers, unexcavated, and this journey into the labyrinth seems to demand some extra depth from her. The thread that she sent Theseus in with, surely that is connected to the spun thread of a mortal life, held by the Goddess—held by *her*, by Ariadne—measured out and finite? She was measuring out his life for him. The Minotaur, also; she measured out his life, sending death in to find him as she betrayed him.

Trinda as Pasiphae enters the labyrinth; she was one who gave birth to the Minotaur. They stand together and talk of his death, and both weep. Later they speak of what it meant to them. Glenn says he felt a deep grief that the Minotaur was excluded from ordinary life for his entire existence, never really seen for what he was, and he felt that he, also, lived much of his life like that. He felt that he was part of the Minotaur, and the experience stayed with him for days, where his understanding had crossed into the personal.

Trinda felt that the two of them stood together in the knowledge of what would happen, not just the death of the Minotaur but the ending of a whole cycle of historical time as the goddess cultures collapsed and were superseded by the patriarchy. As they wept on each other's shoulders, she saw the necessity of it—that this had to happen, and even while she grieved for what would be lost, she also knew the wheel would keep turning and the mysteries the Minotaur and labyrinth represented would return. She understood in that moment all her struggle and resistance over the loss of goddess culture could be surrendered into a trust of the cycle turning.

After this we ran a Samhain ritual; as the heart of it, we asked each person to enter the labyrinth with their offering where the Minotaur paced or waited or wept. In the half-light of the dark night, only candles alight, the shadows thrown by the mask are alarming, but it is an air of somber tragedy that he exudes, and even the children do not hesitate to make the journey. People look at him curiously or speak a few words; some bow their heads in respect, but none greet him as a brother, a lover, or a comrade. The weight of the mask of the Minotaur is separation, and he wears it much as he wears the fur that drapes from his shoulders, part of his beauty and his burden.

The mask we've made has never been stable, the papier-mâché never entirely held the weight of itself, and we have to keep drying it out by the fire as it weeps moisture and threatens to collapse. It doesn't last a year. In the end, after we've tried drying the mask, repainting it, and sealing it, we deconstruct it, remove the length of fake fur, and take what's left into the garden to decompose. It feels like we've released him from torture, set him free from that shape and the labyrinth he was bound to.

Other myths we worked with included Isis-Osiris and Tiamat-Marduk. Later on we worked with Gilgamesh and Enkidu, Artemis and Acteon, Psyche and Eros, Jesus and Mary Magdalene, and Inanna, Ereshkigal, and Dumuzi. With each of these myths we discovered new realms, not just of the myth itself but of ourselves and how we understood the world and of how to work together ritually in this folded, mythic world. We witnessed the others as we saw the archetypal threads that ran beneath the surface in them. We felt this mythic constellation work revealed great truths encoded within the myths, though not necessarily obvious to the casual observer, and that the Circle of Eight encompassed them, giving structure and insight as well as guiding us in our imaginings.

How to Work with Myth
in Your Circle of Eight

Working with myth in your Circle of Eight is a dynamic way to explore archetypes and mythic themes in your life as well as the synchronicities and patterns of story and the way they interact with the cycle of the eight directions. You might choose to explore one myth over a series of meetings or choose a different myth to work with each time or just work with one every so often, when it feels appropriate. We used all of these approaches in our Circle of Eight. Your myth working might be something you keep just within your Circle of Eight group or it might be something you extend out to your families and communities in the form of creating content for a Wheel of the Year celebration or other ritual.

There are thousands of myths recorded from every spiritual tradition. Books and online resources abound in the fields of myth. While it can be useful to read several different versions of a myth before or while working with it, the working is open-ended and most probably you will be straying off the page of the usual interpretations as you explore it.

Some people like to work with fairy tales, as well as or instead of myth and it's also possible to work with an epic poem or a novel which employs or creates archetypes.

There are Sumerian, Egyptian, Greek, Celtic, Norse, Christian, and Indian myths. You may like to work with myths or mythic cycles that reflect your heritage. Cultural appropriation is an issue, so if you are wanting to work with a myth from a living tradition that has been marginalized, colonized, or been a victim of genocide (for example, Aboriginal or Native American myth), possibly even when it is very broadly available and disseminated, it is respectful to seek permission first. It may take a long time and much persistence to find and connect with people carrying the threads of these living traditions. If you are deeply drawn to working with these stories, particularly if they belong to the land you live on or near, this time and energy may be worth it to you, not just in gaining a permission, if that is what occurs, but in developing your relationship to the land and its stories.

There are countless ways to work with a myth; what is described here is how to create an entry point for your exploration. The process can be used to access a deep discussion on the nature and themes of the myth itself, to relate those themes to people's lives, to do personal or group work around those themes or archetypes, or to create dynamic mythic reenactments or explorations. Sometimes one or two people may plan the evening; other times each may bring one aspect of a working and fit them together on the night. One person may have brought a relevant chant, another a guided visualization, another a way to enact part of the story, and another a personal development process using some aspect of the myth. Then you can choose, at the time, which order they work best in.

How to Work with a Myth in the Circle of Eight

1. *Choose a Myth*

One way to choose a myth is to ask everyone for one or two myths they would love to explore. Write these down, putting a star next to those that are mentioned more than once. Then consider which myth correlates with the time of year, or consider the big themes playing out in people's lives currently and choose a myth that resonates with them. Or—if you have been working with myth for a while—choose a myth from a different tradition than those you have already worked with or a myth related to one you already worked with and particularly loved.

2. Look at the Characters in the Myth

Choose which characters from the myth you will work with. This should have some relevance to how many people you have to work them; it's no good choosing six characters if you have only four people. On the other hand, choosing four characters when you have eight people would be fine; two people could work with each character. Sometimes this process involves including quite minor characters and other times excluding characters who would normally be considered part of this story. They can still be involved when you do the working; it's just that no one will have been paying them special attention beforehand. It is possible to group characters together—for example, "the rest of the gods on Olympus"—anything is possible. Use your intuition, your gut feeling, and experiment.

3. Lay the Characters Onto the Circle

This is where you assign characters to a certain direction in your Circle of Eight, usually irrespective of who is holding that direction. You might want to wait to do this until you have turned the wheel, so the people sitting in those positions can get a direct hit on whether or not they feel the character does correspond to the direction. You may be able to do this process just through talking or you might need to write down the names of the characters on slips of paper and move them round the circle. You may choose to make obvious correspondences; the Sumerian Inanna is a goddess of heaven and earth, so you may place her in your Summer Solstice position, with her sister, Ereshkigal, in the Winter Solstice direction. Inanna's consort, Dumuzi, and his sister, Geshtinanna, mark the yearly cycle of descent and return, so they could be placed in the Spring and Autumn Equinox positions. Your assignments may also comment on more subtle characteristics of the direction or the mythic character.

We tended to assign male characters to men and females to women, although not always. Now I would not make it one of the deciding factors; I have seen too many powerful and amazing interpretations of gods by women and goddesses by men. Disregarding gender in assigning roles in a myth opens up the broadest interpretations of divinity and story, as well as allows people to explore many sides of themselves, not just ones that seem to match their human gender.

4. Individual Workings

Each person "takes away" their character or their part of the myth to work with in the time between circle meetings. This working may include research, meditation, inner journeying, creating an altar, art or journaling, and anything else that occurs to you.

5. Creating a Mythic Working

Next time the circle meets, include a round of mythic feedback after your usual openings of sacred space and checking in. Each person gets to share what they have discovered, felt, and understood about the character they've worked with and the myth as a whole.

Then begin your mythic working. Feel free to blend, alter, ignore, or adapt these suggestions:

- *Sound.* Create a soundscape for the story with each character contributing their own sounds, whether vocally or using musical instruments. Play with the soundscape, allowing different characters to be heard and engage with each other.

- *Journeying.* Create a guided journey through the story of the myth, possibly passing it from one voice to another as you go. Describe the setting and events of the myth rather than the feelings or motivations of the characters; this way each person can have their own experience of those, which can be shared later.

- *Reenactment.* This is most powerful when done wordlessly, either in silence with a drum beat in the background or while continuing or creating the soundscape. It can be repeated (also with different people playing the different parts) to explore many different angles and inferences of the myth. Afterwards, discuss your feelings, discoveries, and questions.

- *Aspecting.* Allow each person, in turn, to "draw down," or lightly aspect, the character they have been working with and to speak from that place to the other characters. It is best if only one person does this at a time.

- *Personal work.* Explore where and how each character, or the story as a whole, touches on the life of each person in your circle.

- *Creativity.* Make something together from the mythic working you've undertaken: a group collage or other artwork, a song, masks, a ritual for a larger group, or an altar.

Inner Work

Lying among farmlands, this dam of water is the jewel in the hills. This is a hot inland area, yet here the breeze blows off the water, the trees offer shade, and it seems cooler. Birds own this water; ducks, swans, and water birds of all types glide or skim across its surface. Land-based birds stand at the edges, scooping up water or flying above in the freedom of sky. They behave as if it was built for them, and no one disturbs their ownership of it. Water lilies swarm outwards from the bank, claiming the space as beautiful but unapproachable.

It's a paradox, this place. It's human-built yet kept free of humans— of their fishing, boating, and swimming adventures; free of their rub-bish, petrol, sunscreen and oils and perfumes; free of their shouting and motors and splashing. They don't cut through the water, churn it up to swim laps or dive into; they don't skim across its top on boards or canoes or inflatables; they don't poke rods and lines into it to pull things out to eat or for sport or sale. It's been here sixty years and has settled into the landscape as if it evolved by itself. It's the water catchment for the nearby inland town, but it has the serenity of a lake.

The grounds are maintained like a park: grassed slopes with areas of native trees and brush, picnic tables and toilets. There's a wide causeway you can walk across from one side to the other that admits it's a dam, not a natural lake. Across the causeway it's a little wilder; no picnic tables but still gentle parkland, now with more trees than grassed areas. Looking across the wide water to the far side, there's bush—no paths or lawns there; the eucalypts come down to the water's edge, and it's pristine. The lake invites contemplation of depths: its own or those of its visitors.

It's surprisingly peaceful. On the weekends carloads of people arrive, families with three generations and elaborate picnics; children's parties with balloons and games and birthday cakes; barbeques with sausages and blokes with beer, but that's all contained in a tiny part near the car park. Unlike the beach, people don't spread out and claim the whole thing, and anyone who comes here for peace and quiet only has to walk away from them or come during the week when the place is practically deserted. There's a sense of cool distance, of otherness granted by the water, clean and taboo and yet endlessly enticing in this hot climate; it glimmers with secrets and depths that can't be known except by the birds that sail over it in confident ownership and by the waters themselves.

Below the Surface

As above, so below. As within, so without. First, know thyself.

It's an essential part of my personal belief, magical practice, and world-view that whatever actions we take in the world reflect something within ourselves, and whatever is inside the self will seek to be expressed externally. For me this concept touches on the nature of the soul. I think of soul as being the essential spark each of us is carrying; a spark of life force, of the Divine, the memory of stars and exploding, becoming existence. Thus our souls are intrinsically related to the whole world, an inseparable part of it, although in each of us this piece is expressed slightly differently, just as no two daisies, lizards, or stalks of grain are exactly the same.

In fact, all of our bodies and all the body of this earth is made up of the same stuff: stardust, just expressed in different forms. I believe the division between soul and body is false; I think this essential spark is inherent in that stardust. This living matter of the universe that we are composed of is indivisible from soul, so it is mere form to speak of the soul as separate. But using that concept of *soul* as a lens to focus through instead of a delineation, I experience *soul* as permeable, in constant interaction with the world around it. Indeed, it is literally one with the world around it, just one that momentarily—in the form of a human being, a human life—experiences itself as separate from the whole it belongs to.

So inner work, by definition, is outer work as well. If we do inner work—whether it is meditation, personal development, deep inquiry, therapy, or another form of spiritual, personal, or psychological healing, growth, or exploration—we cannot expect our lives to remain untouched by it. Similarly, things that happen in the external world—the type of work environment we exist within, our relationships and family interactions, events on a larger scale that we are caught up in such as wars, our governmental system, disaster, economic prosperity, climate change—will affect our inner selves. If we have cultivated values of peace and joy, we may find ourselves much less tolerant of the evening news, an abrasive workplace, or an abusive or angry relationship. Our engagement with these external things may then force us to look within again; where within us are the war-monger, the impatient, scathing, dismissive, or angry parts?

Many people have a preference to focus either on inner or outer work; self-enquiry or world-changing, whether that world is the dynamics between themselves and their loved ones, government policy, or an endeavor to make a difference to their community. Both a circle and a wheel teach that neither can be complete without the other. In the Circle of Eight and the Wheel of the Year, opposites balance each other and are equal. Winter is half and summer half; dark and light are half each; the moon spends as much time waning as it does waxing. If one devoted the upward swing of the wheel—Imbolc through to the Summer Solstice—to outer work, to be in balance one would then need to devote the downward swing—Lammas through to the Winter Solstice—to inner work. Or at each station of the wheel one could observe the relative balance of outward and inner and adjust accordingly, but it would still balance out over an entire turn.

All of the festivals and invocations of deity, all of the directional work and even geographic work with the Circle of Eight can have inner dimensions. These things are most powerful when they are mediated and experienced through a human life—a set of events, emotions, and understandings that translate an abstract such as Autumn Equinox, the goddess Inanna, the mountain, or the South-West into human terms. As well as this internal processing of external concepts, there can be time and effort devoted purely to deepening one's understanding of, relationship to, and maturing of one's self. Of course this inner work will not remain inner; once realized, it will strive to be integrated into the outer, just as the outer work of celebrating festivals and working with directions, deities, and geography will prompt internal developments.

A Circle of Eight may act as a support group, a coven, and an experimental place for ritual and magic. Devoting some time to inner work will enrich your circle, both the relationships within it and the nature of the work that evolves from it. Inner work can take many, many different forms. Just as the Circle of Eight is made up of differences that come together to create a whole, so experiencing different forms of inner work will offer the most to your group. Some people love meditation while others loathe it. Some love to discuss and explore dreams while others can hardly remember their dreams and have little interest in them. Some people love emotional processing, whether it is rebirthing, family constellations, shadow work, or deep healing; others barely tolerate it. Some enjoy chakra and energy work, shamanic journeying, journaling, neuro-linguistic programming, Byron Katie processes, Five Rhythms Dancing…the list is endless.

In the Circle of Eight inner work is always informed by and filtered through the direction you are in at the time. Since each person is in a different direction, many different aspects can be brought to each piece of work, not just informed by the personality or life situation of each person but also by the directions themselves. How meditation is experienced in the North, for example, may be very different to how it is experienced in the South-West. Having someone who is sitting in the North lead a meditation followed by a meditation led by someone sitting in the South-West can be informative on many different levels.

When people join a group they bring a whole lifetime of skills, experiences, knowledge, and interests with them. If you check around your group you will find a fantastic pool of resources even before anyone has opened a book or started researching. Asking people to bring techniques, practices, and processes they already know into your circle has many benefits. Your variety of experiences will be far wider than if one or two people were relied on to provide all the workings. Each person is recognized as an authority to teach or guide the group through something they know well. Unusual or unique combinations may evolve as processes from completely different streams are fitted together and new ways of doing things are discovered.

In the Circle of Eight, opposites—and, along with opposites, shadows—are always present. Wherever you are sitting, whichever direction you are holding when you look across the circle, straight ahead of you is the opposite to your own position. Often there is another person sitting there, and it may be easy to see all the ways they are different from you. In a group with a high level of trust and willingness, interpersonal work where relationships and dynamics within the circle are examined creatively, clearly, and intimately can create deep bonding. The circle is well set up to do shadow work, a critical examination of the self where one studies projections, assumptions, and judgments, not as externally relevant but as internal signposts about one's own "dis-ease" with rejected parts of oneself. Experiencing one's brightest, fullest, and most expressive self in the position of the Summer Solstice, for instance, is only a thought away from looking across the circle and seeing or remembering oneself at one's darkest, emptiest, and most inwardly focused.

Shadow aspects can be found within the directions each person secretly (or not so secretly) dreads and equally within the positions that each person loves or finds to be no threat at all. What is it about this direction that is frightening or so easy? Where is that reflected in my life; what am I avoiding, and what gifts are waiting to come to me when I embrace it? If I love a direction, is that because it supports my view of things, posing no threat to my stability and understanding of the world? What shadow does this cast? Why am I frightened of that Lammas position? How do I feel threatened there, not just externally by the change and instability it promises but internally by aspects of my personality that may be revealed, aspects I usually prefer to ignore such as anger, impatience, and self-doubt?

Delving into inner work within the Circle of Eight structure feels very supportive to me, not only due to what the rest of the group brings to the process. The position I am in can also—once I finish fighting with it—lend immense support. Lammas has within it a grace of giving way to the inevitable outgoing tide; once I allow the position to embrace me, I begin to feel this as not just wisdom but literal, almost physical truth, as the position energetically holds me much as I am holding it. Knowing I will move onto another position in a month, then the next one the month after that, is very calming; the structure provides a way for me to continue processing with in-built change. The whole circle sits around me, offering eight different perspectives on any piece of work or internal investigation we are doing, ever present and interactive. Observing this, I am able to see how my current experience is one part, but only one part, of the whole.

The Lake in the West

. . . .

Memoir

I come to the West early in the morning; it's my direction at the moment. We're at the beginning of summer, and it's going to be a hot day. I've brought my reading, my writing, some food, and I don't know what I'm looking for, really, but when I spend time in these places that make up our Circle of Eight always something happens. This particular place—this large, constructed dam that's more like a lake—always seems peaceful to me, its waters undisturbed except by winds and birds, its grounds big enough to lose a dozen groups of picnickers.

I'm so early there doesn't seem to be anyone else here at all. I park and walk down to the water's edge, not the bit closest to the car park but a little way away. There are small islands of trees, shrubs, and native grasses scattered across the lawn, and eventually I sit near one of these, at the edge of the shade cast by the trees. There are three or four of these mini forest patches nearby, and there's nothing special about this one. I gaze at the water for a while; it looks pristine, and I think about the waters of the West.

Mythically, one sets out on those waters but doesn't reach the end. This is the direction of the eternal journey—the journey into death, into the mysteries and other worlds. I think of the west coast of Ireland, gazing off Slieve League; how amazed Damon and I were when we found that place. It seemed like the end of the world. That slow, narrow, winding road with room only for cars in one direction, little passing bays every so often and that after miles of twisting, turning, climbing roads with randomly sprinkled signposts; it was definitely the end of something. We'd come here on a whim; perhaps one of us had seen a picture somewhere or it looked something special on the map and we really didn't know what we'd find.

After an agonizing time on the narrow road, which had helpful little ledges on the cliff side not quite a foot high to show you where the edge was and glorious unfolding banked heather in three shades of purple on the other side, I parked in one of the little bays and insisted we walk the rest of the way, which surely could only be a few kilometers more. I was seriously unnerved at the thought of meeting a car mid-section and having to back along the tight curves, and something about driving seemed entirely wrong; who drives to the end of the world? We were pilgrims, and so we got out and walked, admiring heather and views as we went. We took uncounted photographs that probably all looked the same but close up and live the heather was different, not just in shades of color but in leaf type and density, and together they made a collage on the ground, a composition in purple and green.

We saw Slieve League for a long time before we really saw it; it was in a haze not of distance but of seaspray. The curves of road and land hid all but the top from us, and the top was not the dramatic part. When finally we were standing where we could see it properly, we were silent. All the categories we might have applied to it—*Irish sea-coast; the mythical West; the cliff at the edge of the world*—it filled and more than filled. It was a massively high, straight-down cliff, made black by water and topped with more heather. Waves cracked against its base, vivid in their determination to devour, shear off another face of rock, to pull the cliff down into their grasp. It was brighter, fiercer, more of a trembling vision than it is possible to describe, and if you did not believe that the sea and earth had a language between them until now, or that in Ireland the mythos lies only just behind the spray of water filling the air, you would do, seeing this. It was west of west, the deep Celtic west; west of a thousand visions and poet's journeys, the west of imagining and dream.

This West place in the Circle of Eight, now, is tame in comparison. But it still beckons to memories of that other west, of all wests; of *west* as a place of setting out into the unknown, the beginning of the journey into the mysteries. I read for a while, I write for a while. I'm at a crossroads in my life; I don't know what will happen next. Of course, everything that is already happening might just keep happening; work and raising my son, writing and rituals and magic, and that would be fine. It is fine. Or—something else might happen. I have a sense of that, though I don't know what it is. I have longings, of course, and the West seems a good place to express longings—those yearnings I always carry with me for delight, for fierce intimacy, the depths and shades of love.

I think of all the times I've been here, alone and with other people, and every single time it seems there's that flavor of waiting depths, not inaccessible, just biding their time. I've come here with my son, I've come here with the Circle of Eight, I've come here with lovers. There's always this feeling of walking only on the surface, perhaps because the real spell is in the water and the water's off-bounds. I like that the water too sacred to go into. I like its pristine quality, but I've always been looking for something else as well—for the secret to be revealed.

All the places of the Circle of Eight have different energies, and this one seems the least demanding, or perhaps it is simply that it is peaceful here, whereas so many other directions are challenging, unsettling, fierce, or engaging. I do think there's something more; that it's that stillness we summon up before something large begins to happen, like the balance of the Autumn Equinox, knowing we are headed down, afterwards, into the dark. Vaguely I notice that some other people have arrived; this place is so enormous, there is so much space that I don't pay them any attention. There's plenty of room for everyone, and perhaps that's one of the things about this place: I feel it is receptive, listening, whereas many of the other directions are so caught up in themselves that the most one can do is partake or maybe just marvel at the edges.

The group of people who've arrived are coming closer; they're lugging something between them, folded-up bundles of canvas. I turn the other way, back to the lake. I look at the water lilies, so pretty on the surface, but I know about their stems: those slippery, strong connectors to the floor of the lake, how they grapple and twist with you if you try to swim amongst them or pick one. The lake itself is like that, and maybe the whole place; its beauty laid out on the surface and underneath something more—something connected powerfully to the life force, something that won't let up in a hurry. The scent of those palely purple water lilies is to die for; I think of ambrosia, smelling them; of moonflowers and fairy dust and magical elixirs that can grant eternal life or heart's desire to a mortal.

The men, three men, get closer and closer; I look around irritatedly. Why are they coming so close to me when there's so much room? Haven't they noticed I'm here? They're talking among themselves; eventually they drop their burden on the ground a little way away from me but not very far. One of them approaches me, clears his throat. He asks if I'd mind moving. I look at him, incredulous. I look around—there is huge space in all directions. There is no one else here. Where I'm sitting is absolutely nowhere special; if they wanted to be next to one of these little forest beds, there are plenty of them and nothing remarkable about the one I'm near. I'm not at the water's edge, I'm not close to the path, I'm not at the crest of a rise. Into my not speaking he offers some more words.

It's for a wedding, he says. They've come here early to set up. This is the exact place they want to be. Where I am is where the marquee they've brought needs to be, the one where the wedding will take place.

If I wasn't silenced already by amazement, that would silence me. I think I nod. I gather my things and move back twenty paces farther up the hill and sit down again to watch them. I still don't think there's anything special about that place; looking at it from a little distance, I can see nothing at all to distinguish it from a hundred other marquee-sized places within my scope of vision, but obviously there is something special about it. Something special about me choosing to sit in the place for a wedding, something special about a wedding coming to interrupt me.

From the moment he spoke to me, said the word *wedding*, it was as if I was receiving a vision instead of a request to move; I was hearing voices from the other world. They said to me *wedding* and I was in there with them. I question it; I even try to fight it off or laugh it off or cast doubt over that certainty that visited me in that peculiar parallel-worlds moment, but it still remains, a small but utter conviction that there's a marriage. Not here, not now; but not that far away. I heard it, I caught it, a glimmering flash beneath the water's surface, a moment of truth-telling, foretelling. It's coming for me. And oh, I do want it. For romance and a love to be that deep, that trusting that I could give myself to it; a union of souls. In the West it came to me; how strange but how utterly right. Visions, knowing, dreams; the pause before the change; long journeying.

Sounding the Depths

Myth, ritual, invocation, and inner work all overlap and tide together. A ritual or working may have a huge impact on one person, offering them revelations, insight, and new understanding of their life, while the person sitting next to them may experience none of that. Working with a myth will for one person be a process of delving deeply within, where for another it may have more interest as a commentary on the myth itself or its historical context. These things can't be separated. It would be difficult to run a ritual that excluded personal inner work or to force people to examine themselves deeply if they weren't that way inclined or didn't feel like it right at that moment.

Within particular workings or rituals there may be an emphasis on one of these areas. A Summer Solstice ritual may be dedicated to celebrating the season, with personal or mythic insights as extras, not the focus of the gathering. Or a myth may be worked primarily as a path of inner journeying, with any new understandings of the myth a bonus if they occur. The intention and focus of the group—which may not be the same as that of the individual—directs the types of activities undertaken.

People learn things in different ways, as well as bringing different skills, offerings, and insights to each piece of work, so the ideal is a variety of activities offering different approaches, methodologies, and experiences.

Sometimes a ritual that was intended to be outwardly focused gains strong ground in the inner realms. Recently I was working with a group to construct a ritual inspired by the Norse god Odin, also known as the All-Father, and found we were devolving into a level of personal emotional baggage. When I asked if we could each, in one sentence, speak about our relationships to our fathers, the words we heard were chilling. Fathers were absent, disconnected, uncommunicative, lost. Once we had recognized and named this, we were able to continue our work creating the ritual now at a deeper level, recognizing but no longer tripped up by our relationships with our own fathers. Seeing those relationships as endemic to our whole cultural relationship to fathers and fathering, we allowed this to inform our ritual instead of undermining it.

In the Circle of Eight, Odin's myth was one we worked with in a more interior way. We had decided to focus on him hanging in the tree, his great sacrificial time that resulted in him losing (or offering) one of his eyes and receiving the gift of the runes. Mythically there are many, many layers to this story, including the world tree itself, Yggdrasil; Odin's relationship with magic and the mysteries; the nature of sacrifice, and the part played by the earth goddess Erdda. But we decided to concentrate on the myth from a personal, inner perspective; we would look at where and how we offered ourselves—or allowed ourselves—to be strung up; what we brought as sacrifice and what transformation or knowledge might be granted us.

We began by building the tree magically and energetically. We started with its roots, deep into the darkest part of our circle, our South and the direction of the Winter Solstice. They burrowed down so massively it felt as if they reached through the extent of our planet, as if the earth itself existed only to support this tree. When we began building the trunk we experienced a tremendous upwards force of energy, fed from the bright fires deep below, molten rocks and deep, rich, rare earths, the hidden jewels and underground waterways. The trunk stormed up through the center of the circle, reaching the heights of our

Summer Solstice position and beyond, and also vertically, as if owning the whole width of the circle, the house and land, heading for the sky. Branches sprang outwards, canopying Above, reaching up and out to touch each position in our circle; they were laden in our group vision with bud, leaf, and flower.

Before we began working with Odin we descended into the depths of the tree, the roots, to acknowledge the ancient one, Erdda. We felt her there, hidden, listening, waiting. Then we ascended into the branches and called to Odin. We hung there with him. What will we sacrifice? We took out paper and colored pencils, markers and oil pastels, and each drew a picture of ourselves hanging in the tree. The drawings were anguished, delicate, graceful, serene, ecstatic, violent, chaotic. When we offered them, we stood one by one in the center of the circle, which had now become the center of the tree as well, and we spoke of our sacrifices, what had called out of our depths as we drew and went within. In the center it was as if the tree swallowed each one of us; we could see the force of it consuming the person who stood there, almost transforming them to wood and leaf and sap.

A sacrifice is at least two things. It's a relinquishing, a loss of something, but sacrificing is also *the act of making sacred*. What I hand over to the gods becomes sacred. On that night from the North-East I sacrificed ambivalence. It's nearly ten years since we did that work, and I know my ambivalence must have been a powerful thing to bring as a sacrifice. But looking at the page now, where that's written, I can hardly relate to it. Me—ambivalent? What about? I am not even remotely ambivalent about anything, really; I can hardly imagine that of myself. It's written twice that I said that: on two different pages of our Book of Shadows and in two different people's handwriting, so I have to believe it. And all I can say is, it must have been an incredibly effective ritual; ambivalence is completely gone from me. Something happened: Odin took it, the tree ate it, Erdda accepted it.

Ross, in the South-West, sacrificed control. In his drawing he *was* the tree, lower body rooted in the ground, arms stretching up to branches. He placed a falling upside-down heart to the left of the figure and a many-rayed star on the right. It was as if he was letting things fall away and at the same time rising into growth and light. His control was a shadow characteristic, one that played underneath his easygoing exterior. Glenn, in the East, sacrificed the experience of never feeling loved for who he was, and Cathryn, in the West, sacrificed her softness. These were crucial parts of how Cathryn and Glenn were perceived, not just by themselves but by the rest of us. As Odin sacrificed an eye, they were sacrificing the limitations of how they saw themselves and how others saw them in order to discover a deeper truth. Trinda sacrificed her need to be invisible, to remain less-than, and each of these things—ambivalence, control, not being loved, softness, and being hidden—could have been spoken by Odin, he who came into his power and the depth of his magic on the tree.

We experimented with many different forms of inner work, often combined with ritual, and at different times each person took a leadership role in teaching, facilitating, or guiding the processes. Often during an evening's ritual there would come a time when each of us had a turn in the center while the others drummed, sang, and listened to or mirrored us. This way we could have a few moments of stepping completely into our own story, supported by the others. We would get to see different versions of working the same theme as we witnessed each other, and we would all take turns both in holding the energy for others and being the focal point. This was always powerful, bringing us fully present and into ourselves; standing in the center, it was as if we were stripped bare, supported and seen.

For over a year we focused on inner work. At the Spring Equinox we began as seeds curled up on the floor. We did it one by one and the others fed us the qualities we needed for growth. For one of us was spoken *light, sun, starlight, warmth, care, hope, grace, beauty* and for another *solidity, compassion, warmth, strength, support, nourishment, endurance, stability* and for another *begin again, fresh shoots, inspiration, dynamism, clarity, will, prayer*. During these words we stretched and grew, finding what fed us and turning towards it as the warmth of the sun, allowing ourselves to be nourished and encouraged.

Around Beltaine we stood in the center in turn again, this time to summon up the most powerful rising tide of ourselves, to bring it through our body and voices and feel what it was like to hold and express that much energy to our fullest extent. Just past the Summer Solstice we did a working with opposites, each singing the wordless song of our own direction while focusing with our inner vision and thoughts into the direction opposite us to feel the motion and interaction between the two points and bring ourselves into alignment with it. We brought these two aspects together in our sound and into our body, feeling them marry and join within us.

At Lammas we each traveled out to the place of the direction we were holding to listen. Cathryn went very early in the morning out to the East, listening for the ancient voices of the land and within herself. Trinda set out towards the mountain, the old volcano; she had a sense of traveling and traveling but never quite arriving. We went as a group on an excursion to my direction, the bora ring, so it seemed that the whole circle came with me—not the people necessarily but the circle, all of its angles and directions and possibilities that I carry with me no matter which direction I am in.

At the Autumn Equinox we took turns walking from East to West across the room. Each step we took, someone stood in front of us naming what they imagined might be one of our worst fears. They allowed us to step forward again only when they saw in our eyes, in our breathing and body, that we could meet that fear and hold our center clearly enough to confront it. We spoke later of how much trust was involved to let the others not just call out our fears into our faces, preventing us from progressing, but also allowing them to hold space as witnesses while we met those fears, letting them sense the changes within us as we found a way to meet them. It was absolutely confronting—dynamic and raw and visceral—and yet at the end we felt love, support, and togetherness, as if we had breached the storm together.

Just before Samhain we sat quietly in the circle and shared our hidden selves, our shadow parts that operate below the surface, which we hope to conceal from the world and yet as soon as we named them, they were instantly recognizable to the others. We had met them in awkward moments, caught glimpses of them, felt in our guts that they lay in wait within this person. We named ourselves with shadow names; we became Vicious, Flirtatious, Inadequate, Deceptive, Fearful, and Childish. There was a tremoring sense of night at the edges of the circle; the year had become dark and cold. No extra words were spoken to console or even acknowledge what had been said, but we felt held and seen in the flickering candlelight.

Just after the Winter Solstice we met again for what felt like a culmination of this part of our working. We had been sitting with an area of personal darkness for a month. Each of us brought one of the elements into the ritual: Glenn was in the North-East and brought air, I was in the North carrying fire, Ian in the West with water, Cathryn in the South-West with aether, and Ross in the South brought earth. We sat, one at a time, in the center of the circle, breathing into our darkness. When we felt ready, we called for one of the elements to come to us. The person carrying that element brought it into the center, each time in a different way.

We stayed in the center, breathing in our darkness and calling for the next element, then the next, until we had all five. As fire I brought one person a lit gold candle, to another person I gave the box of matches, for another I put my hand on their heart, to another I spoke loudly *open your eyes,* and to the last person I whispered the memory of summer. For air a harp was played and a song sung, as earth a rock was placed in someone's hands, water was offered to drink or sprinkled like rain, for aether Cathryn applied oil to the crown chakra. It was a beautiful ritual. Each time, for each person, it was a different: the order of elements, the words spoken, the way each element was offered.

At our next circle, nearing Imbolc, we decided to work on our soul purpose: what brought us into the world. First we spent time just breathing and feeling into our own soul purpose, visualizing it. In pairs we shared what we'd seen and felt, and then we created a ritual for each other. The rituals were simple and immediate. Mine was a toning that circled around me, strengthening as it came closer; Cathryn's a visualization that led her to her life force; Ross's and Ian's involved them writing down all the blocks that prevented them traveling towards their goals, then burning the paper in the candle. At the end we gathered together to share our experience. Glenn spoke of vastness and compassion; Cathryn of energy dancing with her; Ross said he felt like holding more of the show.

During our next circle we set out to travel back to our childhoods to reconnect with the spark each of us was born with, then bring that spark and its gifts through time to the present. We divided into men's and women's groups to create containers of trust and witnessing. In the women's group, one by one we entered our childhood story, seeking that beginning spark, and when we found our gifts we spoke them aloud to the others for safekeeping and so they could tell them back to us. We used sound and movement and felt affected by this delicate working, trusting our childhood selves to the others. When we came back together with the men, we found they also were touched by this working but felt they didn't go deep enough. Glenn said later the men were envious when they heard how deep the women's process had been. We agreed that between circles we would do some more work.

The men decided to go to the South together, the earth direction of the waterfall, and the women felt we had to go into the center of ourselves, so we chose the labyrinth. We went one morning, three women and a teenage girl; it was too early for other people to be there except for a gardener adjusting sprinklers. We walked the labyrinth in all our different styles: slowly pacing it out, striding long-legged and eager, gently and meanderingly, purposefully. We met eventually in the middle and sat down, each in our own direction. Our ritual was as much about coming together as women in both the inner and the outer worlds as anything we spoke of.

At the next circle we moved into the time of our teens and twenties, looking at paths we didn't take, things we missed out on but now wished to incorporate or reexamine. Some of us are pleased with choices we made; others find longings for parts of themselves that got weeded out or neglected. Again we worked with sound and movement, energetically reconnecting those threads we'd let go of. Then we took out pastels and cardboard and each drew the story in segments of our seed self, our childhood gifts, the paths we chose. The pictures came out dense and beautiful; we left three segments blank for more pieces of the working.

After that it was nearly Beltaine, so it seemed a perfect time to reincorporate our passions—those initial passions of the seed-spark, of childhood gifts and the later passions of paths chosen and not chosen— and trust that our magic will bring them into our lives. We created rituals in pairs. Ian and Trinda began by listing their passions and analyzing the fears that blocked access to them, then moved into asking for help with this and concluded with a visioning of bringing those passions into life. Ross and Cathryn started with toning, building energy between them until words of passion began to bounce out of the sound, bursting forth and manifesting themselves almost as solid things. Glenn and I began with a conversation and a ritual that seemed to create itself, an enactment of each other's passions, anchoring them into the body. We drew our rituals into the next segment of our pictures.

The next circle was after Beltaine, and we decided to seek the outward spiral: how we would translate these findings into our actions in the world. Again we divided into pairs, choosing people we hadn't worked with earlier. Cathryn and Glenn talked, then danced, then talked again before arriving at action plans. Ross and Trinda created an altar to the elements in four pieces and then stood in the center of it. They tested each other's resolution and strength to stay centered and grounded. Ian and I sat in silence, then both sounded together through the four stages. We wrote lists of limitations and plans; I resolved to make a lot of noise.

We brought our resolutions into spontaneous ritual; each one of us became our own resolution. We danced with each other, drummed and made noise; we surrounded Trinda, whose resolution was to say *yes* in her life, with shouted and whispered and sung *yeses*, the noise spiraling up and around, supporting her. For her this whole process had represented her relationship with her art—that she hadn't gone to art school because it wasn't thought suitable and how her artistic expression, which had been natural when she was young, had been locked up inside even later, when she had gone back to university as an adult. The six-month process helped her to get beyond her fears; the final picture she drew was two feet to remind her *step by step, breath by breath, just now and now* does change happen.

Cathryn's journey was about feeling enough in herself to be equal with others. Through the months she found a new level of confidence, a feeling of worthiness that led to her final spell to dance *with* her life. It meant she was growing free, prepared to be seen, and she made a commitment to dance every day as a way to continue to bring this through. Glenn was challenged throughout the process by having to look at his childhood and the paths he hadn't been able to take, by having to draw, and by his own desire to search for grounding in his life. He felt he resisted the whole way but some growing came out of it, almost in spite of himself.

The final segment of our pictures was dense and emblematic, six months' worth of working and searching and discovery patterned into them; each totally different but with the same journey unwinding. My final picture was a many-rayed star in purple, pink, and gold. Cathryn's final drawing was a woman dancing with the moon, Glenn's a tree-becoming-a-man bursting through the center of a pentacle, and Ian's a five-pointed star with the points named *creativity, love, authenticity, dreams, imagination*. Trinda's drawing showed a lit candle in the center surrounded by the word *yes* written dozens of times, along with the script *yes to knowing, yes to not knowing, yes to painting*. Ross's showed a tight spiral bursting into colored rays that spread to the edges of the square. We took our pictures home to hang on our walls, place on our altars, or paste into our journals.

How to Explore Inner Work with Your Circle of Eight

There are too many types of inner work to list all of them. There is meditation of all types. There are the resources of psychology, expounded in literally hundreds of self-help books. There are physical disciplines and explorations: yoga of many varieties, different forms of dance, various types of therapeutic massage and touch. There are programs for spiritual growth in books, online, and taught directly. There is shadow work, breathwork, dreamwork; journaling and art as inner exploration. There is dynamic exploration of spiritual or magical models, such as the Kabbalah, the Iron Pentacle, and the chakra system, applied to inner understanding and development. There are spiritual, religious, and personal growth teachers, gurus, and leaders of all types currently alive and teaching online, in person, around the world and through books and recordings.

So much is available to us via the vast reaches of the Internet, relatively easy travel, and a culture that, while it doesn't focus on or particularly encourage inner growth and spiritual exploration, certainly doesn't condemn or limit it. In the last twelve months, for example, and among other things, with a group of five others I have completed a ten-month working of *Twelve Wild Swans*, a Reclaiming-based book aimed at facilitating personal and magical growth. I've attended a day-long workshop of Deepak Chopra's in London with a thousand other people. I've been to two Reclaiming WitchCamps, one as a teacher and one as a camper (of four and six days, respectively); listened to a lecture series on sacred relationship (twelve ninety-minute lectures online) and followed that up with listening to further talks on relationship (again online) from Judith Ansara and Robert Gass; and I've participated as a student in an online six-week course on Reclaiming's Pearl Pentacle. I've done some personal processing with Byron Katie's Work and Four Questions; attended half a dozen Five Rhythms Dance evenings, and begun a seven-month chakra working. I've seen a counselor several times over my relationship breakup and spent four months working on an intense personal level with the characters from the Norse goddess Freyja's story. I've kept a personal diary every day and journaled at more length on areas of personal growth and challenge. That's not including rituals I've done by myself and with others, or the courses and workshops I've taught.

Every person in your circle will be a resource for the whole circle. In their journeys through life, their spiritual exploration and personal development, they will have learned meditations and personal processes, attended Rebirthing intensives and tantra workshops, been part of dream groups, twelve-step programs, and co-counseling groups, and learned a huge variety of techniques, skills, and practices. Each person, also, will have been through difficult and challenging times in their lives, dark nights of the soul, and during or after those times they will probably have reached deep understandings about themselves and have sought out resources and support and healing. They now have these resources to potentially share with a group. They will have read books and attended lectures, workshops, or events on different aspects of spirituality and personal growth, at least some of which will have been inspiring, educational, or intriguing. These may be directions they can follow up or offer as explorations or starting points for group process, learning, or discussion.

How to Begin Inner Work Within the Circle of Eight

1. *Agreements*

Before you embark on intensive or focused inner work within your Circle of Eight, forming agreements among yourselves helps create a container both energetically and practically. You may already have agreements about magical work, frequency of meetings, level of commitment, and behavior during circles; these agreements can be revisited and added for this inner work. Agreements of this nature really need everyone to be a part of their creation; if you have new people join, revisit your group agreements.

Some discussion points that may lead to group agreements include:

- What is confidential within the group, and what may be discussed outside the group? How does this work on a practical and energetic level? I often work from the basis that skills, techniques, and processes are not confidential, and one's own experience can be shared any way one chooses, but no one can discuss or reveal another person's experience, words, or sharings. Some people like to add that people within the group can't even talk about what they witnessed with others also in the group, or that they need to check it out with the relevant person before doing so.

- What types of inner work are appropriate, preferred, and of interest? Is the group mainly interested in psychological processing and not meditation, for example, or is the group open to experimenting with many different types of inner work?

- Who should teach or lead this work, and how is it preferred to be taught or led? Does the group wish to rotate leadership and teaching so everyone has a chance to present what they have learned or are interested in? Should sessions be co-taught between two or more people? Should the style be experiential, informative, informal, or a mixture of these?

- What avenues exist or may be put in place for dealing with issues that arise during this work, either personal or interpersonal? How will the group support each other?

2. Material

Create two lists, possibly on large pieces of paper so everyone can see them easily. One list is for "skills and practices," where each person lists all the skills they have in areas of inner work, including things they know only a little about or have just begun exploring. They can indicate their level of comfort and familiarity with each item on the list. The second list is for "areas of interest," where everyone lists what they are particularly interested in exploring with the group. Rather than repeating items on this list, place ticks next to each item to indicate the number of people interested in each one.

3. Outline Sessions

Looking at your two lists, there may be an obvious starting point. For example, two people may have indicated they have some experience with dreamwork and four people that they have an interest in exploring dreams. Your first session could therefore be an introductory dreamwork session. If it goes well, the group may wish to extend that into several sessions or return to further dreamwork later.

There may be something attracting strong interest that no one feels equipped to teach or lead. For a session on this topic, some research can be undertaken by one or more people. It's also possible to begin exploring that topic from a discussion base or approaching it from angles you are already familiar with. For example, if the group was interested in Jungian archetypes, you could begin with visualizing or shamanic journeying with an archetype, followed by free drawing or writing, rather than from an academic knowledge of Jung's work.

A great session for becoming inspired with inner work is to have each person bring a fifteen-minute process, experience, or presentation on any area of inner work. Thus in one meeting you may get to do a meditation, take a glimpse at shadow work, do some breathing practices with a few yoga poses, be introduced to inner-child work, play with some tarot cards, and hear about a self-development book someone read. This is a great stepping-off point; it may be that the group decides to do much more shadow work, possibly incorporating conscious breathing; that others want to read the book described; that meditation is introduced for ten minutes at the start of each session; and that creativity and play are requested to become a stronger part of circle work.

If you have a collection of confident, trained, and experienced people in your circle, you may want to make one position—for example, the South—the teacher's position. Then for one round of the circle—eight meetings—allow the person holding that position to lead a session in whatever they are best at, whether that's by negotiation or decided by them. Alternatively, two people—for example, those sitting in the North and South—may hold one session between them; this would take only four sessions to complete a round.

4. Use Feedback

After each session it's great for the group to give feedback, especially on how they felt this type of work went in your particular group. Be sensitive to those who have spent time and energy presenting it, and praise what you felt worked best. Unless this is part of your agreement with each other or it has been specifically requested, don't enter into strong critique. Speak honestly about whether you want to continue this type of inner work within the group or if you feel it's time to try other things.

Speak for yourself, that is *I felt this work was exciting* or *I found it hard to go very deep with this*, rather than speaking for the group with "we" statements such as *We didn't like this*. Be encouraging; after all, you want people in your group to continue to participate and offer what they know. Be as specific as possible in your praise: *I loved the visualization you led us on* or *I learned a lot from the introduction you gave* or *I was impressed by the level of trust you inspired*. If it has been agreed to offer feedback, make sure it is constructive, such as *I found it easiest to hear when you spoke really loudly* or *I felt safest the times when you explained what the purpose of each exercise was before we did it* or *I could tell you knew a lot about the subject and I would love to hear more of your thoughts about it*.

5. Experiment

Perhaps no one anywhere ever before has combined a Kabbalistic pathworking with yoga poses and breathwork, followed by free drawing and expressive dance—but you might. Perhaps dreamwork, shadow work, and inner-child work overlap and merge for months in your circle, without anyone needing to separate them or choose one over the other. Perhaps you propose a topic such as intimacy, anger, or life purpose that everyone works on in different ways, either individually or as a group. One person might guide the group creating artwork, another person teach journaling techniques, another lead a shamanic journey, and another offer an interactive process. Since you are in a Circle of Eight, you might combine your directions with your offerings in ways that possibly no one has ever thought of or tried before.

Dive in…

Release

It's a peculiar weekend, and we are out of sorts with each other. There are seven of us in a four-bedroom holiday beach house; you'd think it would work, but it doesn't. Glenn wants a room by himself, I won't let any of the men share a room with the teenage girl, there are two double beds but only one couple, and the only person I'll agree to share a bed with is my teenage son, who's not too happy about that. Someone ends up on the couch as a result of all this. Also, we seem to be in the middle of suburbia, not on the beach at all, and there is some muttering about misleading real estate agents and other places that would have been better and why didn't I check it out more thoroughly. I am slightly sick and not in the mood for rituals, beaches, or other people.

Cathryn insists we make masks. It is approaching Samhain and we have come away for a weekend together, choosing this location down the coast for its proximity to the bora ring. It's almost always me who insists we do things so I am astounded and impressed that it's Cathryn, but I don't feel remotely like making a mask, not one bit. I feel cross and headachy, and the task of dealing with cardboard and paint to try to work a concept into a wearable mask seems far too great and awkward for me. At Cathryn's coaxing I agree to sit in the room where the masks are being made and eventually, of course, it wears off on me and I concede that I will have to make a mask; we are all making them for the ritual next week.

I'm currently holding the direction for Samhain. I want my mask to be an animal or a bird; nonhuman, anyway. But I also want it to be simple, stark; almost violent with impact. I sketch a few ideas idly, then I'm suddenly gripped. There's a piece of very heavy black cardboard, white on the inside, far too thick to fold or shape, and I've suddenly seen how it can be transformed into a bird's beak by cutting out a V and sewing the edges together, forcing the rest of the shape to bend in response. There's some thick glittery gold thread: I seize it and the cardboard and a cutting blade and find a skewer to make holes for sewing, and I wrestle and pierce and yank the thread, forcing it into the shape I've seen. I end up with a ferociously piercing triangular-shaped black bird mask. I paint simple eyes on it, but I see where I'm going by looking down, since the mask sits on top of my head. I'm enormously pleased with it and even help make another one so there can be a pair of these almost cockatoos, almost ravens.

That evening we drive to the bora ring. It's a full moon and the sky is clear. It's deserted and seems even emptier than in daytime, as if the winds blowing over it are the winds of tens of thousands of years and we are in no particular time at all, certainly not a special or momentous time. And we are no particular people at all, certainly not special people. Usually this is one of the aspects I like about this place, the reminder of the immensity of time in the bora ring and of imminent mortality in the cemetery before it, but at night it is more disconcerting. We haven't devised a ritual; usually when we visit these places we let the mood dictate, the place offer its own suggestions, and that results in very simple, almost emblematic rituals. And we've been here as a group before but never at night and never with the full moon.

We park the car a little way away and walk over towards the bora ring, not directly beside it and certainly not in it, but nearby. We've brought a drum, and we begin to sing and drum. It is a simple ritual and perhaps doesn't meet our expectations. There's too much discussion, not enough focus, and we don't have a plan, so in the end it is mainly the fact of us being there in the moonlight. As we finish the police drive up; a nearby resident has alerted them to our drumming, but once they see how few we are, they're disinterested.

I pick up some twigs thick with gum leaves to jam into the masks and form the crests of these black birds I've summoned out from between the worlds. Creatures of night, of the air, of movement between one place and the next. And I've always seen this stand of very young gum trees as guardians, current reminders of the ancient landscape when this was not paddocks and roads and houses but rises and dips in the living land, folded truths settling upon one another around and around the ages. I notice they've been allowed to grow—or been planted, even, in the west—so the setting sun cuts through them in stripes and shadows across the bora ring. I think of them as holding a promise that we're returning to a time when we remember the sacred—not remember it as history but as the living now. The gum leaves are a memento of this world, a symbol of the South-West, a whisper on the wind.

Letting Go

Beginnings are so easy, compared with endings. And surely it's true that each ending casts a new beginning, but it's hard to see at the time. An ending seems so monumental, full, and heart-rending—the loss of an irreplaceable thing; whatever is coming is slender in comparison, barely begun, with no shape or consequence as yet, no conviction in it. In both the wheel and the Circle of Eight, endings and beginnings literally overlap as the ending of every festival gives way to the next festival and the cycle, once completed, is endlessly and seamlessly begun again. Each festival has degrees of endings and beginnings in its composition, just as it has dark and light. Imbolc, for example, is a festival that falls within the darker half of the year, though it is a festival given to the light. Beginnings are one of its strongest themes, but the ending of winter is in there too—the ending of all that depth and knowing into something simpler, plainer; new.

When we work the Circle of Eight we know that each time we dedicate ourselves to a direction—for a month or a moon or maybe only a week—we will have to leave it again. Just as we are always arriving in a new direction, greeting it with wariness, desire, or dread, so we are always leaving the direction we have by now become familiar with. Sometimes there is only relief—to escape from a hard lesson or an uncomfortable challenge, to move on from a place we felt didn't represent us at our best—but mostly there is some level of regret, of loss; a tearing ourselves away from what has become a part of us, an unmarrying from the direction we have been bonded to while we saw the world from that perspective and spoke as its voice.

Traveling round and round the circle over time, this may lessen as we learn each direction is always there for us again, catching us in its arms as we arrive and allowing us to fall into it, each time a little deeper, more immediately. We also learn that those directions we've left are never really gone from us; not only do they lie ahead of us on the endless circling, but there are pieces, reflections, and commentaries on each of them within every direction. We start to become more like the circle ourselves, holding all of those refractions within ourselves while just that one—that particular one we are holding at that moment—catches the light, to be seen more brilliantly and be the filter for our experience right now, but knowing it is only an aspect of the whole or, indeed, that the whole is always present, just viewed from different angles.

Still, with all that knowing and within that body of feeling, still there is goodbye. Like leaving a lover at an airport; yes you will meet again, yes you have plans and trust and are as certain of future meetings as one can be of anything; but will you be the same people then? Even if it is only weeks or days away, will you still be the same person? You cannot be—it cannot be—not exactly the same. And in that inexactness, in that growth or change or merely time passing, there is the sadness, the loss, letting go—the surrender that happens endlessly, second to second, highlighted suddenly by a moment at an airport or this moment of leaving one direction to move to the next or this moment of moving on to a different piece of life.

Our Circle of Eight had twelve different participants over its lifetime of five years, not counting the six children in the Phoenix Circle. People came and left. One of them left, came back several years later, and then left again. Always when we turned the wheel that first night without them, it felt as if we left them behind inextricably in time, that its endless movement results in constantly leaving things and people behind.

The circle moved on without them, through the directions they had held and even replacing them; we noticed their absences, the shape they had left, for a while, and then enough other things changed and shifted so that it blurred. They became part of the background of the circle, the whispers and ghosts held just beyond the boundaries of the visible; part of our learning, our knowing, our experience of the circle, but indistinct. We might remember them more strongly in one direction than the others, even briefly see them there when we sat across from that direction or feel them momentarily when we moved into it ourselves. We might miss them when we came to sing a song and noticed their voice absent or when we created a ritual for a particular festival and remembered the way they had held the God at this festival last year or the year before or the altar they had built or the passion they brought into ritual.

Choosing how people can join is one dynamic of a group; coping with and allowing people to leave is another. Our Circle of Eight often worked on eight-month commitments, or the length of time it took to travel around the whole circle. People rarely left in the middle of these eight-month terms, but there's leaving and leaving. There were people whose energy dropped to half-level, who skipped meetings or rituals, hanging on until the eight months would be up and they could leave within the agreed terms.

When anyone left we asked them to come to a final meeting. We sat with them in our current directions and each person spoke, sometimes at length, to the one leaving about what it had been like to be in the circle with them, what they had learned and understood from that person, what they felt their connection to be, and what it was like having them leave. Then the one leaving spoke to each person in turn about what they had seen and learned, what their connection was, and what they would take forward from that into wherever they were going. And then we turned the wheel and the person leaving stepped out of the wheel, not moving to the next direction but stepping off our rotation onto a path of their own. The wheel turned and the world looked different; we found ourselves in a new arrangement but still letting go of that person, whose echoes lay barely under the surface, their shapes and patterns interwoven with ours and still distinguishable.

Bora Ring

. . . .

Memoir

This place holds the start and end of my relationship.

We come here in the afternoon, right at the beginning of things. Over the phone he stammered and choked; I wanted to reassure him. I told him I needed to go to the bora ring, my direction of the South-West. I brought the pages I wrote a week or so ago where I tried to get down, finally and definitively, what I felt for him. It was easy after I started—all those years of friendship and connection flowing out of me into liquid words, my emotions less complicated than I imagined. In the end there is mainly love, although I do recall stages of confusion, uncertainty, thwarted communication, and misunderstandings; those long years where I put barriers firmly around any intimacy or friendship, and the more recent years when he cast me adrift.

I don't think I've got anything to lose; I feel remarkably free. I was about to move to the city to find my son a fiercer, more testing education for his last few years of schooling and just to be somewhere different. This man has stopped me in my tracks, demanding my attention, and told me not to move to the city just yet, and on one level I hardly believe him—I never thought he had any interest in me; not in that way, not romantically. But I've seen him once a week for a few weeks now, and gradually this new reality is filtering through to me. Not enough for me to be invested, not yet; but enough to start that entrancement that, once it really kicks in, nothing can compete with. Not even the city.

We drive out to the bora ring. It's quite a way, and we talk unendingly; he talks a lot and is shocked at himself in it, he says it is not like him, he should shut up. We talk literature and politics and ideas and families; we intrigue each other, fascinate with the unknown, the partly known, the yet-to-be-revealed. It's a fine day although it's mid-April; in fact, it is more or less the time associated with this direction, Samhain. So it's the time of year, it's the position I'm in, it's the place we're going to. It's odd to be starting a relationship in the evening of the year, the drawing-in, but the Celts celebrated their festivals from the evening before; their days began with dusk and ran through to the next dusk. Samhain is associated with beginnings as well as with endings. And this is a beginning.

When we are there, I show him the simplicity of it. There's almost nothing to see, really, once you've driven through the cemetery; it's more in the depths of the place, what it holds and has seen and symbolizes. There's that stand of gum trees; the bora ring a faint raised circle in the ground, surrounded by a low pine-post fence and a few little, lonely graves nearby, out of the cemetery proper and nestled near the bora ring as if seeking its shelter. There's a wide view, it's a high point in the land; you can see fields, the road, stands of trees here and there, the hills in the distance; nothing in particular, but the wind blows through.

I make offerings. I've brought honey for the ants and water from my spring for the land, and we sit in silence for a while near the entrance to the bora ring. It is a place holding its own history and magic that has nothing to do with us. I work my rituals and musings nearby, parallel, like the few graves placed oddly near. Seeking connection but not imposing. There is a majesty here, a dreaming thousands and tens of thousands of years old, and it's as if such depth doesn't need to be marked very deeply on the land; it carries all the energetic layers though all the worlds. I can imagine this bora ring stamped through time and into the million realms of the multiverse, the same; simple but unendingly itself. A fixed point in existence.

We sit on the ground in the shade of the trees on the faded pink picnic rug I have had for years; we have to keep picking ants off it. There are a lot of ants and they're investigative, keen explorers and hunters and gatherers. They're like the business of life and death itself, their jaws munching up and recycling the discarded and the dead into their eager, bustling lives of order and increase. They are the busiest thing here, otherwise the place exudes peace and timelessness, punctuated mainly by visitors who look around for five minutes waiting for there to be something more dramatic to see and then, in its absence, leave. It is only sitting here quietly for an hour or more, an afternoon, a day that the place begins to make itself seen, to hint in the wind at a secret or two.

We eat some lunch, and I read him the piece I wrote. I don't feel nervous, not anxious, though it lays my deepest feelings bare; anticipatory, maybe, and I think there is a good chance it will turn him off completely, repel him by my intensity or truth or willingness to be open. But as I read I feel the shifts in him. I feel his eagerness for it, his acceptance; as if he has swallowed me up already, these words and all I will say in the future. I can't believe it's that easy; I am not, after all, making a declaration of forbidden longings, just exploring, piece by piece, the history of our connection. But it is as if it reaches him on some much deeper level, reminding him, perhaps, of all the length and breadth of our history; reminding him of himself.

Of course I love him. I have always loved him; it has been simple to love him. I have loved his intensity, his interest in me and the world, his easy generosity with so many people, his occasional flamboyance and the ferocity of his opinion, his original way of viewing complex issues. I've always thought he admired much the same things in me, with variations; I thought he marveled at my daring in relationship, where he has been so much more conventional. But now he is the daring one, leaping forward, and suddenly we are already there, in a deeper flow of connection than I expected or anticipated.

This is the real beginning, here at the bora ring; a beginning ten years past that other beginning. I remember seeing him for the first time at a party, laughing and with his arm around his lover; when I was introduced to him, a clear, unbidden thought came into my head: *stay away from this man*. I attempted that for several years while he sought me out, determined to pursue conversation, connection. He remembers a later day, in someone's kitchen, where he tried to engage me in a debate on feminism. But I still had those words pounding through me, *stay away from this man*, and I gave curt answers and more or less ignored him, fueling his interest. Both of these remembered meetings have a powerful awareness of the other and all the reasons why we couldn't and shouldn't connect. But now, here, there are none of those reasons. Here, now, is another beginning, and I don't have to stay away.

I am aware of the time of year, of the place. Still I decide to trust, to let the wheel turn with me and into this new place. What choice is there, after all? It's as obvious as the change of seasons; past summer there can only be autumn, followed by winter. It doesn't go any other way. Past youth there is middle age; past that, old age and dying. That's what we live with: simple truth, as simple as the bora ring. Here is this man I've loved as a friend, with tenderness for who he is in the world and how he's been with me, in a clarity that came from not being involved with him. Now suddenly we are swept forward into relationship; like the waterfall falling off the cliff, it's all different now. We've begun again.

I hardly know where I am in it, but I do remember it is Samhain. Our relationship begins as the veils between the worlds part, as the year slides into the other realm. Our relationship begins among the ancient vibrations of the bora ring, resonances that ripple outwards, unendingly. This is a place deeper than the rest of our circle, the place circle is born from, the dark vortex from which life emerges, the ending of worlds where all is swallowed. I feel small here, small and human and not certain of anything but the present moment. It is a beginning mired in history. His past relationships, mine; my child, his children; our ages and all of our histories; the fact that, though we've known each other for ten years, perhaps we don't know each other very well at all.

Six years later, the bora ring is where he comes after he's left me. It's nearly that time of year again, a little earlier. March instead of April, the equinox and the stepping into darkness rather than the time of deep mysteries. I don't know what the weather's like, what the mood is, how the trees have grown, because I'm somewhere else. It somehow seems appropriate that he comes here to explain himself rather than to me. Of all the directions it's been my favorite; the time of year I was born, given to the mysteries, stamped by them as I entered the world of the living. The shadows have always beckoned me, those other worlds sung into my ears, my eyes have been entranced by things just beyond the visible. It's the place of the liminal where realms overlap, one into the other, dreams into truth into mystery, dancing the eternal dance of becoming and unbecoming, loves and endings.

He comes to apologize, or that's what he tells me later—to apologize for hurt and who knows what else; the failure of relationship. Maybe to seek comfort or lay memories to rest, with all those other memories that are laid here; those countless rituals. All those lives the cemetery holds such slender memories of, all the feet that have danced this earthen ring, the voices that have sung and chanted through it. Maybe he's drawn here on a thread, the thread that takes you round the circle and round again, completing what you've begun and winding back and back to the beginning, as well as on and on to the end. I don't know because I'm not there. I can't say I understand any of it, unless you see it purely as the turn of the wheel, not in human terms. If he's going to vanish, I suppose this is a good place to do it; sacred, circular, complete. Samhain and the South-West are places of endings, after all.

Endings in the Circle of Eight

Every year at Samhain we made a practice of letting go. We named our dead for the year, lit candles for them, spoke of their lives and our connections with them, and then released them. We drew our year onto cards for fortune telling and dropped them into the cauldron; good or bad, momentous or ordinary, we left that year behind. We exited out the west door, leaving the house, the upperworld and the selves we had been. We put on masks, letting go of our faces and names, and journeyed to the spirit realms. We met with our beloved dead, saw their faces and heard their voices one more time, then returned to the dark lawn, the quiet night.

We entered the room through the east door and it was transformed to a labyrinth marked upon the floor; we walked into the unknown. We paid a price to enter: our name or our willingness or our wish to transform, and stepping out onto the path we left behind our companions, our children and friends, our partner or parents, and as we walked we left our history behind us. In the center of the labyrinth we laid down the gift we had brought: a piece of our hearts. We offered dreams and youth; we left promises and lovers and paths we would never take. We died a little, then, leaving our old selves behind; when we stepped forward, that was gone from us and we weren't quite sure who we were anymore. And the labyrinth released us not into new life but into the dark stretch of the year that lies between death and birth, the utter unknown, the limitless reaches of the void.

We picked out a card from the cauldron to offer guidance or glimmers of the future, but we didn't know what it meant. We'd released meaning back there in the labyrinth; now everything was unknown, and we acknowledged each other briefly, almost like strangers on that side of the labyrinth, having passed through. Those on the other side—we could see them and remember them—and those making the journey now, through the winding paths; our hearts went out to them in their innocence. When someone reached the center, our breath caught to see their face lit by candlelight as they stood unaware, offering their hearts like fools, like mortals; it was hard to look at. Many times I wept. But then when they came towards us, the ones who had crossed through already, then we didn't know them anymore.

There's a letting go that comes from being in a magical circle or a coven or grove or temple with others. It's a letting go of the ordinary world; a release, for a time, of the daily roles of parent and worker and spouse and child and whatever other roles we might wear out there. It's not just for a few hours while the circle is actually happening, though that's the illusion. *No, you can't call me; I'll be in circle.* In fact, to be part of a magical group we offer up our identities and our outside lives as the working material of our magic; we don't remain the same. We are challenged and changed again and again; maybe every time we do a magical working we are changed. Each direction and each ritual and each festival leaves us a little different than we were before. We enter into and participate in the constant flux of the universe; we do it willingly and knowingly, and we do it in the company of other people.

It can be hard for those who expect you to remain the same to stand on the edges of this, to observe without partaking in it. In a way, we are continually asking not just ourselves to release who we have been into the transformation of the circle, but asking those who love us to constantly release us as well. There may be only certain points they are willing or able to do this, or a certain time-frame within which they can tolerate or support it. When those points are reached, a dilemma is reached. Will the person choose to stay in the circle, asking for further release from the expectations or requirements of relationship, work, or family, or choose to leave the circle?

Within our Circle of Eight we experienced many aspects of release and ending. People left. The Phoenix Circle—the children's circle—was born and also it finished. Many of us watched our children grow up during our time in the Circle of Eight; some of them to become strong Pagans and ritualists in their own right but others to discard or put aside the magic and ritual we had taught them. The nature of a circle, of the wheel, is one of rebirth, realization, release, and return, and that was echoed endlessly in our rituals, our workings together, and our relationships. A few of us came and went; I traveled overseas most years for a couple of months, and most of us had, on occasion, a child or family-related crisis that meant we suddenly couldn't attend a particular ritual or circle, though it may have been planned months in advance.

During one meeting in the darkest time of the year, after Samhain but before the Winter Solstice, I remember we lay around on the floor in our circle with only a single candle for light. The room was massive, dark and looming around us; the walls and ceiling were a long way away. The fire was lit but didn't warm the air convincingly. We spoke our fears, going round, speaking simply and not detailing the reasons or the history behind them, just naming one and moving onto the next person, naming another when our turn came again, around and around.

There was a mounting sense of dread as fear after fear emerged to palpably enter the room and hang in the vast darkened air all around us. At the same time the process gathered momentum; it took on a conviction of its own as each one of us wove another thread, another fear into the mix, a tapestry of them, and I could well imagine wolves outside the door or ghosts or unkind spirits pressing against the windows, knocking at the edges of what now felt like the tiny circle we had cast. We went around five or six times with this growing sense of doom, of looming darkness, until Ross started laughing; he had run out of fears and in the absurdity of wondering whether he should make one up when it was his turn again, his laughter had burst out.

After he'd explained himself and the rest of us conceded that we had named all the important ones anyway, we sat up and gathered ourselves. Somehow it didn't seem as dark. We didn't feel as weighted, burdened, or frightened; most of those fears we'd named seemed quite forgettable now; as for the others, we acknowledged them but their power was reduced. The room was still large and not very well lit, but it felt spacious and airy, filled with potential. The ghosts had gone, the wolves receded to their forests; we looked at each other and remembered who we were. We'd let go of those fears, though for a moment they'd had us, binding up our space and thoughts, channeling our energies into a narrow race with quickened heartbeats, anxiety, and shortened breath. We'd released them into the night, the time of year, the gap between endings and the start of the new, and it didn't feel as if they were waiting around the corner; it felt more as if they'd been seen and were satisfied, with no need for further action right now.

One time we held a circle knowing Ian was going to leave. We'd been six people for a while now; six very committed people doing deep work together and holding the circle, holding the eight festivals and working the geographic Circle of Eight. Ian had been part of the circle for years, and it felt a little strange: he said he wanted to move in other directions spiritually. He stayed through to the completion of a cycle, for him; he came in at the West and he was leaving while holding the West. We sat together for the final time and he spoke of a deep sea of emotions, of the challenges he'd experienced being part of the circle, of feeling regrets and of the recognition he'd found in this group. But he said he was ready to find his own path and leave the circle.

Shockingly, with no warning, Ross said he was going to leave, too. He'd been part of the circle for four and a half years and we were all amazed; half-incredulous. It didn't seem like he'd considered it at all; more like a moment descended upon him and he'd seized it. We were ready for Ian's leaving—we'd thought about it, adjusted, and accepted it—but this! We were taken off guard completely. We asked questions, and to us the answers were unsatisfactory; we thought he was leaving because of pressure from his new relationship, but in the end it wasn't our place to choose.

Ross wept as he spoke of the loss of the circle from his life. He said he had to focus on other things, to cut down the number of distractions in his life. And of course we bridled at being called a distraction, thinking our work was profound, even that it was of service to the community, but he had moved somewhere else. From the moment he spoke those words he left the circle, and nothing we could say or do would bring him back. That's the thing with endings and leave-takings; they're already done once they've happened in someone's mind. The rest of us might be struggling to catch up, but he's gone. He's moved on, leaving us behind.

We spent the rest of the circle sitting with them. We spoke of how we had seen them grow, what challenges we saw them face, and our feelings on them leaving. We spoke slowly, measuredly; we didn't rush. They spoke to each of us as well, acknowledging us and the part we had played in this unfolding circle, this exploration of land and spirit and place and relationship. I loved that we attended to it so gravely, so carefully; that we all sat there together, even knowing it was the last time, and spent such thought and care upon each other, at the parting. I loved that people can be acknowledged fully for what they have done even as they are moving onto the next thing; that we were somehow grown-up enough to part this way.

We had spent the evening earlier, before this leave-taking, singing— singing and singing and singing, song after song, layered into and over the top of each other, raising and dropping energy, weaving patterns of voice and words, passing the drum between each other, and finding new ways to sing old songs. At the end, when we were ready to turn the wheel, we rose and started singing. We stripped ourselves, energetically, of the directions we'd been holding for a month. I was in the North; so many times I had been in the North. I laid it down again, all its fiery power, its immediate-seeming access to the center of the circle, its unequivocal stance and out-thereness, and I turned to face the next direction, the one I used to dread: the North-West.

Oh, the North-West with its coming of the dark, its looming, broken-off volcano peak, its fire and water, its unpredictability and a power not like the strengthening heat of the North but more like a sideways blast, unpredictable, often unpleasant, what you avoided or dreaded or hoped not to face. I faced it as we sang the song we always sang to turn the wheel, and our singing was stronger and more assured than it ever had been. We placed our left hands into the center of the circle to make the spokes of the wheel and we took that first tiny step onwards, turning with the wheel. The song was loud and vibrant, shimmering with its own life, the glimmerings of the great wheel itself, far beyond our circle, the wheel of stars, the universe, of time and life and the tides of death and rebirth.

We were barely moving as we inched around the circle, each of us moving only a few feet around the edge, but the song swirled up and out as if we were a spiraling dance among stars, rapid beyond thought, space spinning about us and spiraling in and out at the same time, the forces of the universe meeting in the center and us holding to the edges, carving out a space within space, and in this swirling, turning, dancing sound and motion two of us rotated off, stepped out of the turning, off the edges of our universe and onto their own paths, separate while our turning takes us forward and our hands are still joined at the center and I arrived at the North-West. We let our hands drop, we let the song drop, we turned to face each other, and we were only four.

The next time we came together the circle seemed shockingly small in that vast space, this space that holds universes and the whole of the year, all possibilities, and only us four to guard the edges. We were positioned oddly, like an inverse pendulum; three of us together over the North-West, North, North-East, and one down the bottom in the South. None of us wanted to move, to make the arrangement more even; we all felt married to our particular circuits, to this exact progression of the directions; maybe we were holding onto what we still had. We didn't talk about the two who'd left but instead decided to apply that process we used with them to ourselves, turning our minds and attention to who's still here. We spoke to each of the others, in turn, and named how we had seen them grow in the Circle of Eight. We told them what we appreciated and what we felt our relationship with them was. In this way we returned to the strength and connections that remained to us rather than the rips of what had gone.

Samhain's always been the direction of letting go. There are others that speak to it, but this is the big one. For me, this is my home. If you lay the months and days of the year out over the circle, my birthdate falls into this sector in late autumn. And my life has always seemed dedicated to the themes of this direction: secrets, mystery, dreams, and the other worlds—that place of mythos that lies so close to the surface in me, where my writing and imagination surface from. The inner realms and all the amazing extensions they offer.

My house has tall windows in the south-west that look out at the valley and the ridge beyond. The windows carve into the landscape and the sky, bringing a vertical section of outside into the house. Our circle met on the new moon; when the sky is clear, we see the moon's crescent in the south-west. We see its tilt, how thick it is, how many days past the dark. We see it further to the south or further to the north, depending on the time of year. Sometimes we see a planet there as well; Venus, Saturn, or Mercury like a beauty mark, emphasizing this side of the moon or the other; the outward curve or the invitation of the open inner curve, or the planet sits above or below the moon, accenting it, leading, following. Occasionally we see the moon with two planets, seeming to make a diagram between them, cryptic to us but surely understandable by those who read such things.

A native fig tree sits at the south-west corner of the lawn. It marks the boundary between the civilization of house and lawn and the wilderness of forest, weed, and boulder and the rocky stream that runs only in the wet; the border that separates the animal realm from the human one. Here the wompoo pigeons come to feast and gossip, swoop and court; pademelons emerge to nibble grass, preferably freshly mown; here the gateway lies for feral cats to slink through, packs of wild dogs to vanish into, leaping out to hunt and kill and raid and then removing themselves again, invisible, into their jungle. The fig itself is a strangler; the type that encloses and eventually kills its host tree, hatching its splendor and the richness of its fruit through the realms of death.

It's in the South-West that I have one of my most emblematic visions of the Circle of Eight. I'm sitting, waiting for my turn to speak. Since we always begin in the South-East and head around the circle the other way, I have a long time to wait. I become aware of the vast, shimmering circle that lies just below the surface of the wheel, black and cold and bigger than the mind can grasp. I see the stars dotted out among the thick, swirling folds of it, dancing there. Inwards, I look towards the center, the place where the spokes of the wheel converge. I can't see them as solid objects, but in my mind they carve through infinity to reach each other like lovers, creating reason, time, and the ordering of days and thoughts.

But when I look to follow them back out again, to where I sit on the edge, they sweep right past me—they are immediately already past me and heading out, outwards, infinitely far into the nothing. There's a chill at my back as I feel it; the enormity of the South-West. When I look forwards to the center, I'm looking at just a tiny piece of a segment, but behind me lies the entire segment, all of it, the depths of the South-West, the South-West of the South-West. It just keeps getting more and more South-West until—I don't know—until the edges of the universe are reached. And maybe then it folds around, this South-West, to meet its opposite, the North-East, or maybe it just vanishes off the edge; how odd that now it seems the universe is more or less flat, while we ridiculed earlier ages for imagining the earth was, but for them the earth was the whole world, and perhaps they knew something after all.

I feel the South-West at my back. It's as if I am flayed: my very cells seem open to it, receiving the pulse of it, the dense, knowing darkness of it into my being, no barriers as it penetrates and owns me, claims me for the South-West forever. My spine is a column of light, sparking, sending, and receiving starlight out into the blackness; I am a radar, an antenna; my cells are realigning, and their loyalty is not to me or this little earth we sit on but to the vastness. There's nothing to hang on to here; only the thinnest of threads holds me to the vision forward, this little group of bodies and light, this tiny Circle of Eight we've carved into the hugeness of space; all of the pull, the gravity, the importance and loudness and booming enormity is behind me and perhaps it comes through me, into my face or my voice, as I sit here holding the South-West and attempting to represent it.

Forget being human. Forget anything much but starlight, dust and chemical and physical reactions; the pull of fusion, the splitting of fission. What human life can stand beside this? What human concern is worth even a second's consideration? Death and birth are bound together from the first unto the last; the death of stars is the birth of stars with planets incidental, any beings or landscapes on those planets less, even, than that; talk in nebulas and black holes and dark matter and—don't talk—show me in implosions and spawning clouds of galaxies and long-ribboned rivers of stars gushing forth from the body of the Goddess, black night herself. Taste that, the cold brilliance; be seared by that, consumed by that. Offer the moment that is your life, it will not be noticed except by you, as a prayer, and it will drop, an uncounted drop into the infinite.

When it's my turn to speak, I just stammer. I think I manage to say something about how the whole universe of the South-West stretches behind my back, spreading out and out in an endless devouring triangle of immensity, and to convey my conviction that this direction is vaster than everything else, or it contains everything else, or perhaps they are all equally vast but that this one, now, has swallowed me and I can't ever return properly, having seen and felt this, but probably someone just records it as *Jane says the South-West is big* and I can never really, even here with the luxury of written words, convey what it is to me, what I became aware of in that moment.

Release. I have to release that vision or how could I function? How could I go about my human concerns, raising my son and trying to hold the house and land together, run a circle? Why would I do anything but be absorbed in the longing to dive headlong into that outer space, to spend a second tumbling outwards before being swallowed, a speck of dust returned to the dust we came from, my life's brilliance a spark unjoined and lost as I vanished, was consumed utterly by this dark mother that eats everything, that gives everything? Release; I cannot live there in the coldness of the South-West, the vastness of it; I have to live here, in this house and this body and on this earth. Release the grandeur, the comfort, the sheer knowledge sweeping through me, release it back to where it came from, the South-West.

The ending of our Circle of Eight came quickly, unbidden and unexpected. There had been only four of us for a while, though all of us were strong and had been in the circle for many years. Cathryn was about to move away, leaving the area. We met for the final circle with her, and she didn't make it to the meeting. Suddenly, with only three of us, it didn't seem so viable, so necessary to keep this going. Glenn spoke his uncertainty, and when we turned to address it—and it was like turning a corner in a narrow corridor, with no idea what would be ahead except the expectation that it would be much the same as the territory we had already passed through—it was a completely different terrain. We were at the back door, and it opened out onto a different landscape.

We did our working for the night and it still held power, we all felt there was a lot of potential that could be worked, perhaps in a little while, perhaps in another form, but we agreed—almost as an experiment—to lay down the Circle of Eight, as it had been for over five years. We turned the wheel as always and decided to hold our new positions for a month and then do whatever seemed right to us: continue turning with the wheel or let it fade away or something else altogether. We agreed to discuss the circle again in a few months; perhaps by then there'd be some more people or it would metamorphose into a new form.

It was an ending without trauma. It was upon us and we rose to meet it. We were all a little shocked, saddened at the loss; there's not enough ritual in our lives, we all felt that, and to let go of such a huge involvement in ritual seemed momentous. We were on the last few pages of our Book of Shadows as we spiraled off; a confirmation, if we needed one, that this was the time to let it go. We recorded our final meeting on the remaining three pages. I did feel grief to be releasing it;

this circle had underpinned and dominated my inner life for years, but as I moved that night from the South-West into the South, I felt it was sowing seeds within me—that the waiting time had come, and I knew other things would hatch, be born, arise, and so I let it go, spinning off on its own out into the universe, knowing I will always carry with me its structure and vision and immense presence.

How to Release
Your Circle of Eight

Being part of a Circle of Eight involves continual release and letting go as every position one holds is then released. This is agonizing sometimes, to leave behind a position one has felt happy, safe, or productive in and move into the unknown or possibly to a position one imagines as frightening, destructive, or difficult. It can feel like leaving a lover or best friend behind, knowing you won't see them again for a long time.

This continual release and letting go is a commentary on our lives, for each year we live is one we won't have again, and things are always changing; friends move overseas, we change jobs, a relationship finishes, a family member dies. We move house, complete a project, our children grow up, something we took for granted suddenly vanishes. The Circle of Eight offers sustained and profound practice in this continual letting go that is such a fundamental—but often unrecognized—part of things. It teaches us about our own attachments, how we handle loss and change and letting go; in practicing this in the circle, we can then apply what we've learned more broadly in our lives.

As with any group, coven, or collective, over time people leave. They leave for a variety of reasons, including moving away, changing their focus, completing their commitment, ill health, external demands, or the group not proceeding the way they wanted. In a group that is structured so particularly—where people sit in a certain relationship to each other, continually, over time—an absence is immediately noticed; it is a spatial issue as well as a personal one. They leave an energetic hole behind them. The circle continues, the wheel still turns, but it is emptier and now unfamiliar. How we deal with the readjustments—both individually and as a group—can show us how we cope with loss and change in our lives, and potentially it can teach us healthy ways to do this.

How to Release in the Circle of Eight

1. Releasing a Direction

An essential part of the Circle of Eight process is moving around the circle. It's a continual meeting, union, and parting with the eight directions and thus with all aspects of life and death, change and growth. To move on effectively from one direction to the next and not be energetically trailing pieces behind oneself requires some discipline.

I like to do this ritual the same way each time. The repetitive nature of it builds its strength, and as one's connections become stronger and deeper to each direction over time, then the strength of the releasing balances the strength of the connection. This is part of turning the wheel, usually done towards the close of a ritual or meeting, when each direction has been fully expressed and experienced by the person holding it. I like to do it simultaneously; everyone there does it together, releasing their directions and hovering energetically on the wheel but not locked into any part of it, before turning the wheel as a group and moving around to the next direction. One person may speak the process through as it is happening or just before it happens, or each person may speak pieces of it as they feel and experience it. When the circle is well practiced in this process, it can be done silently.

For releasing the directions it is important to stand up, to begin removing oneself from the seat and holding of that direction. Gather all your thoughts, feelings, and experiences of the time you have spent in this direction and acknowledge and thank the direction, internally. Now imagine the energy of that direction flowing physically off you as if it were water clinging to your skin. Brush it downwards, from your head down your arms and off the rest of your body. Imagine it pooling at your feet, that directional energy returned to its direction, releasing you. You might imagine it as colored light or particular sensations. Other images you may choose to work with include unzipping a body-suit and laying it at your feet, peeling off a layer of psychic skin, or diving upwards out of the pull and texture of that direction.

Now you are hovering there, still *in* the direction but no longer *of* that direction. If there are any last pieces of it clinging to you, brush them gently off. Feel yourself as a creature of starlight, a creature bound to the life-and-death cycle, one who turns on the wheel. Look up and see the others of your type around you, also shimmering free of the directions, and reach your hand out to them. If you are in the Northern Hemisphere, it will be your right hand you place into the center of the circle; in the Southern Hemisphere it will be your left hand. Begin chanting, breathing together, or speaking a mantra. Then, as you begin your journey around one-eighth of the edge of the circle, be aware of leaving that direction behind and approaching the next direction.

2. Releasing a Person

Each time a person leaves the Circle of Eight will probably be under different circumstances, so each time of release will be different. If possible, sit with the person as a group and talk about the time you have spent together in ritual, magic, and process; this makes for a clearer release. During this meeting, each person can speak to the one leaving of what they have appreciated about them, how they have seen them grow, and what they have learned from them. The person leaving can speak of their time in the circle, their connections with each person there, and what they will take forward from the Circle of Eight into whatever they are doing next. When the wheel is turned, that person steps out of the wheel, which continues turning without them.

For all sorts of reasons, sometimes this isn't possible. Part of the process can still be done in the person's absence, where each remaining person still addresses what they appreciated about the person who's left, how they saw them grow, and what they have learned from them. If the circle feels fragile, emotionally unstable, or uncertain, it's great to extend that process to the people who remain, with each person speaking to each other person of their connection, gratitude, and learning. When the wheel is turned, add into it an energetic layer of allowing that person to leave the circle and their place to be washed over by the turning of the wheel, leaving it empty and open for the next person who joins.

3. Releasing the Circle of Eight

Perhaps you are the one leaving the circle or the circle is dissolving, finished, or going into recess. You can ask for a group ritual, create your own private ritual, or follow the simple acknowledgments suggested above. One thing to consider is if you personally wish to step off the wheel of the Circle of Eight or just out of this particular circle. If you have been, for example, turning the wheel every new moon for three or four years, moving into the next direction each time, for possibly many new moons to come that impulse and energy will still be triggered in you. You may still feel the threads of connection to others in the circle as living things or still be bound up in the magic you were working together.

It is possible to continue the Circle of Eight work on your own; to continue holding and changing directions and working magic within that framework. Your emphasis will gradually change over time; from seeing others in the directions you are not holding, you will come to see them as held by different aspects of yourself or more purely as directions with no human representative. Both of these can be very interesting and powerful explorations. You may find your understandings and workings transform or develop into something entirely different if you work the Circle of Eight on your own.

If you wish to step out of the circle completely, a ceremony of release may assist. On your own, if it is only you who is leaving or with the whole circle if it is ending, create a ritual where you move into each of the positions in turn. Spend some time in each one while you remember its impact and the feeling of holding that particular direction. Thank it and acknowledge how the themes and energies of that direction continue to play a part in your life. Find some way of releasing it; this might be through drumming, prayer, blowing out a candle, offering a blessing, or anything else that seems right to you. Finally, stand in the center of the circle, acknowledging all the directions and feeling the wheel all around you before stepping out of it entirely.

Conclusion

This book is only the beginning of local magic. If you create a Circle of Eight and work with it, the land, the people in your circle, and the directions themselves will begin to speak to you about the nature, flavors, and seasons of magic where you live. Your magic and ritual may look remarkably like what is commonly written about in books and the most popular versions of the festivals of the Wheel of the Year. They may be broadly similar but infused with local scents, sensibilities, and understandings. Or they may be completely different, even in a style of difference I cannot begin to imagine sitting here and writing this, listening to the cicadas ramping up their summer sound as the skies around me gradually clear from the smoke of early bushfires and we head towards a hot, dry summer.

What is written in this book is a series of inspirations, experiences, and open instructions designed to send you onto your own land with all your senses wide open—to send you off into your own imagination, asking questions, and to send you out into the directions as they exist in your locality to discover what magic they hold. What is contained within these pages is neither prescriptive nor exhaustive; I expect this to be only the starting place for your own explorations and discoveries.

Perhaps you have worked a form of local magic for many years; I hope you will find this book supportive. Perhaps you haven't known where or how to begin; I hope you can find instruction here. Perhaps you've struggled to get your festivals, rituals, or magic to conform to what is given out as the fundamental pattern for Pagan rituals, correspondences, and festivals; I hope this book can offer you inspiration to find your own path.

It's only when our local magic is strong and definite—when we know the places we live in, are sensitive to them and can lend them our magic and work with theirs, and as we create dynamic ritual relationship with them—that we can begin to find our way towards a more global Pagan understanding of the earth's patterns and seasons in their entirety. When we can layer the understanding of my Beltaine over your Beltaine over a dozen other, different Beltaines, then we will begin to see something of the essence of Beltaine. When we know how to work local magic, we can link effectively and vibrantly into global magic.

The Circle of Eight is designed to merge Pagan understandings and markers of elements, directions, and festivals with what is real on the patch of earth where you live. It is an overlay, a structure with no content. The content that you bring, find, and create will be taught to you by the place where you lay the structure down: your own backyard, your immediate surrounds whether that is a shire, suburb, or city or a wider region.

There are no qualifications required to participate in the Circle of Eight; the ideas of the Wheel of the Year and the compass directions can be taught in an hour. Children can do it, people with spiritual backgrounds other than Pagan can do it, people with no particular spiritual affiliation but instead a political, ecological, or other interest can be as creative and fully participate in it as those who've been practicing Paganism for years. The Circle of Eight offers opportunities to work deeply in the fields of personal development, group ritual, magic, mythic exploration, spell work, celebrating the seasons, and many other areas. It will contain and structure what you bring to it. I believe it will give you back more than you could have imagined possible when you first opened this book, set up a circle of eight cushions or chairs, and began thinking about local magic.

Jane Meredith
Beltaine 2013
BLUE MOUNTAINS, AUSTRALIA

Appendix
Casting a Circle, Turning the Wheel, Releasing the Circle

Casting your Circle of Eight is something that is done each time you meet as a circle. Like any circle casting, it involves speaking or calling to the directions; in this case, eight directions plus Above and Below if you include them (or Center, if you prefer). In the Circle of Eight, people always call to the direction they are currently holding. If you change places, or turn the wheel, during the ritual, then when you release the circle you will be releasing a different direction than the one you called to.

I believe the space—the land, the air, the cosmos—is already sacred whether or not a circle is cast and independent of that. Casting a circle is not an asking of the directions to be present; the directions are already there. We humans are the ones who move about, who have to locate ourselves in space and time—who, when we come together in ritual, need to formally remind ourselves of sacred space. As human beings we speak this offering to the Divine, to sacred land, to the wheel our Circle of Eight is based upon. If we are working with particular places in the directions, we may call out to them from wherever we are casting the circle to honor them, to remember their unique qualities and invoke a little of their presence.

The emphasis in the Circle of Eight is not so much on the individuals who are calling to the directions and their unique relationship with them as on the directions themselves in relation to the whole circle. In this way, the peculiarity of calling to one direction in the casting and then releasing a different one at the conclusion of the ritual is minimized. The wheel is ever-turning, and the location of individuals within it is less notable than the relationship of the group as a whole to the wheel. The Circle of Eight is one whole thing composed of the people and the directions together. It contains a shifting pattern of relationship, but all is held within the dynamic of the Circle of Eight itself.

The Circle of Eight is called in a complete circle; that is, whichever direction begins the calling also completes it so there is not a gap left in the energetic ring. I like to anchor my circle into the South, in the Southern Hemisphere, and the North in the Northern Hemisphere. This becomes the beginning and ending point, echoing the cycle of growth and the Wheel of the Year itself, beginning at the Winter Solstice. Some other circles like to begin and end in the East; others in the direction that corresponds to the nearest festival. If you were doing this on the Autumn Equinox, you would begin and end in the West.

Before you begin, choose which direction will anchor the circle, whether you will call Above and Below (or Center) as well as the eight directions, and whether each person will remain facing their own direction once they have called to it or turn to face each of the remaining directions as they are called. You can try different methods until you find what works best or continue experimenting and making changes. If you want to work with a particular format for calling the directions— to have words that each person says at the beginning and end of their calling, for example—or to focus on a theme such as light and dark or growth and decay, mention that before you begin casting.

Ask each person to reflect their direction in their calling by their voice and manner. So the person calling to the Imbolc direction may call in a breathy whisper while the person calling to the Summer Solstice direction can shout it out. You can practice this sounding before the casting, having the whole group turn to face each direction and experimenting with sounds, volume, pitch, and cadence. This soundscape can help provide a clearer sensory picture for people who may not otherwise feel confident shouting, whispering, or calling out in a voice different from their normal speaking voice, encouraging them, for example, to use a very high- or low-pitched voice, or to call in a quick staccato or sing a few simple words. The more you work with casting, the stronger your group will become in it.

If you've come together to work the Circle of Eight, I would always call to eight directions, even if there are not eight people present. This is especially important if you are also going to be turning the wheel. However, if you've come together to celebrate something else, such as a full moon, festival, or other occasion, and you don't have eight people to do the casting, it is fine to call just to the four most appropriate directions, possibly having two people in each direction or two in some directions and one in others, depending on your numbers. For a cross-quarter festival—Imbolc, Beltaine, Lammas, or Samhain—always call to the cross-quarters, whereas for the equinoxes and solstices, call to the quarters. For other celebrations, use what feels right to you.

Where there is no one standing in the position that you are calling or releasing, you can:

- all turn to face that direction and call or release together
- have the person directly across from the empty space call or release that direction, calling *through* the circle from across the other side
- have the person who called the previous direction take a few steps to the empty position and also call to that direction

How to Cast a Circle of Eight

Time: 10–15 minutes

Optional: drums and rattles or other musical instruments

1. Grounding in Your Direction

Everyone stands in the direction they are currently holding. Take a few minutes to ground, either as a group or individually, reflecting on the feelings, presence, and awareness of that direction.

2. Calling In the Circle

All turn together to face outwards to your own direction. It is most beautiful and synchronous if you all turn in the direction of the circle casting—that is, in the Northern Hemisphere turn clockwise, to the right, and in the Southern Hemisphere turn anticlockwise, to the left.

Begin in the anchor position, or Winter Solstice direction, of your circle; that is, North for the Northern Hemisphere and South in the Southern Hemisphere. The person in this direction "anchors" the casting by making a sound (drum beat, rattle, or wordless call) or gesture.

The next position, the Imbolc direction (North-East in the Northern Hemisphere, South-East in the Southern Hemisphere) now calls to their direction.

To call to your direction, breathe deeply and open your eyes. Inwardly summon the senses, memory, and impressions of this direction that you have gathered while you have held it and that you experience in this moment as you stand there. Taking another deep breath, allow those impressions and feelings to move through your body and out through your voice. You may include song, drumming or rattling, spoken word and movement. Speak or sound loudly enough for those behind you to hear.

When the Imbolc person has finished their calling, they remain facing their own direction while the rest of the circle is called, until it is completed.

Call to all eight directions, finishing with the anchored direction of the Winter Solstice. When the eighth direction has been called to, everyone turns together (still in the direction of the casting, so right or clockwise in the Northern Hemisphere and left or anticlockwise in the Southern Hemisphere) until everyone is facing inwards.

If you are calling Above and Below, or Center, all together take a step forward. Raise your arms and faces for Above and as a group tone or call a few words out towards Above. For Below, crouch down on the ground, lay your hands flat upon it, and again tone as a group or call a few words downwards. For Center, reach your hands into the center of your circle, as spokes into the hub, and again tone as a group or speak a few words. When you are finished, step back into your directions.

You can move into a group toning, sing a song, or speak a few words to signify that the circle is cast and you are now in the sacred space of the Circle of Eight.

How to Turn the Wheel in a Circle of Eight

Time: 10–15 minutes

You will need: an appropriate song or chant, drums and rattles or other musical instruments (optional)

1. Stepping Free of the Wheel

Everyone stands in their current position. Gather up all of your thoughts, impressions, and sensations of this direction and imagine them leaving your body, placing them down at your feet, returning them to the position itself. Thank this position for anything it has taught you or shared with you. Now imagine the energy of this position sliding off you like rain to pool at your feet or letting the cloak of it slide down your body to the floor.

Feel yourself standing on the position but no longer a part of it, still touching but ready to move, as if you were hovering above it on the wheel.

Conjure into your head an awareness of the wheel, constantly turning. Feel its directional pull, its life force, its relentless endlessness.

2. Moving Around the Wheel

Facing each other, begin singing your chant or song. Allow it to strengthen and grow between you, tuning in to the energy of the wheel itself. When you feel locked into the power of the music, words, and wheel, reach your hand into the center of the circle—right hands if you are in the Northern Hemisphere, left hands if you are in the Southern Hemisphere.

Still singing together, turn to face around the wheel in the direction of the turn (clockwise for the Northern Hemisphere, anticlockwise for the Southern Hemisphere). You can touch fingertips, layer your hands over each other, or just all reach inwards without quite touching. If you like, you can stretch your other arm out, away from the hub of your circle.

Continuing and even strengthening the song, start to slowly move together as a group. Feel yourselves treading the rim of the circle, transiting from one position to the next. Feel the wheel beneath you, through you, all around you.

When you reach the next position around the circle, stop. Turn and face inwards, all together. Look for a moment at your circle. Allow your arms to drop. Then sit—or remain standing, if you prefer—arriving fully into this new direction.

3. Arriving in Your New Direction

Spend a few moments in silence. Allow feelings, images, and thoughts to come to you if they will.

Beginning with the anchor position (North in the Northern Hemisphere, South in the Southern Hemisphere) and going around the circle, share in just a few words your very first impression of the direction you have moved into.

How to Release a Circle of Eight

Time: 5–10 minutes

Optional: drums and rattles or other musical instruments

The circle is released in the reverse order that it was cast, regardless of who is in which position. If you finished with Center or with Above and Below, then release those first, followed by all eight of the directions, beginning with your anchor position (North in the Northern Hemisphere and South in the Southern Hemisphere) and traveling the opposite way from which you cast it (anticlockwise in the Northern Hemisphere, clockwise in the Southern Hemisphere).

Releasing the circle is not a further invocation, so the thanks and honoring spoken to each direction are simpler and shorter than during casting. The directions are not being dismissed (they will still be there), but the release of the circle is acknowledging that the time for being together in sacred space is finishing for now.

Everyone turns together for the releasing of the circle, facing the anchor position to begin with and all turning together to each successive direction as it is thanked. Once the final direction has been honored, break the synchronicity of movement so you don't all turn back at the same time or in the same direction to complete the release.

Shake yourselves, stamp on the ground, share some food if you like, and blow out any candles that were lit.

RITUALS
of
CELEBRATION

Honoring the Seasons of Life through the Wheel of the Year

Jane Meredith

To order, call 1-877-NEW-WRLD

Prices subject to change without notice

Order at llewellyn.com 24 hours a day, 7 days a week!

Rituals of Celebration
Honoring the Seasons of Life
Through the Wheel of the Year
Jane Meredith

In order to give her family and friends a deep experience of earth-based spirituality, author Jane Meredith holds eight rituals per year, celebrating the solstices, the equinoxes, and the cross-quarter festivals. *Rituals of Celebration* provides accounts of the most memorable rituals she's organized, as well as how-to instructions for creating the rituals. Discover the deeper themes of each festival as Meredith offers meaningful reflections about Imbolc, Beltaine, Samhain, and the changing of the seasons as they correspond to personal growth and challenges. Create the craft projects that go along with each ritual—perfect ideas for artistic expression whether you are practicing alone, with a group, or celebrating with children.

Honoring differences of place and spirit, the rituals are inspired by Pagan, Druid, and Goddess traditions, and a variety of other perspectives. Beginners will learn how to construct altars, invoke deities, and perform basic tasks, while experienced ritual organizers will learn new techniques for planning meaningful rituals in challenging or unexpected circumstances.

978-0-7387-3544-3
6 x 9 • 336 pages

Sacred
Practices
of
Unity,
Power
&
Earth
Healing

ECOSHAMANISM

JAMES ENDREDY

To order, call 1-877-NEW-WRLD

Prices subject to change without notice

Order at llewellyn.com 24 hours a day, 7 days a week!

Ecoshamanism
Sacred Practices of Unity,
Power & Earth Healing

James Endredy

In a society riddled with rampant consumerism and unsustainable technology, it's easy for everyone, including shamans, to lose touch with the natural world. James Endredy, who has learned from tribal shamans around the globe, presents a new philosophy of shamanic practice called ecological shamanism, or ecoshamanism. Designed to deliver well-being and spiritual harmony, ecoshamanism is the culmination of the visionary practices, rituals, and ceremonies that honor and support nature.

Exploring the holistic perspective of shamanism, Endredy encourages readers to establish a rewarding connection with sacred, life-giving forces using shamanic tools and practices. The author describes more than fifty authentic ecoshamanistic practices-including ceremonies, rituals, chanting, hunting, pilgrimage, and making instruments-that reinforce one's relationship with the natural world.

978-0-7387-0742-6
7½ x 9⅛ • 360 pp.

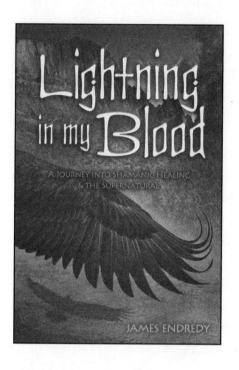

To order, call 1-877-NEW-WRLD

Prices subject to change without notice

Order at llewellyn.com 24 hours a day, 7 days a week!

Lightning in My Blood
A Journey into Shamanic Healing
& the Supernatural

James Endredy

James Endredy invites you on a wondrous journey into the shape-shifting, mind-altering, and healing magic of shamanism. For decades, Endredy has worked with wise tribal elders around the world, participating in their sacred ceremonies and learning from powerful animal guides and spirits. Here he relives these profound experiences, including his first meeting with a spirit guide that led to the seer's path, a terrifying lesson in using his ethereal body in the Sierra Madre mountains, how he outwitted an evil sorceress, and his incredible inauguration into shamanic healing.

Grouped by shamanic medicines, Endredy's captivating accounts highlight a fascinating tradition and the extraordinary journey of a modern shaman.

978-0-7387-2147-7
6 x 9 • 240 pp.

GEDE PARMA

ecstatic
witchcraft

magick, philosophy & trance
in the shamanic craft

To order, call 1-877-NEW-WRLD

Prices subject to change without notice

Order at llewellyn.com 24 hours a day, 7 days a week!

Ecstatic Witchcraft
Magick, Philosophy & Trance in the Shamanic Craft
Gede Parma

Many modern Witches yearn for a deeper, more primal, and more authentic form of witchcraft. This timely book by award-winning author Gede Parma invites Witches, Wiccans, Pagans, and other seekers down a shamanic path that embraces the ecstatic, the wild, the gnostic, the transformative, and the visionary.

This unique guide presents a shamanic craft apprenticeship that readers can incorporate into their own spiritual journey. It includes techniques and rituals for fundamental shamanic practices, including drawing down the gods, working with spirit allies, moving between the worlds, ecstatic spellcraft, healing, and divination. It is designed to deepen and enhance the path already being followed by the reader.

978-0-7387-3299-2
6 x 9 • 264 pp.

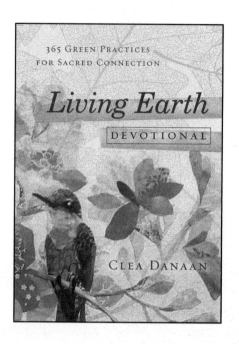

365 GREEN PRACTICES
FOR SACRED CONNECTION

Living Earth

DEVOTIONAL

CLEA DANAAN

To order, call 1-877-NEW-WRLD

Prices subject to change without notice

Order at llewellyn.com 24 hours a day, 7 days a week!

Living Earth Devotional
365 Green Practices for Sacred Connection
Clea Danaan

Tune in to nature, care for the sacred earth, and grow spiritually. *Living Earth Devotional* offers 365 earth-friendly activities for deepening your physical and spiritual connection to nature.

These practical, soul-centered tasks—meditations, craft projects, gardening and outdoor activities, journal exercises, and more—are organized by the Wheel of the Year. Bridging green spirituality with ecological action, this day-by-day guide will help you tune in to the energies of the changing seasons and build a deep appreciation for the earth's beauty, power, and wisdom. Reduce your carbon footprint, recharge your creativity and intuition, and cultivate a connection with the earth that inspires spiritual growth and personal transformation.

978-0-7387-3658-7
5 x 7 • 464 pp.